# JOHN UPDIKE'S NOVELS

BY DONALD J. GREINER

*The Notebook of Stephen Crane* (editor)
*Comic Terror: The Novels of John Hawkes*
*Robert Frost: The Poet and His Critics*
*American Poets Since World War II: Ammons through Kumin* (editor)
*American Poets Since World War II: Levertov through Zukofsky* (editor)
*The Other John Updike: Poems/Short Stories/Prose/Play*
*John Updike's Novels*

# JOHN UPDIKE'S NOVELS

Donald J. Greiner

Ohio University Press
Athens, Ohio   London

**Library of Congress Cataloging in Publication Data**

Greiner, Donald J.
  John Updike's novels.

  Bibliography: p.
  Includes index.
  1.  Updike, John—Criticism and interpretation.
I. Title.
PS 3571.P4Z683      1984        813'.54        84-7213
ISBN 0-8214-0780-5
ISBN 0-8214-0792-9 pbk.

*This book is once again
for Ellen
And for three men besides my father
who have mattered in my life:
Grant Bennett
Frank Logan
Vincent Miller*

# TABLE OF CONTENTS

## ACKNOWLEDGMENTS

Acknowledgments are a pleasure to write. George L. Geckle, Chairman, Department of English, University of South Carolina, and Chester Bain, Dean of the College of Humanities and Social Sciences, provided the released time necessary for research and writing. My graduate assistants John Cobb, Lisa Hyman, and Ken McLaurin energetically checked references. Jane Thesing and Donna Nance, Reference Librarians, Cooper Library, University of South Carolina, tracked down fugitive sources. My secretaries Carol Cutsinger and Carolyn Cobia did all of the typing after having learned to decipher my questionable handwriting. Professors David Cowart and Matthew J. Bruccoli, colleagues and friends, read parts of the manuscript and eased the frustration of the struggling author. I am grateful to be a member of the Department of English at the University of South Carolina, a department that supports our efforts to do our work.

Grateful acknowledgment is made to Alfred A. Knopf, Inc. for permission to quote from the copyrighted works of John Updike.

Don Greiner
1 October 1982

# PREFACE

This book is called *John Updike's Novels* for two reasons. First, it does not discuss the other volumes in his astonishingly varied canon. My companion study, *The Other John Updike: Poems/Short Stories/Prose/Play*, was published by Ohio University Press in 1981 and suggests the shape of his artistic career outside the novel. Second, this book does not impose a thesis on Updike's development as a novelist. Several critical books with descriptive titles have already attempted a thesis-approach, among them Alice and Kenneth Hamilton's *The Elements of John Updike* (1970), Rachael Burchard's *John Updike: Yea Sayings* (1971), Larry Taylor's *Pastoral Patterns in John Updike's Fiction* (1971), Joyce Markle's *Fighters and Lovers* (1973), Edward Vargo's *Rainstorms and Fire: Ritual in the Novels of John Updike* (1974), and George Hunt's *John Updike and the Three Great Secret Things: Sex, Religion, and Art* (1980). While these books are always interesting and often instructive, I wonder if a thesis should be forced on an author as prolific, as gifted, and as unpredictable as John Updike. His interests are so varied and his career so far from concluded that one never knows what the topic of his next book will be. Who, for example, could have foreseen *The Coup*? My primary goal, then, is not to urge a thesis on the canon but to offer an informed and careful reading of the novels in order to isolate and discuss the qualities that make Updike a great writer.

To this end I have examined hundreds of reviews and essays and have briefly outlined the highlights of the criticism to define not only the reception of each novel but also the critical controversy that is all but guaranteed each time Updike publishes a new title. Steady publication, occasional best-seller sales, literary awards, and critical debate keep Updike's work in the public eye more than one might imagine for such a major author. One might expect a writer of Updike's stature to be discussed only in the seminar room and the pages of the *Hudson Review*, to be unknown to general readers, and to be limited to respectable sales to serious book-buyers and academics, but such is not the case. John Updike is an easily recognizable name. Three examples will suffice for the moment. In a *Time* cover story titled "The New Baby Boom," the epigraph to the essay is a generous quotation from Updike's short story "When Everyone Was Pregnant." Similarly, in a *Time* article on the current mania for collecting rare books, Updike is mentioned prominently as a contemporary American author whose volumes already bring high prices.[1] Finally, *Time* featured Updike on the cover of its 18 October 1982 issue. His popular appeal is clear.

Critical attention is equally evident. The unbelievable extremes of the response to John Updike's novels will be discussed later, but several examples will illustrate the spectrum. Writing about the Updike of the early 1970s, Brendan Gill notes, "We are lucky to have the example of a life so unfaltering in the increase and deployment of its powers, and if, now and again, we miss the prankish young literary showoff . . . the loss is small next to the possession of a writer looking out upon the world with the freshness of the first time and the comprehension of the ten-thousandth and finding in it much to rejoice at, something to praise."[2] George Steiner echoes the approval: "John Updike has been an enviable problem. Gifted at once with a supremely alert ear and eye for the pulse and sinew of contemporary American speech and with a passion for the rare word, for the jewelled and baroque precisions still vital beneath and around the current of common idiom, he has been able to write about literally *anything.*"[3]

These comments are high praise indeed, but the negative evaluators are just as quick to pick up their pens. Updike's decades-long skirmish with *Commentary* will be discussed in the following pages. It is interesting to note, however, that some of the negative opinions appear in unlikely places. In Larry Woiwode's novel *Poppa John* (1981), for example, a character implicitly criticizes an author, probably Updike (or John Cheever), for being a writer of slick domestic fiction associated with the *New Yorker:* "A couple of years before this, Poppa John had read a story in *The New Yorker* by one of those Johns he could never keep straight, though it was one of the ones who wasn't Scots or Irish, about a family in a restaurant saying TV slogans to one another as they ate. . . ."[4] Perhaps even more superficial is John Gardner's attack on nearly every contemporary American novelist for not writing what he, for some reason, calls "moral" fiction. Presumably only Gardner himself and a few select others write the kinds of novels he approves of, but "John Updike worries no more about his characters and his readers than does Rabbit about his women. . . . The novels, properly understood, may be too much like sermons."[5] Reading such comments, one assumes that Gardner believes himself to be the only critic capable of "properly" understanding Updike's work.

Updike does not agree with Gardner, and neither do I. Responding with nice irony, Updike says that he admires anyone who can coin a phrase that becomes popular, like "objective correlative" or "moral fiction." He then defines *his* sense of fiction's morality to be "its truth, its will toward truth, from accuracy in minor factual matters to fidelity in matters of form and style to the author's intimate intuition and sense of things." Surely he is correct when he says that no two people—including authors—view experience the same way: "Any effort of individual truth-seeking and -stating of course will involve refusals . . . a refusal to heed the pious strictures and fulminating vocabulary of literary critics, however obviously intelligent and honorable, including demands to write 'moral fiction' in any sense but that I have tried to describe."[6] To accept Gardner's definition of moral fiction at the expense of his own is to compromise his personal sense of truth.

Updike insists that he is not an avid reader of such commentary, that he reads only what crosses his desk. Some reviews may anger him for a day, but the author has no choice except to return to his work. His primary obligation is to write for himself and an elusive Ideal Reader: "I try not, in my head, to satisfy reviewers or to placate Norman Podhoretz [of *Commentary*] or John Aldridge or the late Alfred Chester or any of the people who have been really out to puncture me. I think they can't be placated and that you do your readers the best service by trying to please yourself and some imaginary faceless reader who doesn't write book reviews."[7] In the perfect world, says Updike, one would not write at all because there would be no need to try to change matters or to compensate for problems, but, given the human condition, the author still has the difficulty of writing novels: "You don't know exactly what you're trying to do in a novel. You kind of try to jump at it and hope that something is there."[8]

Updike is also aware of the handful of readers who argue that he writes like an angel but has nothing to say. This censure surfaced especially in the middle 1960s and early 1970s when the call went out to authors to follow the lead of such activist artists as Norman Mailer and to write about civil rights or the moonshot or Vietnam. But, as Updike explains, to heed that suggestion would be to observe someone else's sense of truth. If ideas were his sole concern, he would not write novels: "If I had a mind to deal entirely in ideas, I suppose I wouldn't be a writer of fiction. Any writer of fiction has some appetite for the circumstantial, for the material, for the sensuous and the accidental, and so I can't think of any fiction of mine in which the germ was an idea. But once an image or a notion takes root, of course, I suppose ideas to some extent nurture it."[9]

What does interest Updike, however, are accuracy and love. Time and again in his comments about the craft of fiction he urges faithful observation and the centrality of romance. In his speech upon accepting the National Book Award for *The Centaur,* for example, he calls for a "habit of honesty" in the writer:

He must, rather athletically, instill his wrists with the refusal to write whatever is lazily assumed, or hastily perceived, or piously hoped. Fiction is a tissue of literal lies that refreshes and informs our sense of actuality. Reality is—chemically, atomically, biologically—a fabric of microscopic accuracies. Language approximates phenomena through a series of hesitations and qualifications; I miss, in much contemporary writing, this sense of self-qualification, the kind of timid reverence toward what exists that Cézanne shows when he grapples for the shape and shade of a fruit through a mist of delicate stabs.[10]

This commitment to accuracy, to the delicate stab through a mist, applies also to the author's concern with love.[11] Good readers and writers, says Updike, are "members of a conspiracy to preserve the secret that people *feel*." Explaining that he is not describing pulp fiction or trash, Updike cites such modern masterworks as *Remembrance of Things Past*, *Lolita*, and *Ulysses* as supreme examples of groundbreaking fictions that are also about love: "Perhaps the reason Stephen Dedalus is slightly tedious . . . is that he is not in love. Not to be in love, the capital N novel whispers to capital W western man, is to be dying."[12]

Many of Updike's characters—Harry Angstrom, Piet Hanema, Jerry Conant—suffer from the same concern, from the fear that falling out of love means plummeting toward death. For all their selfishness, their crises are real. Creativity is one way to hold off the void, as his characters know, and for Updike himself every new novel is a renewal: "Every novel is a departure for me; I find I have no firm conception of what a 'novel' is, and every one is in a sense an experiment. For every novel I have published, by the way, there exists one, or a fraction of one, that I have scrapped."[13] Part of his sense of life as he writes comes from the pleasure of creation, from the conviction that the artist brings something into the world that was not present before and that does not destroy something else in its making: "That still seems to me its central magic, its core of joy."[14] For this reason he is conscious of his achievement, and he has all his books and their translations arranged in chronological order. But though he admits to being "canon-minded," he knows that "you can't keep tasting them. That is, you do have to move on and try to do the best you can with each, and then more or less forget it."[15]

Yet for all the success, for all the variety of a sustained career, Updike wonders if his writing gets lost in the current proliferation of published material. He knows that "some writing at least has a chance of getting through," but he suspects that sensitive readers are inundated with more reading matter than they can manage.[16] He may be correct. One key to being read amid the glut is observing the unspoken agreement between reader and author: "But any reader who picks up a work of fiction enters into a contract whereby he purchases with credulity satisfactions of adventure and resolution that his lived life denies him."[17] In other words, fiction engages the imagination, but the reader must be prepared in the complex business of ambiguity and metaphor. Those who are not ready fall a little farther behind in an increasingly sophisticated world. Although Updike is on record as charging the school systems for failing to teach people how to read, he does not fear for the written word: Reading "is elitist. The alphabet is a code, and large numbers of people, either through lack of opportunity or ability cannot decipher it. It is less accessible than oratory, or music, or cinematic imagery. In this country, *Publisher's Weekly* estimates, only five percent of the population ever buy a book. The written word, nevertheless, is not easily dispensed with, and those without it are disadvantaged in all but the remotest corners of our shrinking world."[18]

From the dozens of other equally pertinent comments in Updike's essays and speeches about reading and writing, I have selected a few additional examples that suggest the range of his interests. Many of his observations have the memorable pungency of proverbs and may in due time assume an authority commensurate with that accorded the pronouncements by our great nineteenth-century novelists:

For a book to be great in a reader's life it is not enough for the book to be great; the reader must be ready.
    (*"Remembrance of Things Past* Remembered")

Fiction must recommend itself or remain unrecommended.
    (Foreword to *Olinger Stories*)

Not counting journalists and suppliers of scripts to the media, hardly a hundred American men and women earn their living by writing.
    ("Why Write?")

*To remain interested*—of American novelists, only Henry James continued in old age to advance his art.
    ("Why Write?")

What we want from fiction, and what fiction is increasingly loath to give us, is vicarious experience.
    ("Bombs Made Out of Leftovers")

The contemporary attempts to shake off the heavy spell of realism, however seemingly formless and irresponsible, are a worthy phase of man's attempt to educate himself through literature.
    ("Honest Horn")

The bourgeois novel is inherently erotic.
    ("If at First You Do Succeed, Try, Try Again")[19]

I have isolated these quotations not to fabricate an aesthetic theory but to illustrate some concerns. As my comments on *Bech: A Book* show, Updike is not given to pontification about the state of fiction. Unlike his contemporary John Gardner, he does not attempt to preach to other novelists about how to write.

Yet he does care just as fervently about his art, and he has not hesitated to comment on his own books in interviews and conversations. These opinions will be noted in the chapters that follow, for it is always instructive to know how an author views his own writing. Still, I agree with D. H. Lawrence's admonition to trust the art and not the artist, and thus I use Updike's comments as a context rather than as a guide. Similarly, the critical reception of a novel is instructive, especially when the author is as prolific as Updike. For this reason I have discussed the appropriate reviews and essays as they indicate the response to Updike's fiction for the past twenty-five years. From everybody's bright young man to watch, to the celebrated established author to evaluate, Updike has received almost as many critical blows as he has plaudits. Examining the range of the criticism, I am astonished not only by the extremes of the opinion but also by the intensity of the tone. Few commentators take Updike's achievement lightly. Whether it be panning him for his ideas or praising him for his style, the reaction to Updike's novels reverberates with strong convictions forcefully expressed.

The focus of this study, however, is not the critical judgment or the authorial commentary but the novels themselves. I have grouped the novels to suggest the broad outlines of Updike's interests, and I have avoided the temptation to impose a thesis or a biographical interpretation. Still, certain concerns are evident in this close examination of Updike's fiction, and the reader may want to keep them in mind as loosely-defined boundaries within which the development of my study takes place. Needless to say, the theology of Karl Barth and the notion of belief versus busyness are always at issue in Updike's books and have been well documented by other critics whose ideas will be duly noted. When appropriate I discuss Barth, belief, and busyness. Similarly, adultery is a major concern. Updike's couples swap beds; it is not news to say so. Yet the impulses behind the swapping are important, and for this reason I have touched on the relationships between adultery and fiction, transgression and art.

I have also found the stately ghost of Nathaniel Hawthorne hovering in the background of Updike's work. Influence is not an issue, but the connections between these two authors are of interest when one is discussing certain of Updike's novels. The same may be said for the relationships among Hawthorne, Updike, and the troubling term "Romance." Not to be confused with the Romantic literary movement or with the concept of romance as love, the Romance as a specialized branch of the novel was first argued in American literature by Hawthorne and William Gilmore Simms. Since Updike has pointedly used the term to define one of his novels, I have investigated several theories of Romance as they suggest an approach to some of his work. An offshoot of the problem of defining fiction is the intransigence of language itself, clearly a fascinating notion for any writer. The fascination attracts Updike. Like many of his more experimental contemporaries, he occasionally creates fictional characters engaged in the business of creating fiction. They, as well as he, find that language is always the stumbling block. A final concern that the reader may look for is the overview of the Rabbit saga. Rabbit Angstrom is always close to Updike's imagination, even when he is not mentioned in a specific novel. Happily for me, Updike published the third Rabbit novel as I was beginning this study and thus indirectly granted the opportunity for a comprehensive look at one of the most important characters in all American literature.

As I wrote in *The Other John Updike*, I should much prefer to meet Updike—and Rabbit Angstrom—for a round of golf, a sport that I find as spiritually satisfying and as physically maddening as he shows it to be in his fiction and essays. Like Updike, I too wonder if there is "life after golf." In lieu of that opportunity, I have written this study. The primary concern of *John Updike's Novels* is not what he should write but what he does.

## NOTES

1. "The New Baby Boom," *Time*, 22 February 1982, p. 52; "The Clothbound Collectibles," *Time*, 26 April 1982, p. 83.
2. Brendan Gill, "A Special Case," *New Yorker*, 8 January 1972, p. 84.
3. George Steiner, "Scarlet Letters," *New Yorker*, 10 March 1975, p. 116.
4. Larry Woiwode, *Poppa John* (New York: Farrar, Straus, and Giroux, 1981), p. 125.
5. John Gardner, *On Moral Fiction* (New York: Basic Books, 1978), p. 99.
6. "A Writer's Forum on Moral Fiction," *Fiction International*, no. 12 (1980), pp. 21-22.
7. Richard Burgin, "A Conversation with John Updike," *John Updike Newsletter*, nos. 10 and 11 (Spring and Summer 1979), p. 8.
8. Burgin, pp. 4, 11.
9. Burgin, p. 7.
10. John Updike, "Accuracy," *Picked-Up Pieces* (New York: Knopf, 1975), p. 17.
11. For a discussion of Updike's commitment to mimesis in fiction see my *The Other John Updike: Poems/Short Stories/Prose/Play* (Athens, Ohio: Ohio University Press, 1981), pp. 229-239.
12. John Updike, "The Future of the Novel," *Picked-Up Pieces*, p. 20.
13. Lewis Nichols, "Talk With John Updike," New York *Times Book Review*, 7 April 1968, p. 34.

14. Charles Thomas Samuels, "The Art of Fiction XLIII: John Updike," *Paris Review,* 12 (Winter 1968), p. 117.
15. Burgin, pp. 9-10.
16. Burgin, pp. 10-11.
17. John Updike, "On Such a Beautiful Green Little Planet," *New Yorker,* 5 April 1982, p. 197.
18. Donald Sanders, "Author Charges U. S. Schools Fail to Educate," Columbia (S.C.) *State,* 9 December 1976, p. 16-C.
19. "Honest Horn" may be found in John Updike, *Assorted Prose* (New York: Knopf, 1965); the Foreword to *Olinger Stories* is in John Updike, *Olinger Stories* (New York: Vintage, 1964); the rest of the essays are in *Picked-Up Pieces.*

# CREATED LANDSCAPES

*The Poorhouse Fair* (1959)

*The Coup* (1978)

# The Poorhouse Fair

*"There is no goodness, with-*
*out belief. There is nothing but*
*busy-ness."*

—*The Poorhouse Fair*

*The Poorhouse Fair* (1959), John Updike's first novel, is his second book, following *The Carpentered Hen and Other Tame Creatures* (poems) by one year and published in the same year as *The Same Door* (short stories). His astonishing success in several genres was evident at the beginning of his career, but it is fair to say, despite the general excellence and even superiority of his short stories, poems, and essays, that Updike's high reputation rests on his novels. The appearance of each fiction after *The Poorhouse Fair* has usually been an occasion for spirited disagreement and substantial sales. The publication of a novel by John Updike is an event.

Yet in recent years that event has also become an invitation to "assess" Updike or to "place" him, as if an author of more than two dozen books had to be ranked and filed away despite being only in mid-career. Instead of reading to appreciate, many critics read to worry. The reason may be that while Updike is generally accorded the stature of a major author in command of an exquisite style, he is not, like Melville with *Moby-Dick*, Hawthorne with *The Scarlet Letter*, Twain with *Huckleberry Finn*, or Fitzgerald with *The Great Gatsby*, known as the author of one particular novel that towers above most on the shelves housing the canon of American fiction. Thus while J. A. Ward could say in 1962 that *The Poorhouse Fair* is Updike's most successful book, others today might nominate *Rabbit, Run* (1960), or *Of the Farm* (1965), or *The Music School* (1966), or *The Coup* (1978).[1] It seems to me, however, that not a single stunning success but the exceptional quality of a long career sustained for dozens of books should be the final measure of his achievement.

That achievement in fiction begins with *The Poorhouse Fair*, a first novel that illustrates the bones of contention motivating many of his supporters and detractors to take sharply defined stands: the scintillating style, the figurative language that consciously calls attention to itself, the lavish care expended to tell the tales not of heroic men but of little people living little lives, and the general concerns with either nostalgia for the small-town, rural past or delineation of the small-town, urban present. The embarrassments of middle-class individuals, usually momentary but always painful, trigger the conflicts in Updike's novels.

As early as 1961, following the publication of his second novel *Rabbit, Run* in 1960, commentators were attempting to summarize Updike's career. A typical generalization is the following by Evelyn Geller, who also describes *The Poorhouse Fair*: "Despite the cleverness of his verse and the possibly overcivilized restraint of his fiction, Updike avoids a simply facile sophistication through his acute awareness of the dislocations of modern life and his religious sensitivity. . . . It is the aged, living close to death, freed from the urgency of the flesh and the debasement of economic pursuits, who have an ultimate concern."[2] One can already detect in these sympathetic comments the tendency to separate style and content when discussing Updike, a tendency that develops, as the Updike canon grows, into the clichés that either he writes like an angel but has nothing to say or he has plenty to say but ruins the prose with an overly ornate style.

Most of the reviews of and comments about *The Poorhouse Fair* are laudatory, but it is disturbing to note that even at this early date some observers were already attacking his work with the relish usually reserved for an established writer who may have slipped a peg or two. In 1959 Updike had not even scaled the middle pegs of fame. Yet, unlike most authors with a first novel just published, he had a growing reputation because of his short stories in the *New Yorker,* and he was thus considered fair game for perennial detractors. Norman Podhoretz is one such perennial. Only readers conversant with the past twenty-five years of Updike criticism are aware of the negative stance consistently taken by *Commentary* in general and Podhoretz in particular. In the case of *Commentary,* the attacks on Updike are nearly always linked with criticism of the *New Yorker. Commentary's* review of *The Poorhouse Fair* is a case in point.

Norman Podhoretz, an editor of *Commentary,* did not write this notice, but the reviewer David Fitelson successfully mimics Podhoretz's tone: "The failure of *The Poorhouse Fair* lies largely in its adherence to established *New Yorker* convention regarded in many quarters as rather OK." Fitelson does not mind the urbanity of Updike's prose, but he does resent what he calls "that *New Yorker*-like critical remoteness." In other words, Fitelson wants Updike to resolve the conflict in *The Poorhouse Fair* despite the author's effort to suggest that resolution is unwarranted: "the conflict between Conner and the inmates is neither continued nor resolved. It is just neglected. . . . It is a sign of an inability to deal—beyond a certain point—with ideas and the problems that ideas create."[3] Podhoretz saves his own attack for *The Reporter,* but his review revels in the same preachy arrogance that characterizes his—and other—comments about Updike in *Commentary.* Going for a knockout, Podhoretz uses such phrases as "utter failure" and offers advice about what Updike will have to do if he plans to become a "good novelist." He despairs of Updike's joyful use of language, branding it an "excessive Mandarin elegance," and he recommends that the novelist stop avoiding process to admire pattern: "The last thing Mr. Updike wants anyone to do is get exercised over anything. . . . but if he is ever to become a good novelist he will have to give up his easy Olympian superiority and take the risk of defining a stand. Such a step would undoubtedly ruffle the phenomenal composure of his prose style, but it might also provide him with the means of perceiving the *process*. . . ."[4] Reading such comments, one wonders if Fitelson and Podhoretz compared notes and adjusted poses before advising Updike on the nuances of making it.

Later attacks by Podhoretz and *Commentary* correspondingly increase in vehemence as Updike's reputation grows. An author has little opportunity to respond in kind to such ill-tempered notices, but when Updike does react he has the grace to do so with wit. A good example is his creation of a relationship between *Commentary* and his imaginary character Henry Bech. In *Bech: A Book* (1970), Updike includes a bogus appendix of articles about Henry Bech's books and attributes one of them to Norman Podhoretz with the revealing title, "Bech's Noble Novel: A Case Study in the Pathology of Criticism."[5] A year later he conducted an imaginary interview between Bech and himself during which, in what has become a well-known dismissal of reviewers, he wonders about the way "all the little congruences and arabesques you prepared with such anticipatory pleasure are gobbled up as if by pigs at a pastry cart."[6] Readers familiar with Podhoretz's campaign against Updike will notice the witty retaliation with the help of Henry Bech. Updike explains: "to be candid, the bibliography was also a matter of scoring off various grudges, a way of purging my system. I've never been warmly treated by the *Commentary* crowd—insofar as it is a crowd—and so I made Bech its darling. Norman Podhoretz has always gone out of his way to slam me, and this is my way of having some fun with him."[7]

Updike's fun is consistently laced with wit. Sentences shine, memory is recalled, and the reader responds to the affirmation of technique that balances the often despairing theme. Hook's meditation in *The Poorhouse Fair* may not revise Conner's blueprints, but the old man is still hopeful, still grateful at the end. As Updike observes, one goal in his first novel was not to take a stand about the problems of old age in the bureaucracies of the great society but "to write well, in a way I hadn't written before, making syntax and punctuation my own, rather than have them, to an extent, manipulate *me*."[8] The other goal was to honor his grandfather and thus indirectly to comment on the changes in American society between then and now:

I was home in Pennsylvania in March of 1957, having completed a 600-page novel which I had just decided not to rewrite, but to chalk up to practice. . . . At the end of the street where I had lived in Shillington, there had been an enormous poorhouse, complete with farmland, pigstys, etc., which was being torn down to make way for a lot of little houses. I suddenly wished to write a memorial to it, a book about America changing. I had lived with two grandparents while growing up, and I had no fear of writing about old people. . . . I was trying to say something about what I felt the condition of America was in 1957. I was personifying, and in a way purging, some personal emotions of my own. I was trying to make an oblique monument to my grandfather; who in the guise of Hook I wished to treat with a tenderness I had never shown the old man himself.[9]

Yet even with these generous comments about the genesis of *The Poorhouse Fair* in hand, the reader must not make the opposite mistake of Podhoretz (who demands that Updike take a stand) and read the novel as autobiographical revelation. Calling *The Poorhouse Fair* "an anti-novel," Updike insists on the primacy of the fiction, reiterating that "my life is, in a sense, trash, my life is only that of which the residue is my writing. . . . I tried not to force my sense of life as many-layered and ambiguous, while keeping in mind some sense of transaction, of a bargain struck, between me and the ideal reader."[10] The reader who accepts the bargain will approach his novels not as pontification but as meditation, not polemic but poetry, not directives about ideas but reactions to textures and things.

Some reviewers of *The Poorhouse Fair* do just that. Richard Gilman, for example, lauds the urbane style, noting that the novel relies more on language than thought: "Updike sees and hears before he judges or constructs; his prose aims at the immaculate immediacy of things perceived and at the freshest rhythms of intuited life. . . . This supple, most accurate prose is also capable of delights beyond itself—knowledge, insight, the restitution of truth displayed by sentiment."[11] Guerin La Course recognizes that the quest for love and the threat of time are central themes in Updike, but he wonders if his method, his tendency to "harvest" the responses of the heart in lieu of a "more embracing vision," is at once a staple and a shortcoming of his genius.[12] Leigh Buchanan says "no"; the language *is* the genius, especially in such a novel as *The Poorhouse Fair* where Updike's concerns are not those of Aldous Huxley or George Orwell in making a statement of social prophecy despite the novel's setting in the future, or in speculating, as Podhoretz would have it, about the fate of the current generation. Complex imagery is more important than complex action; language more important than debate. The fate of heroes is not at issue, but the predicaments of little people are. As Buchanan notes, "the reader is continually stopping to admire the clarity of [the novel's] conception. . . ."[13]

The point is that even at this early moment in Updike's career he was judged a writer's writer, a phrase which, if it means anything, means an author who lavishes so much care on his prose that its very intensity approaches poetry. A writer's writer writes for an educated audience blessed with an initiated eye. Whitney Balliett has such an eye. Titling his essay-review of *The Poorhouse Fair* "Writer's Writer," Balliett praises the novel as "a kind of poetic vision, tied loosely to earth only by its outward form of narrative prose." He worries about the cost of such exquisite prose to the emotional center of the book, but he correctly notes that Updike's recall of the vital past in conflict with the bureaucratic future does not degenerate to sentimentality because "it is continually ringed by a feeling of dread that is never allowed out of the reader's mind."[14] Indeed it isn't. That feeling of dread, indicated by the caged parakeet, the mangled cat, and the crashing storm, underlies Updike's unhappy sense of the nation. *The Poorhouse Fair* ends with an unanswered question and with the suggestion that if an answer is forthcoming, which seems unlikely, painful but unintentional wounds could be healed. Unfortunately, the pain will probably remain intact behind the bedroom wall.

That sense of hurt and loss, of time lived through without lessons learned, animates Updike's short stories and novels. Exquisite prose does not mean empty ideas, nor does being a writer's writer imply that the writer has nothing to say. Readers who support Updike's fiction see the complexities at work beneath the gorgeous surfaces. In a commentary that counters Podhoretz's, Donald Barr notes that the truth of *The Poorhouse Fair* resides not in any one character or idea or narrative stance but in the clashes among them: "No one is morally annihilated in this brilliant book. No one is a mere convenience of argument. Here is the conflict of real ideas; of real personalities; here is a work of intellectual imagination and great charity."[15] As these comments illustrate, Updike criticism runs to opposing extremes.[16]

Another concern of those who first noticed *The Poorhouse Fair* is the structure of the novel. Short and sustained, a series of scenes and details of dialogue rather than a complex of actions with panorama or scope, *The Poorhouse Fair* seemed strange to many readers in 1959. Even as seasoned a critic as Granville Hicks called it "deliberately and even self-consciously offbeat . . . often hard to follow."[17] For those weaned on the intricacies of James Joyce and William Faulkner and reared in the post-1959 world on the difficulties of Thomas Pynchon and John Hawkes, Hicks's opinion itself seems strange. How, one wonders, can a novel that reads so easily and delights so readily be considered hard to follow? Yet recall that Updike himself describes *The Poorhouse Fair* as an "anti-novel" and that he suggests its association with the "cool surface of some contemporary French novels."[18]

Neither he nor Hicks elaborates, but the point may be reader expectation of what constitutes a novel. Peter Salmon, for example, apparently believes that *The Poorhouse Fair* should have been a collection of sketches: "That they do not cohere into what we ordinarily think of as a novel is probably attributable less to the author's ability than to the publisher's insistence upon the novel form."[19] It seems unlikely that the publisher's insistence had anything to do with the structure. The key word in the previous quotation is "ordinarily," for it exposes the reviewer as the kind of reader who expects the venerable staples of developed character, recognizable setting, and resolved plot when he picks up a novel. Variations on the tradition are consequently viewed with suspicion. Even more disturbing is Bryant Wyatt's charge that the focus of *The Poorhouse Fair* is "capricious," that Updike's psychological concerns in his novels lack structure. Inadvertently revealing his preference for conventional fiction, Wyatt is uneasy with novels that alter the traditional limits of the genre. He claims that the want of "a proper focus" leads to a "structural undoing," and he urges Updike to center his attention on one of three themes: family, time and death, or identity.[20] Evaluating such statements, one can only judge them questionable and ask the critic to reconsider in light of not what the reader expects but what the author offers. John Updike offers a great deal.

The dust jacket commentary for the first edition, first printing of *The Poorhouse Fair* echoes with Updike's own prose rhythms and wit, and it points to some of the concerns of his first novel:

Animals haunt the landscape, and inanimate objects—a sandstone wall, a row of horse-chestnut trees, a pile of pebbles—strain wordlessly toward the humans, who act out their quarrels of tradition versus progress, benevolence versus pride, on a ground riddled with omens and overborne by a massive, variable sky.

One sees the emphasis on inanimate objects, from pebbles to sky, and notes how their wordless straining toward the humans is so much gentler than the quarrels that animate the world of men. This sense of a silent plenty has been a highpoint of the Updike canon since the beginning, and it is nowhere better explained than in the foreword to *Olinger Stories* (1964), where Updike recalls a boyhood impression of being surrounded by "an incoherent generosity." The connection between the following passage from the foreword to *Olinger Stories* and the jacket commentary for *The Poorhouse Fair* is clear:

. . . a quiet but tireless goodness that things at rest, like a brick wall or a small stone, seem to affirm. A wordless reassurance these things are pressing to give. An hallucination? To transcribe middleness with all its grits, bumps, and anonymities, in its fullness of satisfaction and mystery: is it possible or, in view of the suffering that violently colors the periphery and that at all moments threatens to move into the center, worth doing? Possibly not; but the horse-chestnut trees, the telephone poles, the porches, the green hedges recede to a calm point that in my subjective geography is still the center of the world.[21]

The stability of the past, suggested by the permanence of trees and stones, remains, because of memory expressed in art, the still point of Updike's present. It is also the still point for the inmates of the poorhouse, old folks who, like Updike, use their handiwork, their quilts and pincushions, to express their sense of constancy and grace. This wordless plenty contrasts with the human "quarrels of tradition versus progress, benevolence versus pride" in *The Poorhouse Fair* and suggests a small but significant loss as the modern world lurches noisily toward plastic perfection. As Updike explains elsewhere, "I describe things not because their muteness mocks our subjectivity but because they seem to be masks for God."[22]

Although Updike may not be responsible for the jacket material for his first novel, he did comment on the Dick Cavett Show (15 December 1978) that he often wrote the blurbs for the dust wrappers of his books. If he did write the jacket material for the first edition of *The Poorhouse Fair*, he foresaw the complaints from some reviewers about his untraditional technique: "While *The Poorhouse Fair*, insofar as it regrets the decline of patriotism, handcraft, and religion, carries a conservative message, its technique is unorthodox; without much regard for fictional conventions, the author attempts to locate, in the ambiguous area between farce and melodrama, reality's own tone." Technique is thus part of theme, for the contrast of unorthodox technique expressing conservative message illustrates the clashes in the novel between silent things and noisy humans, long tradition and questionable progress, and, most of all, meaningful individualism and muddling bureaucracy.

Updike grins while simultaneously acknowledging the special favor that many authors grant their first novels. In 1977, nearly twenty years after the publication of *The Poorhouse Fair*, Knopf reissued the novel in a sixth printing that contains a previously unpublished fourteen-page introduction by Updike. Once again the jacket commentary rings with his wit, for he smiles and offers an in-joke in the guise of the ever-helpful Henry Bech: "Though the future has degenerated into our present, and Updike's later work is better known, such critics as Henry Bech have hailed this little novel as, still, 'surely his masterpiece.' "

Mr. Bech is not, however, the author of the 1977 introduction which, although written long after the 1959 first edition and thus offering the fresh perspective that memory creates, is valuable for its account of the genesis of Henry Bech's favorite novel on the Updike shelf. Despite the shadows and turns that the expanse of two decades inevitably brings to a recollection in the present of an event in the past, Updike maintains in the introduction the insistent contrast between now and then that enlivens *The Poorhouse Fair*. Staring at the "parabolic and luminous splendor continuously and coolly on fire" that the skyline of East Cambridge, Massachusetts, presents him with one night in 1977, he recalls a moment twenty years earlier when he stood by a wall in Shillington, Pennsylvania, his birthplace, and "looked down at the razed acres where for all of my boyhood the poorhouse had been."[23]

The destruction of the poorhouse, ironically memorialized by a hole in the ground, spurred him to write what he calls "a futuristic novel" to commemorate the fair that he had attended there as a child. A description of the way the poorhouse looms in his memory may be found in his autobiographical essay "The Dogwood Tree: A Boyhood":

At the end of our street there was the County Home—an immense yellow poorhouse, set among . . . orchards and lawns, surrounded by a sandstone wall that was low enough on one side for a child to climb easily, but that on the other side offered a drop of twenty or thirty feet, enough to kill you if you fell. Why this should have been, why the poorhouse grounds should have been so deeply recessed on the Philadelphia Avenue side, puzzles me now. . . . But at the time it seemed perfectly natural, a dreadful pit of space congruent with the pit of time into which the old people . . . had been plunged by some mystery that would never touch me. That I too would come to their condition was as unbelievable as that I would really fall and break my neck.[24]

The contrast between the fate of the old people in the poorhouse and the assurance of the young boy at the edge of time did not last, Updike recalls, when he turned from the future of old age to the futuristic novels of H. G. Wells, George Orwell, and Aldous Huxley. Reading *The Time Machine* at age thirteen, he realized that while he might not break his neck in a fall from the poorhouse wall, he would nevertheless one day die. The tomorrow of the poorhouse and the future of science fiction merged.

Written as "a deliberate anti-*Nineteen Eighty-Four*" with a "political ambiance" that avoids Orwell's "dire absolutism," *The Poorhouse Fair* offers a vision of the future that Updike describes as showing how "in our mundane reality it is others that die, while an attenuated silly sort of life bubbles decadently on" (x, xi). The poorhouse administrator Conner, whom Updike calls a cousin, "perhaps," of Orwell's O'Brien, is not the feared bogeyman of *Nineteen Eighty-Four*. But he is a man of the near future, a man who believes in comfort and passivity rather than eccentricity and life, and thus he represented to the Updike of the late 1950s the American bureaucrat of the late 1970s.

Yet if Updike's portrait of the government do-gooder successfully caricatures today's government meddler, some of the dating in the first edition, first printing of *The Poorhouse Fair* is not so accurate insofar as Updike's intentions are concerned. As he explains in the 1977 introduction, for example, he wanted the time of *The Poorhouse Fair* to fall short of 1984, but he made a mistake in the first printing when he associated John Hook's graduation from normal school with President Taft's administration (1909–1913). Since Hook is ninety-four years old, the time of the novel would have to be around 1984. Realizing the potential confusion, and still hoping to avoid the reverberations surrounding the date made memorable by Orwell, Updike changed the presidential references from Taft to the first Roosevelt (1901–1909) when Modern Library published an edition of *The Poorhouse Fair* in 1965.[25] A similar change was made in a comment about the anniversary of the St. Lawrence Seaway which was opened in 1959 (x–xi). With both alterations Updike nudged the time of *The Poorhouse Fair* back from the allusions to 1984 that the first edition, first printing inadvertently encourages, and toward the middle 1970s that the 1965 edition and the 1977 printing make clear.

Although the 1977 introduction is Updike's most thorough commentary on *The Poorhouse Fair,* his brief foreword to the 1965 Modern Library edition clarifies an anachronism that he let stand in all editions:

*The Poorhouse Fair* was written in 1957 and was supposed to take place twenty years hence—that is, in 1977. I meant the future it portrays to be less a predictive blueprint than a caricature of contemporary decadence. Though I expected that some details would be rendered obsolete, I did not imagine that Hook's rhetorical question . . ., "Isn't it significant, now, that of the three presidents assassinated, all were Re-publican?" might abruptly become impossible. I have let it stand, as a vivid anachronism.[26]

But such anachronisms as well as the absence of references to computers, drugs, Vietnam, and television—strange perhaps for a novel set in the 1970s—are not important to a careful reading of *The Poorhouse Fair.* As Updike points out, his primary interest was not a "predictive blueprint" of the future but a caricature of the present. Visions of tomorrow are invariably streamlined models of today; drugs and computers were not prominent in the 1950s. One concern, then, was not to rival the predictions of Wells, Huxley, and Orwell, but to create a poetic rendering of current foibles: "It is such a future, an unpredictable one wreathed in mists as of nostalgia, a fuzzy old-fashioned non-future of a future, that I tried to render in this novel, imitating not the science-fiction classics mentioned above but the obscure poetic *Concluding,* by Henry Green" (xiv).

Rereading the novel after twenty years in order to write the 1977 introduction, and noting the borrowings from Green and Wells, Updike calls attention to the affirmation that many commentators miss in their preoccupations with the dead end that the old people face in the guise of dreariness or death. Not the finality of dead ends but the motions of life shape the novel. What Updike calls his "philosophical ambition" at work in *The Poorhouse Fair* is "an attempt, no less, to present the meaning of being alive, as conveyed by its sensations. Our eager innate life, rebounding from the exterior world, affirms itself, and the quality of affirmation is taken to be extrinsic, immanent, divine. I needed God to exist" (xvi–xvii). Yet balancing this desire for an extrinsic confirmation of intrinsic needs is a realization that life itself is flux, that "nothing lastingly matters" (xix). Examining his first novel from the perspective of middle age, Updike recognizes that the lack of certainty shaped by a sense of ceaseless loss came more naturally than affirmation to the youthful author of *The Poorhouse Fair*. Even old Hook, for all his lively self-knowledge, feels, when praying, that his mind is swamped by an "infinitely thick blanket." The claustrophobia of the mind reflects the claustrophobia of the poorhouse which, in turn, mirrors the claustrophobia of the universe.

Updike concludes his extraordinary introduction with an admission that is also a lament—that he could not write *The Poorhouse Fair* now but "will respect the man who could." What he calls the "innocently bold eclecticism" of his youth rouses his envy today, but the demands of newer days call for different visions, other views: "The future is now; it is as if, standing by that poorhouse wall, I threw myself down, into the pit of time, and, my neck unbroken, find myself here" (xx).

Where he finds himself in terms of his fiction is the Diamond County Home for the aged in northern New Jersey, an imaginary institution that he creates to investigate the future by glancing back over his shoulder at the past. Having grown up with grandparents in the house, he is aware of the uncertainties that punctuate the lives of old people, of how stairs give them trouble and obituaries give them news. The uncertainty suggested by the epigraph from Luke 23:31—"If they do this when the wood is green, what will happen when the wood is dry"—pinpoints the menace of the future that lingers in time to threaten all men, especially those cast loose from once useful lives to find dubious harbor in a home for the aged. Updike establishes on the opening page the tension between anonymous authority and pride of individuality as he invites the reader immediately into the conflict: Someone has placed name tags on the old folks' porch chairs and thus denied them a sense of choice. The time is the middle 1970s; the welfare state that Updike glimpsed in the middle 1950s is in second gear; and the old people, holdovers from the first three quarters of the century, are out of place. Time, says the state, has passed them by.

The irony, of course, is that the wood is not yet totally dry. Perhaps dry at the extremities and now surely brittle, most of the old people still show green at the core. During the course of one day, the span of *The Poorhouse Fair*, they protest the name tags, drink a bottle of whiskey, import a mangled cat, and stone the prefect—hardly acts of dried-up old fogies. But their protests do not alter the general situation, and they know it. They are in a strange land.

That sense of strangeness is indicated not by time machines and big brother but by how they view their world. Northern New Jersey is a real place, but Updike describes it in such a way as to make it seem created: "Despite the low orange sun, still wet from its dawning, crescents of mist like the webs of tent caterpillars adhered in the crotches of the hills."[27] Similarly, Lucas' view of the operating room recalls the mad surgeons of science-fiction novels:

Even more than black death he dreaded the gaudy gate: the mask of sweet red rubber, the violet overhead lights, the rattling ride through washed corridors, the steaming, breathing, percolating apparatus, basins of pink sterilizer, the firm straps binding every limb, the sacred pure garb of the surgeons, their eyes alone showing, the cute knives and angled scissors, the beat of your own heart pounding through the burnished machinery, the green color of the surgeon's enormous compassionate eyes. . . . (31)

The description continues further; one might be reading *The Island of Doctor Moreau*. Even the clouds seem other-worldly: "Upon the terraces of these ranged clouds blackish embryos of cumulus stood on their tails like sea horses or centaurs performing" (165). This aura of strangeness occasionally affects young Conner, the prefect who believes in a future society with each in its ordered place: "He hated beds; they were damp and possessive, and when he lay down, words, divorced from their objects, floated back and forth, like phosphorescent invertebrates swaying in the wash of the sea" (49). Updike's sentences shine; they are rhythmical, imaginative, and clear. More important, all the glitter, what negative critics mean when they say that language may be more significant than thought, supports theme. Words appearing like phosphorescent invertebrates and clouds like performing centaurs dance along the borders of Updike's futuristic poorhouse. One-eyed monsters and little green men are not needed.

These clouds and mists and surgical instruments are what Updike has in mind when he comments in the dust-jacket copy how "inanimate objects . . . strain wordlessly toward the humans. . . ." The world is "riddled with omens," all watched over by a "variable" sky that promises rain. Men of the future like the humanist Conner ignore the straining, the omens, but Updike keeps us in touch with the progress of this eventful day by periodically describing the approach and growth of the impending storm. As the day of the poorhouse fair moves from dawn to dusk, the squall glimmers in the eastern sky, crashes down during midday, and sweeps away in the late afternoon. Evening finds the poorhouse grounds crowded with people gathered to enjoy the delights of gossip and quilts.

The threat of rain is everywhere in the first pages as the omen of weather joins the name tags of authority to upset the serenity that the old people need to plan the fair. But name tags from meddling do-gooders are one thing, rain clouds in a variable sky another. The clouds are a mask for God and thus, unlike the tags, are accepted by the inmates as an undesirable but understandable part of the natural cycle. Conner, the man who has lost "all sense of omen," the man who feels "not a shred of awe," stands before a window and witnesses but does not respond to "an appearance of the phenomenon which two millenia before had convinced the poet Horace that gods do exist: thunder from a clear sky" (14, 66). Old, blind, and lovely Elizabeth Heinemann never feels alone when it rains, but Conner faces the rain as his enemy (76). He is a good but incomplete man. The old men do their jobs as if the chores were their sole tasks "for all the time remaining in God's scheme," but Conner sees only fumbling inmates somehow completing their work (24).

Three of the old fumblers are wonderfully alive: Lucas, Gregg, and John Hook. They are distinct personalities whom the narrator generalizes as "the man of flesh, the man of passion, the man of thought" (184). We learn a great deal about them, but some of Updike's critics want more. Recall the negative commentators who are suspicious of a novel that does not adhere to the venerable traditions of rounded character and resolved plot. Fiction that stretches the limits strains their responses. Apparently desiring cradle to grave coverage of the "I am born" school, these readers are uneasy when Updike purposely writes his "anti-novel" and peoples it with characters who enter the tale in old age. Yet if Updike withholds information expected by some, he supplies details admired by others.

We know little about their earlier lives: Lucas has a grown daughter, Gregg is a former electrician, and Hook is a retired schoolteacher who has outlived his wife and children. The point is that their earlier lives do not matter, but their reactions to the uncertainties of fair day do. An innocent source of information for Conner, Lucas is young by the standards of the Diamond County Home. The narrator describes him as a man who knows land but displeases people, and Hook is unsure of his association with him because Lucas seems "preoccupied still with the strings of the outer world" and thus holds himself "aloof from the generality of inmates" (9). But Lucas is not about to waste away despite his interest in those strings. Described as a man of flesh, he deliberately irritates his ear with a wooden match to keep an earache alive. Pain means response, and response means life, but significantly Conner fails to understand. As a believer in the future of welfare states and regimented comfort, he cannot accept Lucas' intuitive association of irregularities and life: " 'Good God, you'll give yourself otomyeosis.' Conner hated, more than anything, pain dumbly endured. Oppression, superstition, misery—all sank their roots in meekness" (20). As the day progresses, however, Lucas, Hook, and Gregg are far from meek.

Gregg, the "man of passion" with foul mouth and mercurial temper, responds to Conner's insulting name tags with the action of the skilled laborer he once was. Reaching to the hip pocket of his shapeless trousers, he pulls out a "black bone jackknife of the old style, with a blade for removing the metal cap from bottles" and begins to loosen the nameplates (4). Gregg's reaction is immediate; he wants nothing to do with Conner's efforts to place the old people. Perhaps a more important point is that his facility with hand-wielded tools develops into a general metaphor that suggests the skilled handicraft of the past versus the plastic molds of the future. Reading such a sympathetic characterization, one might think that Updike sentimentalizes the inmates and caricatures the prefect. Such is not the case. For all of his will to action, Gregg is largely impotent. Lucas correctly says that Gregg lives in a "boy's irresponsible world," and Hook, in a mixture of distaste and affection, describes him as a difficult, unruly student (81). Perhaps the most telling comment comes from the narrator, who calls Gregg a "coward in the face of blunt hostility" (81). He huffs and puffs and uses his mouth but finally accomplishes little. Updike does not romanticize his oldsters, not even John Hook.

If there is one character in *The Poorhouse Fair* who is largely sympathetic, it is Hook, the ninety-four-year-old former schoolteacher, but he is by no means a spokesman for Updike or the norm on whom the "message" of the novel hangs. Updike's refusal to provide such a spokesman or norm angers readers like Podhoretz, who demand that he abandon his "easy Olympian superiority" and take a stand. These readers want solutions whereas Updike presents problems. A gentle irony is that the seventy-year-old Gregg looks up to the ancient Hook as a kind of wise leader, but Hook, though thoughtful, does not have all the explanations. Indeed, his final response to the day's trials is a question that remains forever unanswered.

His life now "empty of material purpose," Hook sees himself as an arbiter among the several factions that snipe at each other on fair day (47). Charitable to a fault, he responds to the inanimate world with love, unshrinkingly musing on the relationship between an endless past and a future that holds only death. He knows that he has apparently "lived without end" (37). But his greatest strength is his sense of awe, his sensitivity to nature's omens, his awareness of rivers and trees. The rain is

Conner's enemy, but to Hook it is a sign of God. Yet Hook's musings are often incommunicable beyond the formalities of debate in which he dearly loves to participate. His wisdom, such as it is, does not translate into action. As the narrator tells us early, "It was Hook's misfortune to have the appearance of authority yet lack the gift of command" (4). Updike's description of him in the 1977 introduction, written twenty years after the character was created, emphasizes Hook's innocence in a life that requires more: "Like a child he is in love with the world and hopes that the world loves him. He is alert for clues, though blind to patterns" (xvi). His clues come from nature or heaven, but his praying never promises results: "His mind seemed a point within an infinitely thick blanket" (39). The blanket gets thicker as life lasts longer, and for Hook it has lasted a long time.

Still, Hook's understanding that Conner's mania for order masks a need for security puts him one step ahead of the other inmates. Frankly jealous of Hook's stature in the poorhouse, Conner fails to understand that though the old man's authority is negligible, his humanity is not. A mixture of grace and flaws, not a formula for security and stasis, permits an examined life. Hook leads such a life. Even a discussion of something as mundane as the weather reveals their differences: The young prefect believes the radio prediction for fair and cooler weather while the old man sees rain in all the signs.

Conner is by no means a bad person, a straw man set up merely to personify the faults of the welfare state. He is genuinely concerned with the condition of the inmates as a group, and he is described, perhaps not without some irony, as "devout in the service of humanity" (14). But this is just the point; he elevates humanity over humans, mass over man. Dedicated to what he terms the "social cause," and trained for the bureaucracies of the state, he thinks in terms of results, forgetting the foibles of process. Updike poses no solutions in the 1950s to what has become a dilemma in the 1970s: Do we leave the indigent and old to their own devices and thus guarantee their individuality, or do we attempt to provide their needs and thus reduce them to name tags? Conner wants to fulfill needs, but nothing better illustrates his inability to accept flaws in the system, resistance from the inmates, than his ludicrous reaction to the threat of rain:

The weather of this one day would be, he felt, a judgment on his work; these people, having yielded all authority, looked beyond themselves for everything—sufficient food, adequate shelter, and fair weather on their one day of profit and celebration. He would be blamed, and strangely felt prepared to accept the blame, for foul skies. (41)

In the perfect society, even the weather should be subject to directives from career men and bureaus. Believing impartiality a virtue, Conner is embarrassed when he is cordial.

How, then, is he to adjust to the eccentricities of men like Gregg and Hook if his primary concerns are sufficient food and adequate shelter? Poorly; and at odd moments he realizes that his basic goodness is not enough. Convinced that the skies are "blank" where Hook glimpses omens; and dedicated to his "dynamic vision: that of Man living healthy and unafraid," Conner yearns for a chance to prove his worth: ". . . he envied the first rationalists their martyrdoms and the first reformers their dragons of reaction and selfishness" (65). Taking care of the aged and the ignorant is a social good, a duty that he performs willingly and well, but receipt of an anonymous, illiterate letter criticizing his efforts ruffles his composure: "When would they all die and let the human day dawn?" (78). With no desire to be loved, he longs for a useful rather than a pleasant life.

Although *The Poorhouse Fair* is free of the rise, fall, and resolution of action that characterize the traditional novel, it does satisfy our desire for a confrontation of words between Conner and Hook. Updike places their discussion in the center of the novel, showing the prefect's embarrassment at entering a room where Hook, Amelia Mortis, and a group of inmates wait out the rain by debating Lincoln's motives for freeing the slaves. Conner believes that his decision to meet them sociably is courageous, an odd gesture on a "dislocated" day, but he inadvertently becomes a comic dupe, trying to light a fire by using for kindling a copy of *Sweet Charity,* which he officially practices but innately lacks. When he finally joins the group for a discussion about the reality of heaven, we understand that Updike has carefully foreshadowed the debate with the earlier descriptions of Hook's sense of wonder and Conner's lack of awe.

Readers must not make the mistake of ganging up on Conner as if he were an insensitive brute. The inmates' views of heaven are, after all, remarkably childlike: Bessie Jamiesson believes she will be beautiful there; Amy Mortis hopes to lose her goiter; Elizabeth Heinemann thinks she will see; and Hook longs to meet his dead children. Such eccentric innocence has its joys. By contrast, Conner's definition of heaven is mundane, even common. Careful not to make fun of their dreams, he describes a bureaucratic heaven on earth. With no sense of mystery, no touch of awe, he lacks sympathy with the flaws and scratches that are the signposts of individuality. To him, evil is merely pain, as his bafflement with Lucas' earache shows, and he misses the connection between ethical concerns and human vitality: "There will be no disease. There will be no oppression, political or economic, because the administration of power will be in the hands of those who have no hunger for power, but who are, rather, dedicated to the cause of all humanity" (106). One might as well add that there will be no more poorhouse fairs. Who needs the rough delicacies of handmade quilts when state administrators give out mass-produced blankets? In such a heaven there may also be no Hooks.

That, suggests the novel, would be a shame. To Conner's argument that virtue is a worthless abstraction when suffering exists, Hook replies like the believer he is, insisting that "suffering provides the opportunity for [virtue's] exercise" (109). More important, Hook defines virtue not only as "obedience to the commands of God" but also in terms of the skilled handiwork he admires: "Virtue is a solid thing, as firm and workable as wood. . . . Now in my own life . . . looking back I perceive a mar-vel-ous fitting together of right and wrong, like the joints the old-time carpenters used to make, before everything was manufactured metal and plastic" (110–111). Inevitably the debate turns to the reality of God, yet the point here is not Conner's lack of belief but his insistence that emptiness is the chief characteristic of the universe, which, if it was made, was "made by an idiot, and an idiot crueler than Nero. There are no laws. Atoms and animals alike do only what they can't help doing" (113). Hook's rejoinder, however naive, is the emotional center of the novel: "When you get to be my age—and I shall pray that you never do, I wish it on no one, but if you do—you shall know this: There is no goodness, without belief. There is nothing but busy-ness" (116). Hearing Hook, one wants to cheer. But one also realizes that innocence and belief will not feed old people who live in poorhouses and like to hold annual fairs in August.

The debate between Hook and Conner is an impressive achievement for an author who was only twenty-five when he wrote it. Avoiding the pitfall of letting the discussion slip into tract, Updike anchors the exchange in humanity by matching the ideas expressed with the tones, gestures, and expressions of the debaters. The novel does not bog down here; it leaps forward toward not resolution but an unanswered question that separates past and future: How can the two men communicate opposed ideas of goodness?

Perhaps they can't, but largely because of this scene *The Poorhouse Fair* has sparked analyses of Updike's religious themes. Alfred Klausler, for example, argues that Updike's fiction reveals faith kin to Pauline despair: "He willingly attempts to dramatize the conflict which Unamuno portrays in *The Tragic Sense of Life:* the presence of religion, an objective impossibility, and the absence of religion, subjectively impossible." Similarly, Kenneth Hamilton, a critic who insists on finding religious messages in all of Updike, calls *The Poorhouse Fair* a parable about "what it means to live in the time of the death of God." Such a reading, however, hints that the novel is not imaginative fiction but religious tract. To date, Bernard Schopen has written the soundest analysis of the relationship between religion and Updike's fiction because he understands that the faith discussed in the novels "is one to which many of the assumptions about the

Christian perspective do not apply—especially those which link Christian faith with an absolute and divinely ordered morality."[28] Not sweetness and light but the theology of Karl Barth shapes the nuances of religion in Updike's fiction, especially the tenet that God is unknowable and that, thus, not God's existence but *belief* in God's existence is the first question. As Updike says, "I believe that all problems are basically insoluable and that faith is a leap out of total despair."[29]

Conner's mistake may be his failure to understand that all human leaps can be futile. This point is a key to *The Poorhouse Fair,* for Updike's emphasis is finally not on Hook's Christian vision but on his individuality as a man. Updike has said that his novels are meant to be "moral debates with the reader."[30] If this is so, then we see that there is no resolution to the debate about morality itself, as Hook's final query shows. This stance frustrates some of Updike's critics who mistakenly judge his refusal to pose solutions as a paucity of ideas. We may like Hook's definition of goodness more than Conner's, but neither man is wholly right. If *The Poorhouse Fair* says anything about faith, it suggests that not moral certainty but moral ambiguity surrounds us.

The man who may best embody the status of flawed but saintly human is not Hook but Mendelssohn, the fondly remembered dead prefect. We learn little about him beyond the recollections of the inmates, and thus evaluations of him are always tinted by the oldsters' tendency to compare him to Conner, whom they distrust. True to the processes of memory and general charity toward the dead, Mendelssohn's errors—his drinking, his neglect of fire escapes, his insufficient medical facilities—are pushed aside when remembrance reconstructs his days at the poorhouse. But Conner does not forget these oversights. He remembers, and he remembers especially well whenever he needs to impress the inmates with the progress of his administration: "Half the county home acres were lying fallow, waste. The outbuildings were crammed with refuse and filth. The west wing was a death trap. When Hook, last autumn, ate that unwashed peach, he would have died if Mendelssohn had still been in charge" (17). But Mendelssohn is not still in charge, and the old folks miss him. It is not that Conner's evaluation is mistaken. It is correct in each instance, but Conner ignores the point.

The point is that Mendelssohn may have been careless with his duties and habits, but he was sympathetic with his gestures and words. He was a good human being. He cared, and caring for his charges on a personal level, he did more for their welfare than the practicalities of fire escapes and medical facilities can provide. For Mendelssohn had a natural faith in life itself. He somehow understood intuitively that embarrassing insufficiencies, be they drinking or goiters or Hook's tendency to hold forth, are part of the definition of being human. The narrator explains early in the novel: "Mendelssohn had in part thought of himself as God. Conner thought of no one as God" (14). It is not that Mendelssohn is right and Conner mistaken but that the dead prefect reacted as a man. He encouraged the inmates' handiwork, he felt their quilts, he sang with them in the rain. As Amy Mortis tells Hook, "You know them when you come across them, rare as that is," and in Mendelssohn they know they had a winner (29).

Unfair to Conner but true to their frustrations, the inmates insist that rain never fell on fair day during Mendelssohn's tenure. Yet the significance of past weather reports is not that the dead administrator had a special magic with rain clouds and storms but that had it rained, as it does on their current fair day, he would have had them singing hymns and shouting while reminding them that all men die. He cried because he cared:

As the songs grew more religious the rims of Mendelssohn's eyes grew redder, and he was dabbing at his cheeks with the huge handkerchief he always carried and was saying, in the splendid calm voice that carried to the farthest corner and to the dullest ear, how here they all lived close to death, which cast a shadow over even their gaiety, and for him to hear them sing was an experience in which joy and grief were so mixed laughter and tears battled for control of his face; here they lived with Death at their sides. . . . (80)

One need only add that Conner never sings and that he hides death away in the west wing. Their memories of the flawed prefect, with his drinking and his bald head—and with his neglect of fire escapes and fields—is part of their faith in heaven.

One of Updike's general concerns is not to exonerate Mendelssohn or excoriate Conner but to flesh out the contrast between past and future. *The Poorhouse Fair* is not a futuristic novel in the sense that *The Time Machine* and *1984* are, but it is set twenty years ahead of the time of its composition and thus it offers a critique of disturbing trends in the present. For this reason Hook's age versus Conner's youth is not just a counterpoint in human terms but also a general metaphor for the goods that the different ages produce. From the perspective of the 1950s, when Updike wrote the novel, American products in the 1970s looked as if they might be shoddy. From the perspective of today, we know they are.

Updike appreciates cross beams and handmade joints and quilts.[31] He cares about craftsmanship and tools and skill. He looks for solidity, for permanence, for sheer lastingness. To him a skilled worker is an artist, and an artist is someone who creates. What happens, he muses, if the craftsmanship of the past becomes the bureaucratic mold of the future? How is one to deal with the quagmires of moral ambiguity and faith if man's work is planned for obsolescence? Hook may not understand the complexities of the dilemma, but Updike does. Yet Hook knows that skill is giving way to plastic: "Modern day workmen are not what they were . . . there are no workmen now as there were in my day. The carpenters of fifty years ago could drive a stout nail as long as my finger in three strokes. The joints that they would fit: pegs and wedges cut out of the end of a beam to the fineness of a hair, and not split the wood though they were right with the grain" (5, 10–11). To Lucas' remark that everything is plastic, Hook responds that today the only chore is to pour the plastic in a mold and watch it harden.

The problem is that plastic products do not help one learn how to read a sundial or evaluate carpentry or sense rain. Pride in workmanship is no longer an issue in a society the major concern of which is to provide food and shelter for those who need: "To let a man choose idleness or labor, on the ground of whim: why in Mendlessohn's time such a thing would never be seen" (24). The irony is that Conner's world considers the old people junk, but only they can still carve little baskets out of peachstones. Nowhere is the art of the past better contrasted with the junk of the present than in the prefect's office.

Beautifully constructed and lovingly made, the office, seventy years earlier, had been a piano room. The piano is still there because the artisans who shaped the room built it around the piano, hoisting it up and placing it when the room was still unfinished: "the system of supports and joints above had been left free, diagonal rafters and slender crossbeams where music could entwine, and the musicians grouped around the piano below could play on and on, feeding the growing cloud above without having their noise press out from the walls and crowd them" (21). Such a room cries for soloists or carpenters, but we know that Conner is not that person. Converted now to an office, the music room caters to "a kind of comfort not proper to executive and clerical work," but the youthful prefect misses the cues (22). He is too worried about arranging the tables which the inmates cannot set up in a straight line. Although his intentions are good, his vision is faulty—with his need for order, he would probably cover the ceiling in the piano room if given the chance. The holiness that Hook finds in carpentry is reflected in rag quilts and carved peachstones, skills of the past which reveal by contrast the sterile plastic of the future. As Amy Mortis tells Conner, "You expect us to give up the old ways, and make this place a little copy of the world outside, the way it's going" (43). Neither Hook nor Amy—nor Updike—likes the direction.

Updike supplies two symbols to illustrate the dilemma facing old people in poorhouses and administrators who provide for them: the mangled cat, which is shot, and the escaped parakeet, which is caged. Lame and grotesque and barely able to walk, the injured cat is, in Hook's words, "hopelessly out of order" (46). We recall the future world's need for arrangement and system, and we compare the disabled cat with the eccentric inmates. Updike's symbol is appropriate if only because Gregg calls attention to the parallel between the mangled animal and Conner's mistaken belief that the old people are helpless. Although Conner honestly protests against hurting the cat, he just as honestly believes that the humane policy is to put it out of its misery. He orders it shot, apparently a standard solution in the world of the future, for Ted, the young truck driver who crashes through the poorhouse wall, says that he would rather be shot than be old.

It is not that Conner resents the cat; indeed, he feels nothing but sorrow for the animal itself. But he resents what it stands for: dirt that needs purging for the world to be clean. There is no more revealing description of his idealism and its unintentional threat to the old folks than his following meditation on the cat:

Conner had no regrets about ordering the animal killed. He wanted things *clean;* the world needed renewal, and this was a time of history when there were no cleansing wars or sweeping purges, when reform was slow, and decayed things were allowed to stand and rot themselves away. It was a vegetable world. Its theory was organic: perhaps old institutions in their dying could make fertile the chemical earth. So the gunshot ringing out, though a discord, pleased the rebel in Conner, the idealist, anxious to make space for the crystalline erections that in his heart he felt certain would arise, once his old people were gone. (64)

One cannot help noting his easy transition from disabled cat to unpredictable inmates. The shooting of the cat, the smashing of the wall, and the crashing of the thunder occur almost simultaneously as if wrinkles and snags purposely foul Conner's order.

Lucas' parakeet plays a similar role. Mrs. Lucas' daughter has gotten rid of the bird just as she has dumped her mother; both end up in the poorhouse. The caged parakeet, with no room to turn around and thus in need of freedom to stretch, parallels the inmates on fair day when they talk, move, and set up as many irregular lines of tables as they wish. Lucas tracks down the escaped bird in the hospital wing, but before he returns Updike gives us the great scene where the parakeet and Lucas are described by an invalid in a medicine-induced stupor as if they were a leaping flower and a growling bear. Some critics do not like this scene, just as they disapprove of a similar scene with a bluejay in Updike's story "Leaves" (*The Music School,* 1966), because they judge it an example of his facile linguistic skills. They miss the point. Updike supplies no transition between Lucas' pursuit of the parakeet and the sick man's marvelous vision, and for a moment the reader is as startled as any invalid who suddenly finds a bird and a strange man in his room. The scene is only one paragraph long, concise, poetic, and surrealistic. But in it Updike suggests the other-worldly quality of life in the poorhouse that such outsiders as Conner and Ted cannot fathom. To us the scene is stunning in conception but natural in description: The invalid responds as in a dream. To the outsiders, however, the scene, had they witnessed it, is fantastic in conception and ludicrous in description: The invalid responds as if merely senile. The parakeet as metaphor is no more unusual than blind Elizabeth Heinemann describing the sounds of silent things like walls, descriptions that Conner cannot accept and thus can attribute only to hallucination. Updike knows, however, that hallucination has nothing to do with sensitive responses to nonhuman otherness. One is reminded again of the words on the dust jacket which note that inanimate things strain wordlessly toward humanity. The drugged invalid, Elizabeth Heinemann, and Updike all listen. Updike's descriptions of the cat and parakeet are set pieces that call attention to themselves, but they are not obtrusive given the form of the novel. Vignettes, descriptive paragraphs, and snatches of dialogue make up the rest of the novel and flesh in the details surrounding the cat, the parakeet, and Hook's debate with Conner. All the pieces are held together by the unity of one day, and everything that happens on that day points toward the fair.

Despite the rain, the hired band appears in shiny uniforms glittering like seraphim, and with their appearance it seems as if life is set in motion again following a slowdown for storms, cats, and arguments about heaven: "It was as if the world had been holding its breath while Hook and Conner debated its condition, and now resumed bumping onward" (121). We already hear the oompah, oompah of a Sousa march. Even Conner feels the joy of working with his hands as he leads the men in clearing away the rubble from the wrecked wall now that the rain has stopped.

But this sense of renewal is momentarily dulled by the extraordinary stoning of Conner as the inmates briefly rebel against his vision of an ordered future that has no patience with their kind of behavior. The rainy day has to sink to its nadir before the joy of the fair can begin. The stoning is unjust, the rocks are harmless, and Conner forgives them all, but the prefect is no Christ figure despite the inviting association. Not Conner but Hook has the intimation of rebirth as the young people stream through the gates toward the bustle of the annual fair: "His forebodings lifted at the sight of their gay-making clothes, the round limbs of the children, the young women holding their bodies so upright. It seemed a resurrection of his students, and he sensed that he would never leave them, never be abandoned by this parade" (144). This is the parade he has been marching in all his life, and he loves it—children and women, the future of America.

The fair revives urban America's need for hand-worked goods that savor of an older nation. Updike understands that trivets, samplers, buttonhooks, and rag quilts cannot keep up with a world of automobiles and plastics, but he also knows that, like the hand-fitted joints in the piano room, these items will outlast the time of the people who buy them. Not profit but pride is the primary motive in their making. Old Mrs. Mortis does not want to sell all her quilts to the antique dealer because a quick sale would deprive her of conversation with the fair-goers. Conner's assistant Buddy says that the people come to see the freaks, but the narrator knows who the real freaks are: "Heart had gone out of these people; health was the principal thing about the faces of the Americans that came crowding through the broken wall to the poorhouse fair. They were just people. . . . History had passed on beyond them . . . the conception 'America' had died in their skulls" (158–59). Updike is by no means apocalyptic in his account of the fair, but he does cause one to wonder how what he terms a nation of pleasure-seekers can ever have the heart of John Hook or the grace of Elizabeth Heinemann. His America of the 1970s has lost touch with its flawed but human past in its rush for a perfect yet boring future.

Nothing better suggests the banality of the fair-goers than their conversations. As if he were strolling among them with notebook in hand, Updike lets us hear snatches of gossip, tidbits of talk. Concerned with sex and rumor and candy, their lives seem trivial compared to those of the inmates. We eavesdrop on them, but they expose themselves. They might as well be walking through the vanity fairs of Bunyan and Thackeray. After listening to Hook and the others discuss virtue, God, ethics, and life, one can only shudder when these people see carved peachstones as merely curios and gossip as communication. Vaguely alarming stars shine down on them all: "Above, the stars were not specks but needles of light suspended point downward in a black depth of stiff jelly" (184). We recall Hook's sense of claustrophobia when praying.

Yet for a while the peace of the fair works its magic. Dusk falls, and the children go home, and the people who remain are a bit more affectionate as their gossip turns to "the past they had in common" (184). But the final note of the novel is ambiguity. The line between peachstones and plastics is too far to go. Waking in the night, Hook gropes after "the fitful shadow of the advice he must impart to Conner, as a bond between them and a testament to endure his dying in the world. What was it?" (185). The novel ends with this unanswered question, and one nods in agreement at the gloss Updike wrote twenty years later: "The poorhouse is fair, I wanted to say, against my suspicions that it is, our universe, a poor house for us" (xix). Hook's dying, when it occurs, will not be a tragedy but it will be a loss. Permanence is not a condition of this world. The days always turn toward tomorrow, but the promise of the future brings a dismissal of the past. Both Hook and Updike wonder how to communicate the vitality of what has been. Never raising his voice in his first novel, Updike glances back over his shoulder to create a vision of what will be.

## NOTES

1. J. A. Ward, "John Updike's Fiction," *Critique*, 5(Spring-Summer 1962), p. 32.
2. Evelyn Geller, "John Updike," *Wilson Library Bulletin*, 36(September 1961), p. 67.
3. David Fitelson, "Conflict Unresolved," *Commentary*, 6 December 1959, pp. 275-276.
4. Norman Podhoretz, "Novels: Style and Substance," *The Reporter*, 22 January 1959, pp. 42-44.
5. John Updike, *Bech: A Book* (New York: Knopf, 1970), p. 205.
6. John Updike, "Bech Meets Me," *Picked-Up Pieces* (New York: Knopf, 1975), p. 12.
7. Frank Gado, "Interview with John Updike," *First Person: Conversations on Writers and Writing* (Schenectady, New York: Union College Press, 1973), p. 105.
8. Judith Serebnick, "New Creative Writers," *Library Journal*, 1 February 1959, p. 499.
9. Serebnick, "New Creative Writers," p. 499.
10. Charles Thomas Samuels, "The Art of Fiction XLIII: John Updike," *Paris Review*, 12(Winter 1968), pp. 97, 116, 117.
11. Richard Gilman, "A Last Assertion of Personal Being," *Commonweal*, 6 February 1959, p. 500.
12. Guerin La Course, "The Innocence of John Updike," *Commonweal*, 8 February 1963, pp. 512-514.
13. Leigh M. Buchanan, review of *The Poorhouse Fair*, *Epoch*, 9(Spring 1959), pp. 252-254.
14. Whitney Balliett, "Writer's Writer," *New Yorker*, 7 February 1959, pp. 138-140.
15. Donald Barr, "A Stone's Throw Apart," New York *Times Book Review*, 11 January 1959, p. 4. See also Mary Ellen Chase, "John Updike's Wise, Moving First Novel," New York *Herald Tribune Book Review*, 11 January 1959, p. 3. Updike calls Chase's review one of "extraordinary enthusiasm and warmth." See John Updike, "Introduction," *The Poorhouse Fair* (New York: Knopf, 1977), p. xix.
16. The British notices are understandably brief since at the time of publication of *The Poorhouse Fair*, Updike did not have a wide reputation in the United Kingdom. Pamela Hansford Johnson does not like the novel, calling it "too whimsical, too much of a stunt. It is too earnest an attempt to get away from the great American terror of the Familiar." This judgment seems curious since Updike is generally celebrated for his perception of the familiar. By contrast the unsigned review in the London *Times Literary Supplement* describes *The Poorhouse Fair* as "a first novel of assurance and achievement: truthful, perceptive and coloured by a spirit of sad, unillusioned comedy, perfectly in keeping with the subject of old age." See Pamela Hansford Johnson, review of *The Poorhouse Fair*, *New Statesman*, 28 March 1959, p. 453; and "Ways of the World," London *Times Literary Suplement*, 20 March 1959, p. 157.

17. Granville Hicks, "Novels in Limbo," *Saturday Review,* 17 January 1959, p. 58.
18. Charles Thomas Samuels, "The Art of Fiction XLIII: John Updike," p. 116.
19. Peter Salmon, "A Slice of Life," *New Republic,* 12 January 1959, p. 20. See also Fanny Butcher, "1st Novel Talented, Tho Haphazard," Chicago *Tribune,* 11 January 1959, p. 4.
20. Bryant N. Wyatt, "John Updike: The Psychological Novel in Search of Structure," *Twentieth Century Literature,* 13(1967), pp. 89- 96.
21. John Updike, Foreword, *Olinger Stories* (New York: Vintage, 1964), p. vii.
22. Charles Thomas Samuels, "The Art of Fiction XLIII: John Updike," p. 116.
23. John Updike, Introduction, *The Poorhouse Fair* (New York: Knopf, 1977), pp. vii, viii. Further references to this introduction will be noted in the text.
24. John Updike, "The Dogwood Tree: A Boyhood," first published in Martin Levin, ed. *Five Boyhoods* (Garden City: Doubleday, 1962) before being collected in John Updike, *Assorted Prose* (New York: Knopf, 1965). This quotation comes from *Assorted Prose,* p. 156.
25. While not complicated, the publishing history of *The Poorhouse Fair* is mentioned here to clarify why I shall be quoting from the 1977 first edition, sixth printing instead of from the 1959 first edition, first printing. There are three significant states of the novel: *The Poorhouse Fair* (New York: Knopf, 1959); *The Poorhouse Fair/Rabbit, Run* (New York: Modern Library, 1965); *The Poorhouse Fair* (New York: Knopf, 1977). For the 1965 Modern Library edition, the fourth edition of the novel, Updike altered the historical references to President Taft and the St. Lawrence Seaway that were in the 1959 first edition. In the 1977 sixth printing, the pagination is the same as the 1959 first edition but different from the 1965 Modern Library fourth edition. For the sixth printing which contains the introduction discussed in this chapter, Updike retained the adjustments in the historical references, liberalized a few of Gregg's profanities that were partly disguised in the earlier printings, regularized the name of the young boy who attends the poorhouse fair, and cleared up some lingering typographical errors. The 1977 printing thus represents the author's latest intention and is more readily available than the 1959 and 1965 editions, both of which are out of print. Readers with access to only the 1959 edition may note these relatively minor changes in some of the quotations I shall use in this chapter, all of which come from the 1977 printing.
26. John Updike, Foreword, *The Poorhouse Fair/Rabbit, Run* (New York: Modern Library, 1965), no pages.
27. John Updike, *The Poorhouse Fair* (New York: Knopf, 1977), p. 6. Further references will be noted in the text.
28. See Alfred P. Klausler, "Steel Wilderness," *The Christian Century,* 22 February 1961, pp. 245-246; Kenneth Hamilton, "John Updike: Chronicles of 'the Time of the Death of God,' " *The Christian Century,* 7 June 1967, pp. 745-748; Bernard A. Schopen, "Faith, Morality, and the Novels of John Updike," *Twentieth Century Literature* 24(Winter 1978), pp. 523-535. For a negative evaluation, see the essay by Richard H. Rupp (who is no friend of Updike's fiction), "John Updike: Style in Search of a Center," *Sewanee Review,* 75(Autumn 1967), pp. 693-709.
29. Jane Howard, "Can a Nice Novelist Finish First?," *Life,* 4 November 1966, p. 80.

30. Eric Rhode, "Grabbing Dilemmas: John Updike Talks About God, Love, and the American Identity," *Vogue*, 1 February 1971, p. 184.
31. For another fiction on the subject of craftsmanship, see "Plumbing" in John Updike, *Museums and Women* (New York: Knopf, 1972).

# The Coup

> "All the languages they used,
> therefore, felt to them as clum-
> sy masks their thoughts must
> put on."
>
> —The Coup

Nearly everyone agrees that *The Poorhouse Fair* is an unusual first novel. How, admiring readers asked in 1959, can an author so young write about people so old? With the dash and assurance of an experienced novelist, Updike reversed the normal procedure of first purging himself with a story of youth and initiation and offered instead a tale of age and belief. *The Poorhouse Fair* is an extraordinary debut.

Just as unexpected as the subject matter was Updike's decision to set his first novel in the near future. Many beginning authors write to find out where they are, but Updike took a guess at where we will be. His guess was uncannily accurate. From the safety of hindsight, it is easy to lament the degeneration of handcraft to plastic, belief to busyness; for shoddiness was not so pervasive in the late 1950s when he wrote the novel. Even more difficult than the forecasting was the necessity of visualizing a world for the people at the poorhouse fair. Representing a landscape is more conservative than creating one because the author may rely on the touchstone of familiarity to keep his readers aware of the setting. *The Poorhouse Fair* is not a conservative novel, just as Updike is not always a traditional novelist. Yet to manipulate the conventions of conservative storytelling is not to insist on the excesses of experimental technique. A writer does not have to resort to pyrotechnical displays of narrative energy to illustrate his delight in innovation. One of the triumphs of *The Poorhouse Fair* is that Updike sets his tale in the strange future and yet keeps his readers in touch with the familiar present. The created landscape seems oddly representational. Such is also the case with *The Coup* (1978), his most surprising novel to date.

The mythical future of the poorhouse gives way to the manufactured country of Kush, but in both cases Updike has gone beyond looking around him to imagining the idiosyncrasies of his created worlds. The result in *The Coup* is a sophisticated comedy of language and disguise. Ask the literate reader to define the normal concerns of Updike's novels, and he is likely to suggest suburbia, adultery, and the crises of middle age. He will be correct. Rabbit Angstrom may not be welcome at the cocktail parties in Tarbox, but he can sympathize with the long-legged wives and the intrigues there. Conversely, Colonel Ellelloû suffers enough grief from his wives and mistresses to understand the pathos and absurdities of both Rabbit and Tarbox, but his tale is not one of suburbia. Middle-class comfort and available lovers may be at the periphery of his problems, but the mystical integrity of Kush occupies the center. The point is that *The Coup* is a change of pace in the Updike canon.

Most commentators recognized the shift in locale and emphasis, and Joyce Carol Oates noticed it better than anyone else. In an essay that praises the novel while indicating its intricacies, she calls *The Coup* "a lengthy monologue that really *is* a coup of sorts, constituting Updike's most experimental novel to date."[1] Oates understands that *The Coup* is as different as *The Poorhouse Fair,* and she correctly insists that while Updike pays homage to Vladimir Nabokov with a virtuoso command of style and voice, he does so without Nabokov's "self-referential props": ". . . the prose Updike has fashioned for [Ellelloû] is even more difficult and resembles nothing so much as an arabesque superimposed upon another arabesque. Motifs, phrases, 'imagery,' coarsely comic details from the 'external world,' Ellelloû's various and conflicting pasts, are rigorously interwoven into complex designs."

As might be expected, not everyone agrees, especially *Commentary*. It makes no difference whether Updike publishes in the late 1950s or the late 1970s; *Commentary* is ready for the attack. Such foolish consistency loses its sting as the attacks drag on with the years, but followers of Updike's career usually check out the *Commentary* review to see what new bases for disparagement the editors have found this time. Pearl K. Bell's essay-review avoids the personal harangue and hysterical tone of past analyses of Updike in *Commentary*, but, of course, her evaluation is finally negative. She admits that the novel is "audacious" and that Ellelloû is a "great achievement," but she mistakenly assumes that Updike tries to write in "blackface" and thus fails to "close the gaps between his alien sensibility and the obdurate reality of Africa."[2] Such a comment ignores Ellelloû's education in America. A graduate of McCarthy College in Franchise,

Wisconsin, he is not likely to write with the metaphors and rhythms of a Kush tribesman. Even more questionable, Bell realizes that the reader should not make the common error of identifying an author's "moral attitude" with that of his characters, but she then turns around and accuses Updike of a "hackneyed caricature" of America even though the comic diatribe comes from Ellellloû: "In its scornful parody of American culture, *The Coup* is clearly a descendant, a particularly simplistic descendant, of that recurrent illusion of paradise."

Harold Hayes, Maureen Howard, Deborah McGill, and Dean Flower also worry about voice. Although most commentators praise the astonishing twists and turns of Ellelloû's sardonic memoirs and bewildered meditations on "the idea of Kush," Hayes argues that the Colonel's language "too blissfully transcends the reality of character."[3] In a word, Hayes wants realism, the kind that will teach him something about African dictators, and thus he is unhappy with Updike's imagined locale. Similarly, Howard wants Updike to write like Nabokov or Conrad, and she decides that the voice of the novel is "all Updike."[4] Deborah McGill hears not Updike in Ellelloû's rhythmical confessions but, incredibly, Jerry Conant, the hero of *Marry Me* (1976). While many readers laud Updike's discovery of Kush, McGill finds that he never leaves suburbia where absolution is unearned, guilt rarely assigned.[5] Finally, in an extremely negative commentary, Dean Flower attacks *The Coup* for lacking conscience, indulging its style, and preaching from the point of view of a narrator who sounds like "every other Updike anti-hero."[6]

One can only grant these readers their say and then reply that Ellelloû does not sound like Updike or his other characters. Surely Rabbit Angstrom cannot speak with the Colonel's rhythm or imagination; he is too busy trying not to grow old in his middle twenties. The same goes for Joey Robinson (*Of the Farm*, 1965), who may be more speculative than Rabbit but who does not come within an unabridged dictionary of Ellelloû's command of language. *The Coup* was greeted with many more cries of praise than howls of derision, as suggested by Peter Collier in, of all places, the *Book-of-the-Month Club News*: "It's not so much 'style' that distinguishes this writer as it is a whole way of seeing. He has the quality which T. S. Eliot found in the works of Andrew Marvell: 'a tough reasonableness beneath a slight lyric grace.' "[7]

To blend lyricism with the remoteness of Kush is in itself a kind of coup. As Updike says, "I've always been attracted to hidden corners." Africa was "the emptiest part of the world I could think of."[8] What is so much fun about *The Coup* is that he fills that emptiness with language. To insist on a correlation between Kush and Chad, or to demand that Updike use his African novel to teach us about African dictators, or to require representational language when the whole point of the novel is that language creates its own realities is to miss a delightful, surprisingly funny reading experience, what Robert Towers calls a "comedy of absurd cultural juxtaposition."[9] In Kush the Third World is in collision as much with itself as with the superpowers, and its leader has only oratory in reserve. While the United States sends in McDonald's and miniskirts, and the Soviets send in missiles, Ellelloû sends out metaphors with such a worried face that the reader ends up laughing. The irony is that the Colonel's concern is legitimate, for he confronts a dilemma of either pure Kush and starving Kushites or debased Kush and swinging Kushites. Another irony is that the people of Kush care nothing for purity. The "idea of Kush" has melted with the vapor and the heat, spinning away with the nomads who cross Ellelloû's path, and it may be that, however unfortunate, the people glimpse the future better than the leader. Paul Theroux has a point: "I did not attempt to give a sense of place to my fiction until I wrote about Africa; it helped me see straight. . . . Updike has done a more difficult thing. His Kush is both real and imagined. . . . More important than the Americans who will read this book are the Africans who will at least understand what it is that they have been trying to say."[10]

Unlike Theroux, I am not concerned that *The Coup* will help Africans understand themselves, but I am bothered by Americans who dismiss the novel as an inaccurate representation of the African sensibility. Such charges not only reveal the reader's avoidance of the excitement of imagination for the safety of verisimilitude but also recall the irrelevant outcry against William Styron's *The Confessions of Nat Turner* because Styron had dared to imagine a black leader's mind and to express it in the first person. The task of the novelist is to create a landscape that is true to the needs of his fiction. In this sense Kush is as much an imagined domain as it is a point of departure for Updike's satiric potshots at what John Hook in *The Poorhouse Fair* calls goodness without belief—"busy-ness." Kush is so destitute, so dispirited, so dry that it is more a state of mind than a nation, but Updike's imagination convinces us of its geography.[11] Who can resist a country that contains ancient caves decorated with a combination of primitive rock-paintings and American graffiti, especially "Happy Loves Candy," the nicknames of Ellelloû and his wife?[12]

The juxtaposition of art and graffiti is one way that cultures collide. War is not an issue in Kush. Yet everywhere Ellelloû turns, he sees both bubble gum and the Koran, hears rock music and the rites of prayer. When he confesses poetically to his wife Candy that he is about to "walk the edge of my fate, and may fall off," she responds as if from another planet: "Don't give me any of this Kismet crap. . . . I knew you when you couldn't tell the Koran from the Sears Roebuck catalogue" (120). Ellelloû is powerless before such bluntness. How can he call on the cadences of language when he knows that his listeners care nothing for words? As Alastair Reid observes, American colloquialism becomes the "language of the infidel."[13] Updike's insight into global politics suggests that not armaments but words are the keys to invasion. Reid's praise of *The Coup* captures its many facets: "Call *The Coup* a caper, an indulgence, a tract, a chronicle, a fable—and it is all these things at different times—the fact is that Updike's sentences can be read with the pleasure that poetry can, and the fingers are more than enough to count the novelists of whom such a thing can be said."[14]

His sentences come from many sources. Although Updike traveled in Africa as a Fulbright lecturer in 1973, he reveals in a page of acknowledgments that he also journeyed there with the aid of books. Along with a series of scholarly studies consulted for the occasion, he lists *National Geographic*, "children's books, *Beau Geste*, and travellers' accounts." Eclectic reading shapes the background of *The Coup*. Accounts of the 1968–1974 drought merge with thrilling tales of the Foreign Legion, and the result is a sardonic commentary on global confusion.

But Updike also used books to travel to Africa before he thought of *The Coup*. As a regular reviewer for the *New Yorker*, he has written essays about such African authors as Yambo Ouologuem, Kofi Awoonor, and Ezekiel Mphahlele. Readers who do not want to track down the separate issues of the *New Yorker* where these and other pertinent essays were published may find them collected under the catch-all title "Africa" in Updike's miscellany *Picked-Up Pieces* (1975).[15] In the essay "Shades of Black," he muses generally on the dilemma that faces Ellelloû in *The Coup*: How does a modern African handle language? Ellelloû is not sure, and while he would not deign to express himself in the pages of the *New Yorker*, he might agree with Updike's understanding of the problem:

The black African moved to literary expression confronts choices a Westerner need not make. First, he must choose his language—the European language, with its alien tradition and colonial associations, or the tribal language, with its oral tradition and minuscule reading audience. Unless his mother and father came from different tribes and used a European tongue as the lingua franca of the home, his heart first learned to listen in the tribal language, which will forever then be more pungent and nuancé; but English and French command the far broader audience, across Africa and throughout the world. So he must choose his audience: foreigners and the minority of his countrymen educated in white ways, or the majority of his fellow-tribesmen, who can be addressed chiefly through recited poetry and theatrical performance. . . . The African writer must consciously choose not only his language, audience, and tone but his reality.[16]

Language, tone, and reality—these are the stumbling blocks for the Colonel. Audience is not an issue because he writes chiefly for himself, but complexities of tone and language have always affected his wanderings through reality as he tries to juggle Islamic mysticism and Western training. A son of the tribe and a soldier for France, Ellelloû is also a student in America and the leader of Kush. No wonder his scheming assistant Ezana describes him as ruling "by mystical dissociation of sensibility" (230). Leaving the practical concerns of running the country to the treaties and plots of those who care, Ellelloû quests into the mysterious wastes of Kush in search of a mystical cause of the drought. What he finds is a parody of himself in the guise of a city crammed with the junk he has labored to keep beyond the borders. The city's name? Ellelloû.

Thus *The Coup* is more than a comic-strip tale of emerging Africa; it is an imaginative commentary on the ridiculousness of power politics, the idiocies of nationalism, and the infinite recesses of language. The difference between Updike and Ellelloû is that the former knows that language is political as well as creative, whereas the latter hopes to separate the two. The Colonel wastes his poetry on glamorous declamations that say, in effect, that America stinks or Russia smells. We know that we have picked up a comic fable about political realities when on the first page we read Ellelloû's outrageous rhetoric about the prostitution of Kushite peanut oil to make American soap: ". . . then the barrelled oil is caravanned by camelback and treacherous truck to Dakar, where it is shipped to Marseilles to become the basis of heavily perfumed and erotically contoured soaps designed not for my naturally fragrant and affectionate countrymen but for the antiseptic lavatories of America—America, that fountainhead of obscenity and glut" (3). Or, when the Volvos of "Swedish playboys'" "forfeit their seven coats of paint to the rasp of sand and the roar of their engines to the omnivorous howl of the harmattan," Ellelloû cries righteously, "Would that Allah had so disposed of all infidel intruders!" (4). But fountainheads of glut and infidel invaders cannot be kept out by rhetoric. Unfortunately for the Colonel, poetic flourishes are all he has. He apparently misses the irony that he spouts the rhetoric of revolution while prowling around Kush in a German Mercedes and worrying about his marriage to an American blond.

Ellelloû's joyous command of language is further undercut by our suspicion early in the novel that he is no longer the leader of Kush. Describing the form of government in his country as "a constitutional monarchy with the constitution suspended and the monarch deposed," he must now face the galling truth that he has also been removed (7). The first clue that a coup has replaced him is the word *here* in the following sentence: "(I am copying these facts from an old *Statesman's Year-Book*, freely, here where I sit in sight of the sea, so some of them may be obsolete)" (6). He does not tell us where "here" is, but he does imply that he is now distanced from the time of his tale.

Narrative distance is a source of irony and laughter in *The Coup*. Writing about a land where even memory "thins," Ellelloû tells his story not to defend his policies but to discover them: "In a sense the land itself is forgetful, an evaporating pan out of which all things human rise into blue invisibility" (23). The people of Kush may think that the Colonel has evaporated, but he still longs to anchor his life. What happened, he wonders. All he has left are language and the past. *The Coup,* the novel itself, will not reinstate his presidency but it will guarantee his memory. So he tells his tale to explain as much to himself as to the reader why he is a victim of a quiet revolution, and he knows that narrative distance is one way to investigate the self: "There comes a time in a man's life . . . when he thinks of himself in the third person" (269).

Although placed late in the novel, this comment is the key to Updike's narrative technique. A student of the Koran, Ellelloû understands sura 76, which Updike uses as an epigraph: "Does there not pass over man a space of time when his life is a blank?" To write his memoirs is to fill the blank, so the Colonel switches, occasionally even in mid-sentence, from third person to first person as a way of indicating both narrative distance and the dual perspective he has of his political career. Needless to say, that career baffles him: "There are two selves: the one who acts, and the 'I' who experiences. This latter is passive even in a whirlwind of the former's making, passive and guiltless and astonished. The historical performer bearing the name of Ellelloû was no less mysterious to me than to the American press. . . . Ellelloû's body and career carried me here, there, and I never knew why, but submitted" (7). The "I" may be passive before the whirlwind of the "he," but the "I" controls the tale of the "he" who acted. All the "I" wants to do now is find out why.

The point is that Ellelloû is a narrator watching his own presence in the story he is narrating. Once, for example, he interrupts the tale to explain that his manuscript is blurred in places by a wet ring from a glass of Fanta. Since he is now drinking such impurities, one wonders about his outburst against American obscenity and glut. The public mask is clearly not the private man when the "I" suffers the effects of the "he's" actions but drinks junk that the "he" would dash to the ground. Ellelloû, of course, claims that not he but Kush acts whenever he declares an outrage or defines a role, but the "I" is not so sure now. After all, Ellelloû has revolutionized a country in which there is nothing to revolutionize. With twenty-two miles of railroad, one hundred seven of paved highway, and two Boeing 727s in Air Kush, this drought-stricken land has little use at the moment for the complexities of ideology and identity. The irony is that Ellelloû prefers the emptiness. While his assistant Ezana negotiates for oil rights and capital, the Colonel fights for mysticism and purity. Money brings meddlers, and meddlers bring modernity, the very things, Ellelloû argues, the country does not need if it is to retain its sense of being Kush. Thus it is revealing when he rants against the American students of the 1960s who only played at revolution, for he knows now that he has also failed to touch the pulse of his people.

Longing to identify with Kush, to see himself as the personification of his country, he plays a series of roles with the various masks he adopts—beggar, singer, laborer—in order to travel the land anonymously: "His domicilic policy is apparently to be in no one place at any specific time" (10). But his determination to know his people by adopting their roles eventually confuses his identity and blinds him to his true relationship with his nation. He can be a tribesman or an Islamic Marxist, but he cannot be both despite his efforts to support tribal purity with revolutionary rhetoric. The closest he comes to knowing who he is occurs when he pays a poignant visit to the Salu tribe and his first wife: "For there lay no doubt, in the faces of these his relatives, that through all the disguises a shifting world forced on him he remained one of them, that nothing the world could offer Ellellou to drink, no nectar nor elixir, would compare with the love he had siphoned from their pool of common blood" (93). What a comedown from that pool of common blood to a glass of Fanta. He can drop his masks with the Salus, who call him Bini, but while he longs for their serenity, he also dreams of a Marxist paradise in an Islamic nation. The two desires paralyze him. Listening to his wife Kadongolimi point out his flaws, he has no answer to her charge that he has forsaken the gods of their fathers for revolutionary zeal: "Have you forgotten so soon? The gods gave life to every shadow, every leaf. Everywhere we looked, there was spirit. At every turn of our lives, spirit greeted us. We knew how to dance, awake or asleep. No misery could touch the music in us" (95).

Ellellou begs to believe, but he finds himself pulled between those like Kadongolimi who trust the old gods of nature and those like Ezana who worship the new gods of consumerism. Unfortunately for the Colonel, most of his people agree with Ezana. Disguised as he travels through Kush, Ellellou watches as rock and roll displaces prayer. The result, he realizes, is not religion in any form—the gods of nature or the gods of the Koran—but entropy:

. . . in the attenuation, desiccation, and death of religions the world over, a new religion is being formed in the indistinct hearts of men, a religion without a God, without prohibitions and compensatory assurances, a religion whose antipodes are motion and stasis, whose one rite is the exercise of energy, and in which exhausted forms like the quest, the vow, the expiation, and the attainment through suffering of wisdom are, emptied of content, put in the service of a pervasive expenditure whose ultimate purpose is entropy, whose immediate reward is fatigue, a blameless confusion, and sleep. (91)

Ellelloû has certainly not abandoned religious belief to the reward of fatigue, but at the end of the novel he approaches a kind of entropy: His ceaseless quests have left him motionless.

The Colonel's religious fervor is part of his faith in the "idea of Kush." It makes no difference to him that the country was once called Noire, or that it is mired in poverty, or that a plentiful horde of diseases is listed among its natural resources. What matters is his devotion to the spirit of his stumbling nation. He does not want his people to starve, but neither does he want the tentacles of American and Soviet aid to squeeze the land. Given the dilemma, he militantly chooses the former and sets out on his quest to discover a religious source of the drought. Purge the dragon and the land will thrive. But there is no dragon, just as Ellelloû is no St. George. All he can do is publicly execute old King Edumu who reminds the assembled witnesses of the contrast between the abundance during his reign and the disaster during Ellelloû's: "If their rule is just, why has the sky-god withheld rain these five years?. . . . I say Kush is a fiction, an evil dream the white man had, and that those who profess to govern her are twisted and bent double. They are in truth white men, though their faces wear black masks" (69). Edumu has a point, for he uncannily sees that Ellelloû models a repertoire of masks. Yet the old king is fighting for his life while the Colonel is struggling for his country. There is little doubt that Ellelloû loves Kush more than Edumu, but the king is cunning enough to throw in the word "fiction" as he denounces his murderer. For Ellelloû's Kush *is* a fiction; no one else has his faith in the mystical power of this wretched land. The final irony is that, for all his devotion, the drought lifts only when he is deposed in a bloodless coup.

All Ellelloû can do is apply to his memoirs the audacious rhetoric that he spouts to his countrymen. Updike, of course, is aware that the rhetorical flourishes in *The Coup* are even more elaborate than those in his earlier novels, and he seems to take a special delight in disturbing the sensibilities of readers who do not share his pleasure in the inventiveness of language. Many of the figurative touches are comic as well as lovely, as when the Colonel describes the king's nose as sitting in "the center of his face like a single tart fruit being served on an outworn platter" (12). In other cases, however, Updike offers self-parody as a way of indicating that the language as well as the landscape of *The Coup* is not rendered but created, made up, a fiction. When Ezana escapes, for example, Ellelloû writes that his assistant makes a series of "knotting, and measuring actions that like certain of these sentences were maddeningly distended by seemingly imperative refinements and elaborations in the middle" (165). Updike jokes of his conscious use of style just as he makes Ellelloû conscious of his intricate twists of narration.

For not Ellelloû but language is the hero of *The Coup,* a source of laughter as well as a means of defining the masks that condition one's perception of the world. Recall Updike's analysis of the dilemma facing African authors as they try to select language, tone, and reality, and then note Ellelloû's description of his conversation with Edumu:

They spoke in Arabic, until a more urgent tempo drove them to French. All their languages were second languages, since Wanj for the one and Salu for the other were tongues of the hut and the village council, taught by mothers and lost as the world expanded. All the languages they used, therefore, felt to them as clumsy masks their thoughts must put on. (13)

Without Wanj and Salu, Kush itself is a fiction; its author is Ellelloû.

The Colonel manipulates language the way he plays with masks, and the results are unavoidable: His constant donning and discarding of masks and rhetorical stances confuse his sense of self. He must write *The Coup* to define not only who he once was but who he now is. The pathos is that he may never know. Is he the President, the Colonel, Ellelloû, Bini, or Happy? Each name is a word, and each word is a mask, and the "I" is not sure what to make of them. When he tries and fails to communicate the reality of the suffering in Kush and the "cosmic refusal" to prevent it, he is terrified at being stranded without the protection of a role: "Held mute in a moment without a pose, a mask, Ellelloû felt the terror of responsibility and looked about him for someone with whom to share it" (14). But there is no one to share it because no one shares his understanding of Kush. Even the people do not know who he is.

One of Updike's ironies is that Ellelloû's command of language does nothing to change his status as little more than a myth in his own country. Some Kushites have never heard of him, some believe he is a slogan, and some hate him for being a freed slave, but no one looks to him to end the drought or lift the famine. Updike's comic touch shapes the narrator's response to his quandary: "Only I expected this of Colonel Ellelloû . . ." (32). But the passive "I" is only the recorder of the active "he's" wanderings. The narrative distance between them is as unbridgeable as the gap between Ellelloû and the people he does not know.

The highpoint of Updike's suggestion that not arms but language is the weapon of power politics occurs when Ellelloû confronts Gibbs, the American do-gooder, before an audience of hungry Kushites. The scene is a set piece of exaggeration, an inspired blowup of two little men sparring with words in front of a mountain of American junk food. Battle lines are drawn, stances assumed, and a war of colloquialisms begins. Gibbs's hip jargon seems insulting before Ellelloû's rhythmical cadences: "Who're you trying to kid? . . . These cats are *starving*. The whole world knows it, you can see 'em starve on the six o'clock news every night. The American people want to help" (39). Offering tons of dry cereal and powdered milk, the very foods Kush does not need since it has no water, Gibbs personifies America's mindless need to be loved. When Ellelloû points out that America's program of cattle vaccination increased herds that in turn exhausted Kush's limited forage, all Gibbs can reply is that he has read about it in a report: "O.K., O.K.—better late than never. We're here now, and what's the hang-up?"

But while Ellelloû's outrage is justified and his anger at American meddling confirmed, he also resorts to catch-phrases and clichés: "The people of Kush reject capitalist intervention in all its guises. . . . Offer your own blacks freedom before you pile boxes of carcinogenic trash on the holy soil of Kush!" (40). We laugh at his rhetoric even as we understand his fury. Here are two men from different countries who realize that the people of Kush are starving, but while they speak the same language, neither can cross the frontier of words to pose an acceptable solution. Updike then adds another twist to this comic scene when he shows Ellelloû slipping into a different mask that undercuts his sincerity. When Gibbs tells Ellelloû that he once read some of the Colonel's essays in a "Poli Sci course" at Yale, Ellelloû thinks: "So he knew of my exile. My privacy was invaded. Confusion was upon me. I took off my sunglasses. The brightness of the lights shed by the torches was surprising. Should I be getting royalties?" (41). Instead of the righteous defender of his nation, he is now a television star worried about re-runs. He cannot control his masks. With his audience expecting action, he torches both the do-gooder and the junk and inadvertently opens the way for American advisors who will travel to Kush to investigate Gibbs's death.

No wonder a Russian advisor is called Sirin, the penname of another master artificer, Vladimir Nabokov. Ellelloû's ornate use of words is one way that Updike smiles at himself in *The Coup*. Like the Colonel, he dances among flourishes and roles, delightfully playing with variations of prose rhythms and figurative language. But, unlike the Colonel, he is aware of the laughter. Ellelloû takes every conversation seriously, so that while Updike and the reader laugh when Candy calls her husband "the most narcissistic, chauvinistic, megalomaniacal, catatonic schizoid creep this creepy continent ever conjured up," Ellelloû muses on how Americans indulge in "the endless self-help and self-exploration of a performance-oriented race that has never settled within itself the fundamental question of what a man *is*" (123–124). Satirizing Americanese, the Colonel fails to hear the silly pomposity of his own rhetoric, which hampers his search for an answer to a similar, fundamental question: who is he? The act of writing *The Coup* may tell him.

But it will not tell him what is happening in Kush so long as he avoids reality for mysticism. During his first important journey to the myste-rious north, he glimpses two sights that should not be there, a solitary flatbed truck carrying crushed automobiles and odd golden arches that turn out to be a McDonald's hamburger joint. Ellelloû has no idea why they are there, and he would not know how to confront such infidel intrusions even if he could define them. They do not fit with his idea of Kush. Sadly, his people prefer Big Macs and mini-skirts to his notion of purity.

Ezana agrees with them. Identified by his language, as are most of the characters in *The Coup*, he speaks with what Ellelloû calls "the rhetoric of Poli Sci." He is the perfect bureaucrat, a man who sees no need to trek the far wastes of northern Kush in search of mystical explanations for the country's disasters when the lure of American aid is just around the next friendship treaty. For all of Updike's laughter, he recognizes the disintegration of tribal customs and traditional lives if modern men like Ezana assume control. Ezana wants to urbanize the nomads and negate their way of life, arguing that a nation cannot "withdraw into sainthood," but Ellelloû sees only blasphemy in such plans. He realizes that Ezana can produce facts and figures for any situation because the assistant lacks "that inward dimension, of ethical, numinous brooding, whereby a leader bulges outward from the uncertainties of his own ego and impresses a people" (55).

But how does one impress a people if their stomachs are empty and their wells dry? Ellelloû looks for a Marxist explanation for Sittina's hairstyle, while Ezana shifts statistics in hopes of enlisting American money to build offices for Kush's bureaucracy and to translate the Koran into Braille. He will destroy their roots, but he will give them burgers and french fries. Foreseeing not entropy but peace, he argues with Ellelloû that life must be lived in the present:

The fading of an afterlife—for it has faded, my friend Ellelloû, however you churn your heart—has made this life more to be cherished. When all is said and done about the persisting violence on our planet . . . the fact remains that the violence, relatively, is small, and deliberately kept small by the powers that could make it big. War has been reduced to the status of criminal activity. . . . This is a great thing, this loss of respectability. . . . Hatred on the national scale has become insincere. . . . The units of race and tribe, sect and nation, by which men identified themselves and organized their youth into armies no longer attract blind loyalty. (116)

What can a linguistic artificer do against such pragmatism? Ellelloû's response that the units of sect and tribe were mankind's "building blocks" and that Ezana's explanation predicts not peace but entropy cannot stop the invasion of flatbed trucks and jukeboxes. Denying religion, war, and nationalism, three uncertainties that Ellelloû believes in, Ezana does not worry about a world-wide drift toward sameness that will eradicate the idiosyncrasies of languages, cultures, and countries. Religious meditation gives way to an "alien rhythm" complete with words "repeated in the tireless ecstasy of religious chant": *"Chuff, chuff,/ do it to me, baby"* (82). The Top Forty has crossed the borders of Kush.

So Ellelloû travels once again to the north, this time to confront the mysterious talking head of the executed king. The journey is his version of the quest, his plunge into the heart of Kush where he hopes to locate the curse and exorcise it. To his surprise but not to ours, since we know that he is writing from the perspective of narrative distance, he finds that *he* is the curse on Kush and that he has already been exorcised. Oil has been discovered in the Ippi Rift, and American plenty in the forms of drilling rights, free beer, and apricot halter tops has ended the drought, restored the land, and indirectly deposed the Colonel. In the wasteland of northern Kush, nearly dying of thirst and heat, he stumbles to a cave that houses not the grail but graffiti. The nuances of language, his primary reserve, cannot sink much lower.

Ellelloû's spiritual self is clearly not pleased when Sirin's Russians rescue his physical body and escort him to the land of the talking head and McDonald's. Feeling a "guilty sensation of something undone, of something disastrous due," he sees the unexpected sight of a "newly built funicular railway" that he does not know is there (191). His disaster has a quiet irony about it that points back to his eradication of the American Donald Gibbs, for just as the ridiculous Gibbs has been turned into a martyr and will have a library named after him in Kush, so the elegant Ellelloû has been deposed and will have a plastic city named after him—also in Kush. The toppling of the bungling "he" is all too obvious to the observing "I."

The contrast between the Colonel's idealism and Ezana's facts is located once again in language. While Ezana hopes to develop a "plausible pragmatism," Ellelloû travels "westward to the Ippi Rift; but as this new leaf of adventure unfolded before him he felt only an exhaustion, the weariness of the destined, who must run a long track to arrive at what should have been theirs from the start: an identity, a fate" (219). Despite his rhetoric, he finds only a parody of identity: Ellelloû the man comes face to face with Ellelloû the city. The nuts and bolts of Ezana's materialism are everywhere, for when Gibbs dies, a victim of the Colonel's right-eousness, all Ezana does is welcome another "Gibbs" with the name of Klipspringer.

Stunned by the go-go city named after him, Ellelloû casts about for a Marxist explanation for what he calls the "blue-collar stink" brought by money. None is forthcoming. Deprived of his identity as president and Colonel, he survives, as always, by dipping into his repertoire of masks: a parking attendant and a short-order cook named Flapjack. The America of his student days has transported itself to Kush, and Ellelloû is back in the confusion of the all-American drugstore with its maze of sunglasses and notions, magazines and cards. All he discovers in his search for identity is that he ceases to exist: "I, submerged in posthumous glory, immersed in the future I had pitted all my will against, relaxed at last" (263).

Just as significant as the expulsion of Ellelloû is the erasure of language. For all along, language has identified both the Colonel and his fears that the modernization of Kush will eradicate the distinctive rhetoric of this unusual land. His fears are justified: "A loss of tension, of handsome savagery, was declared also in their accents, which had yielded the glottal explosiveness of their aboriginal tongues to a gliding language of genial implication and sly nonchalance" (263). Glottal explosiveness and handsome savagery give way to the jukebox of "Cry Me a River" and "A Whole Lotta Shakin' Goin' On," and America wins the war of words without firing a shot. Ezana feels at home with "The Naughty Lady of Shady Lane" and the Donald X. Gibbs Center for Trans-Visual Koranic Studies, but Ellelloû is baffled. Kutunda, his mistress, tells him what we already know: "You have run out of masks" (279).

Exiled to France with a pension, a wife, and his children, he masks himself with NoIR sunglasses and sits by the avenue writing *The Coup*. At the end of the novel, Updike reemphasizes the narrative distance between the teller as he tells the tale and the actor who has acted it: "He does not appear to be the father of the variegated children who march at their sides. . . . It gladdens the writer's heart, to contemplate the future of his girls" (297–298). Thus Ellelloû observes Ellelloû writing the story; the "I" watches the "he." Holding down a sheet of paper, remembering behind his sunglasses the details of the coup, he retains his audacious rhetorical flourishes and pens "long tendrils like the tendrilous chains of contingency that have delivered us, each, to where we sit now on the skin of the world . . ." (299). Language remains his primary companion, his constant joy. The final sentences call attention not to story but to technique: "The man is happy, hidden. The sea breeze blows, the waiters ignore him. He is writing his memoirs. No, I should put it more precisely: Colonel Ellelloû is rumored to be working on his memoirs" (299). Updike's final comic touch is that Ellelloû is the main character in a novel in which he plays the role of an author writing a memoir in which he is the main character. Such doubletalk is Updike's little joke on his own highly conscious, highly rhetorical art.

*The Poorhouse Fair* and *The Coup* remain Updike's most unexpected novels. It is not that they are militantly experimental as are John Hawkes's *The Cannibal* or Thomas Pynchon's *Gravity's Rainbow*, or that they transport the reader to such unfamiliar locales as Kurt Vonnegut's Tralfamadore or

Robert Coover's Universal Baseball Association. Strangeness is generally not an issue in Updike's fiction. But for these two novels, this most polished author, long admired for his lyrical discourses on the unhappy bedrooms and rapidly aging lives of suburban Americans, turns from the subject matter that his audience expects and creates landscapes that have little to do with the serious domestic crises of the middle class. The problems of belief in a secular age that rankle the spirits of John Hook and Felix Ellelloû have thematic importance in other Updike fictions, but their significance in *The Poorhouse Fair* and *The Coup* is that they support a perspective on where we are going more than on where we are. Imagining locales that permit him to stand outside, as it were, his familiar fictional territory, Updike invents two settings and the languages that humanize them in order to visualize the drift of the world.

## NOTES

1. Joyce Carol Oates, review of *The Coup, New Republic*, 6 January 1979, pp. 32-35. See also Oates's comment in "How Is Fiction Doing?", New York *Times Book Review*, 14 December 1980, p. 3: ". . . a world of precarious sentences, astonishing as a city built of pick-up sticks."
2. Pearl K. Bell, "Imaginings of Africa," *Commentary*, (April 1979), pp. 74-76.
3. Harold Hayes, "Updike's African Dream," *Esquire*, 14 December 1978, pp. 27-29.
4. Maureen Howard, "New Books in Review: Eight Recent Novels," *Yale Review*, 68(Spring 1979), pp. 436-437.
5. Deborah McGill, "Boy's Life," *Harper's*, 258(January 1979), pp. 87-89.
6. Dean Flower, "Picking Up the Pieces," *Hudson Review*, 32(Summer 1979), pp. 300-303. For further dissent, see Charles Truehart, "Updike Fashions African Mask," *Chronicle of Higher Education*, 11 December 1978, pp. R7-8; and Walter Sullivan, "Model Citizens and Marginal Cases: Heroes of the Day," *Sewanee Review*, 87(April 1979), pp. 343-344.
7. Peter Collier, "Author's Choice," *Book-of-the-Month Club News*, (Spring 1979), p. 21. See also Wilfred Sheed, review of *The Coup, Book-of-the-Month Club News* (January 1979), pp. 2-3: "John Updike is such a good miniaturist—the fine golden hairs on a girl's leg, the slap of a sneaker on cement—that his talent sometimes tends to linger too long at the microscope, and we forget what a wild, rambunctious talent it can be. In *The Coup* he lets it run. . . ."
8. James Atlas, "John Updike Breaks Out of Suburbia," New York *Times Magazine*, 10 December 1978, p. 60.
9. Robert Towers, "Updike in Africa," New York *Times Book Review*, 10 December 1978, p. 55. See also "Editor's Choice 1978," New York *Times Book Review*, 31 December 1978, p. 3, which lists *The Coup* as one of the best books of 1978.
10. Paul Theroux, "Updike in Africa," *Bookviews*, 2(December 1978), pp. 36-37.
11. See David Brudnoy, review of *The Coup, Saturday Evening Post*, 251(May/June 1979), pp. 86-87; Brudnoy suggests that Kush is a nation "so believable that the U.N. should admit to membership now."

12. John Updike, *The Coup* (New York: Knopf, 1978), p. 186. Further references will be noted in the text.
13. Alastair Reid, "Updike Country," *New Yorker,* 25 December 1978, pp. 65-69.
14. The British reception of *The Coup* is largely favorable. Although D. A. N. Jones claims that he is "bored, irritated and uninformed," other commentators are impressed. John Ryle likes the novel but wonders if Updike the "parodist and pasticheur comes to the fore" too often. Claire Tomalin praises the "extraordinary virtuosity and elegance." David Lodge says that the novel is "daringly conceived and brilliantly carried off" and that "perhaps the greatest achievement of this novel is that it allows us to enter imaginatively into the consciousness of such leaders and see the unflattering image of ourselves there." Tom Paulin and Paul Ableman are even more enthusiastic about *The Coup.* Calling the range of Updike's imagination "extraordinary," Paulin says that "this fine novel is eventually a parable of the imagination as usurper, autocrat and failure." Ableman describes *The Coup* as "the finest American novel since *Lolita*": "Social historians of the future may well conclude that this book signified a new maturity in the political consciousness of America. Literary critics will certainly go on regarding it as a superb work of art." See D. A. N. Jones, "Kismet Kush," *The Listener,* 15 March 1979, pp. 390-392; John Ryle, "Going with the Current," London *Times Literary Supplement,* 30 November 1979, p. 77; Claire Tomalin, "State of Africa," *Punch,* 38 March 1979, pp. 552-553; David Lodge, "The King's Head," *New Statesman,* 23 March 1979, pp. 404-405; Tom Paulin, "Operatic Surface, Deep Politics," *Encounter,* 53(August 1979), pp. 52-55; Paul Ableman, "Poetic Precision, Prose Breadth," *Spectator,* 24 March 1979, p. 18.
15. For a checklist of these essays, see my *The Other John Updike: Poems/Short Stories/Prose/Play* (Athens, Ohio: Ohio University Press, 1981), pp. 277-279.
16. John Updike, *Picked-Up Pieces* (New York: Knopf, 1975), pp. 328-329.

# WHY RABBIT SHOULD KEEP ON RUNNING

*Rabbit, Run* (1960)

*Rabbit Redux* (1971)

*Rabbit Is Rich* (1981)

# Rabbit, Run

*"They've not forgotten him:
worse, they never heard of
him."*

—*Rabbit, Run*

Published more than two decades ago, *Rabbit, Run* (1960) continues to upset the unprepared reader. It is not the explicit description of sexual activity, which was uncommon at the time of publication, or the shocking account of the baby's drowning that disturbs readers, but rather the simultaneous reactions of distaste and sympathy that Updike encourages toward Harry "Rabbit" Angstrom. Why, readers wonder, do they urge Rabbit to keep on running when he inadvertently causes desperate pain with every stride? Should they resist Updike's skillful manipulation of reader sympathy, or should they applaud Rabbit's dash from a situation that crowds him, even if the run results in abandonment and death?

*Rabbit, Run* is Updike's first full-length consideration of the way sexual dissatisfaction and marital tension mask religious questing, as if the betrayal of a spouse is confused with the need for freedom and fluidity.[1] The imperative voice of the title suggests Updike's sympathetic command to his hero to break with confining apartments and mediocre lives, but by the end of the novel both author and reader know that Rabbit's momentum is wistful, his motion sad: Harry Angstrom has no place to go even though he keeps on running.

Rabbit Angstrom is Updike's most famous character, and *Rabbit, Run* his most recognized title. When the novel was published in 1960, Stanley Edgar Hyman called Updike "the most gifted young writer in America," and it is clear from today's perspective that *Rabbit, Run* put Updike on the map. The vacuum left by the decline of William Faulkner and Ernest Hemingway was obvious in 1960, and Hyman, despite some reservations, suggested that Updike might fill the void: "Updike has a first-rate intelligence, a considerable learning, an impressive honesty and a true creative imagination. Writers have achieved immortal fame with less. . . . One awaits his next novel as a child awaits Christmas morning."[2]

What impressed Updike's supporters in 1960 was that Rabbit is not a rebel of heroic stature but a little man refusing to wait for his little life to trap him. And it will trap him if he plays by society's rules of domesticity and stasis. Always running uphill as if questing toward the unseen and thus the unknown, he has what Updike calls "the beauty of belief."[3] He may not use such terms as "beauty" and "belief," but he knows that something, what he calls "it," is up there. Yet a first reaction to Rabbit's haphazard search is likely to be disapproval bordering on despair, for his actions seem vicious. It is not, a reader might argue, that Rabbit intends to cause pain but that he wrecks the lives of others in a selfish break for freedom. The shock and necessity of Rabbit's running are what Updike hopes to convey, for this is a novel of paradoxes. Admitting that many readers think of Harry Angstrom "as a kind of beast, almost a satiric creation," Updike denies the possibility of satire and refuses to take sides for or against Rabbit: "I don't really know about the youth of today or any other day. If the book has any sociological value, that's fine, but it was not the purpose of writing it. There is a certain necessary ambiguity. I don't wish my fiction to be any clearer than life."[4]

In no way can Rabbit call his own life clear. Willing to lose his life in the social sense in order to find his individuality, he does not know how to begin the search. When he denies his guilt in the burial scene, the reader's shock at his apparent brutality is magnified, but Rabbit senses that the true believer in God need feel no guilt. He need only "cast every care on Thee," which is exactly what Harry does. A believer who cannot define belief, Rabbit feels threatened when his family and friends urge him to join their shared sense of guilt for the baby's death, their humanistic ideal that people survive by relying on each other. Guilt is eased when all accept its burden. But Rabbit intuitively rejects their appeal to what John Hook (*The Poorhouse Fair*) calls "busy-ness," goodness without belief. Harry is the only believer at the gravesite and hence the only mourner worthy of asking God to lift his burden. It is not that the reader should judge Rabbit admirable but that he should understand this flawed and baffled man who inadvertently wounds others while he fights to break free of the net.

Conventional saintliness is not an issue for unconventional believers like Rabbit. In an essay on Henry Green, published long after *Rabbit, Run*, Updike describes the English novelist as a "saint of the mundane."[5] Rabbit will never be canonized, but he has a saintly reverence for the mundane details dotting his unexceptional life. Only he notices the leaves, feels the gravel under his feet, recoils from the filthy ash trays, and rebounds toward the park. Only he wants to clean up the apartment, throw out the junk, find life's rhythm. But at what price? Updike himself asks the key question in a preface to the 1977 edition: "Rabbit is the hero of this novel, but is he a good man? The question is meant to lead to another—What is goodness? . . . In the end, the act of running, of gathering a blank momentum 'out of a kind of sweet panic,' offers itself as containing a kernel of goodness; but perhaps a stone or a flower at rest holds the same kernel." Updike refuses to answer his question directly, but he implies that goodness is a large part of Rabbit's make-up when he calls him "fertile and fearful and not easy to catch. . . . wild and timid, harmful and loving, hardhearted and open to the motions of Grace."[6]

Rabbit's harmful, loving pursuit of grace is unsettling because it is a product not of the 1960s, the drop-out decade, but of the 1950s, the tranquil Eisenhower years. As Updike explains in the foreword to the Modern Library edition: "Rabbit, Run was written in 1959, in the present tense. The time of its writing contained the time of its action."[7] That is, the songs and news and styles that Harry hears and sees are those that Updike heard and saw in the late 1950s when he was finishing the novel. His first inclination was to write two novellas about the rabbit and the horse, about quick gratification and steady self-sacrifice; title them Rabbit, Run and The Centaur; and publish them in one volume. But Updike found the tale of angst-ridden Harry expanding, and he began to imagine the story developing as a film would. The influence of cinematic technique is one reason for the present tense of the novel, for in movies every action or thought seems immediate. Originally subtitling Rabbit, Run "a movie," Updike wrote the opening scene of the boys playing basketball as a background for the title and credits of the film, but he realized later that, unlike the novel, the film medium could not show the "shadow of moral ambiguity."[8]

That shadow is a key. Developing ambiguity not only in Rabbit's actions but also in the reader's response to them, Updike discarded the notion to adapt film technique to the novel but retained the present tense. A novel written in the present tense was unusual in 1959, an example of what Updike calls "technical daring" for which Joyce Cary's Mr. Johnson (1939) was the only precedent: "You can move between minds, between thoughts and objects and events with a curious ease not available to the past tense. I'm not sure it's as clear to the reader as it is to the person writing, but there are kinds of poetry, kinds of music you can strike off in the present tense. I don't know why I've not done a full-length novel in it again. I began tentatively, but one page deep into the book, it seemed very natural and congenial. . . ."[9] The present tense also allows Updike to stress the immediacy of Rabbit's sensations, which in turn calls attention to the primary trait of his character: He feels but he does not think. Rabbit reacts to every stimulus, every emotion as if they exist only in the present without development from the past or reverberation toward the future. In this sense he is an extreme product of the placid, hermetic Eisenhower years, a kind of historical artifact. Updike comments: "My fiction about the daily doings of ordinary people has more history in it than history books. . . ."[10]

That history is of the daily rituals of the American middle class. Unconcerned with apocalypse, Updike distinguishes his fiction as focusing on the "excitements of normal, everyday life . . . on investigation of the quotidian": "My subject is the American Protestant small-town middle class. I like middles. It is in middles that extremes clash, where ambiguity restlessly rules. Something quite intricate and fierce occurs in homes, and it seems to me without doubt worthwhile to examine what it is."[11] His examination in *Rabbit, Run* reveals the fierceness. It is not that Janice Angstrom wants to stop being pretty in her middle twenties, or that she means to drink Old-fashioneds while the dinner burns, or that her husband dreams of his past athletic glory, but that they do not know how to cope with the tensions of living as a family on the margin of the middle class. Books and ideas and art are never at issue in the Angstrom home, but whether or not to pick up the car first or the baby from the mother-in-law is. How can they join the middle-class treadmill when they cannot define the middle-class dream?

In *Rabbit, Run* Updike poses a dilemma that results in the ambiguity he aspires to: Should Rabbit define himself by social convention, or should he indulge his yearning toward individual belief? Harry sees the conflict as either a nine-to-five job and dinner in the kitchen or the freedom to run but with no place to go. Updike calls this clash of values the "yes, but" quality of his fiction: "Yes, in *Rabbit, Run*, to our inner urgent whispers, but—the social fabric collapses murderously."[12] Although Rabbit is not intelligent enough to realize it, his problem is unsolvable. We may applaud his refusal to give in, but we shrink from the pain that his running initiates. Updike explains: "There is no reconciliation between the inner, intimate appetites and the external consolations of life. . . . there is no way to reconcile these individual wants to the very real need of any society to set strict limits and to confine its members."[13]

Inarticulate but full of feeling, Rabbit expresses his need to break the limits of society by acting out his yearning in sexual escapades. Updike is well aware of how daring his accounts of sexual activity were in 1960: "Yeah, I meant it to be . . . I think the word is 'courageous,' although there was nothing more at stake than whether or not a book would be published. I thought then, and I still feel, that if you're going to have sex in a book, you really ought to have it. You should go into it enough to try to show what happens, to make it a human transaction. . . . I was aware of predecessors and of what had been done with the language in this area before. The model I really had most in mind was *Ulysses*."[14] It is fair to say that published reactions to these scenes split when the novel appeared. *Time*, for example, called them "too explicit" and "often in the worst of taste," but George Steiner argued that the descriptions have "integrity" because Updike "sees in sexual life the only compensation, the only open terrain, left to human beings cornered in the soul-detergent inferno of American middle-class existence."[15]

But despite the attention focused on the sex scenes in *Rabbit, Run*, the irony is that not sexual promiscuity but lack of useful work is at the heart of Rabbit's dilemma. Once an all-star basketball player, he cannot find at age twenty-six an occupation commensurate with his past days of glory. He looks around and sees that he may peddle used cars or MagiPeelers, and he knows that to sell either is to sell himself. Rabbit cannot express himself on this subject so well as Hook in *The Poorhouse Fair*, but both suspect that the deterioration from handcraft to plastics results in a depletion of personal worth from individual to automaton. "My novels," Updike says, "are all about the search for useful work. So many people these days have to sell things they don't believe in, and have jobs that defy describing. . . . A man has to build his life outward from a job he can do."[16] Rabbit, unfortunately, has nothing he can do except run, so he fashions his life on running to keep his sense of self-worth alive. The sexual encounters are important to him, but in the end he leaves Janice and Ruth too.

Some readers hope that he will never come back. J. M. Edelstein, for example, charges that Updike lacks sympathy for Harry Angstrom, that he sketches Rabbit with a "bitter, almost vicious, hatred and a humorless lack of pity. The poor in spirit, the supposedly resourceless and the desperate in *Rabbit, Run* are only further debased and distorted by him."[17] John Thompson agrees, arguing that Updike damns the efforts of humanity to break free from the drab and dispiriting.[18] The problem with such opinions is that these critics want Updike to take sides, to make authorial sympathy obvious, to persuade the reader to accept the legitimacy of Rabbit's run. But to do so would be to deny the ambiguity that Updike sees at the center of American middle-class life, the "yes-but" quality that lures a man beyond the confines of the living room yet acknowledges the grievous damage done when he steps through the door. Although off target because it implies that Updike attacks his characters, the brief, unsigned review in *Newsweek* is closer to the point than Edelstein or Thompson when it suggests that Updike's picture of the middle class is the fiercest since Flaubert.[19]

As an example of the extremes of Updike criticism, one should compare David Boroff's review with those mentioned above. Calling Rabbit an older but less articulate Holden Caulfield, Boroff praises the novel as a "triumph of intelligence and compassion" because Updike does not glibly condescend to his characters.[20] The point is that the most acceptable analyses of *Rabbit, Run* understand how the reader's unsettled attitude toward the characters is part of the mixture of attraction and repulsion that most of us, including Updike himself, feel toward American domestic life. As Richard Lyons notes, a summary of Rabbit's actions might mistakenly convince someone that Angstrom is hollow and spineless, but a fairer reading shows that Rabbit suffers because he cannot communicate what he desperately longs to say. Living primarily in the present, he experiences moments of great intensity but can only mutter banalities when called on to explain his actions: "What are in Rabbit selfish, physical indulgences become when translated into an acceptable traditional vocabulary respectable and transcendent expressions of saints who have touched God in the night. . . . To be affirmative, to believe in life is at present, I gather, unpopular. To try to project this belief through an inarticulate athlete instead of through a highly articulate mystic, such as Seymour Glass, is to compound the difficulty."[21] Updike surmounts the difficulty to create a character who, in Richard Foster's splendid phrase, illustrates "the dangerous force of utter selfhood."[22]

Rabbit's refusal to allow society to absorb the self may be the courage not to give in, an intuitive realization that what is right socially is wrong personally; or it may be individualism bordering on selfishness.[23] But the rightness or wrongness of his running is not the issue; rather, the novel urges acknowledging the complexity of his dilemma. *Rabbit, Run* does not offer answers, but it does pose problems, and one problem, as illustrated by the epigraph from Pascal, is how does a man find grace when the little demands of living crowd out his life? Harry does not know. The quotation from Pascal reads, "The motions of Grace, the hardness of the heart; external circumstances."[24] Rabbit may be many things, but his heart is not always hard. What he does have is too many external circumstances beyond his control. School, family, work, and church all fail him. The epigraph suggests that either "the motions of Grace" or "the hardness of the heart" is available, and that the relation between action and internal needs is determined by the external circumstances of one's life. Culture shapes personality. Social forces clash with Rabbit's sense of possibilities. The demands of family deny the motions of grace.

It is not that society is malignant or that Harry is a saint but that neither can prevent the slow disintegration of the other. Updike's negative critics want him to take a stand, to blame either social pressures or individual whim, but to do so is to ignore the ambiguity that colors the periphery of these little lives. If Rabbit could understand the harmony of Pascal's thought, he would be paralyzed. Rather than wait for a rational explanation of the balance between external circumstances and internal needs, he runs. Yet even though he runs, he is the only one in the novel to sense the motions of grace. He cannot translate his intuition into words, but his inarticulate yearning is more valuable than the Reverend Eccles' need to demythologize belief to the level of humanistic cooperation and, finally, compromise.

The point is that Harry Angstrom is the sole religious layman in the world of Mt. Judge and Brewer, Pennsylvania, the world of the Reverends Eccles and Kruppenbach and their circle of professed believers. Outside events do not touch these people. Intellectual matters are never broached. But regaining grace, in all its manifestations, is vital to Rabbit, and he does not know how to go about it. All he can do is transfer his need to the realm of athletics where he was once a star with motion and glide. Thus Updike begins the novel with twenty-six-year-old Rabbit crashing a sandlot basketball game with a bunch of kids who resent his intrusion. He is on his way home from work, but the playground is more attractive than the apartment. Twenty-foot set shots or dingy Janice—Rabbit has unknowingly made his choice when the novel begins.

The opening movement of *Rabbit, Run*, from the sandlot game through Harry's aborted trip south, contains the outline of his dilemma. He feels crowded, for example, by the end of the first paragraph: "The kids keep coming, they keep crowding you up" (151). By the beginning of the third paragraph, his vague sense of the relationship between basketball and sex is clear: "The ball, rocketing off the crotch of the rim, leaps over the heads of the six and lands at the feet of the one" (152). And at the conclusion of the third paragraph, the net, which will eventually suggest the cooperative effort to trap him, comes into play: "It drops into the circle of the rim, whipping the net with a ladylike whisper" (152).

Crowding, sex, net—they all mix together in Rabbit's mind. At various times in the novel, he feels "pinned," trapped by a "shark," "glued-in," "manipulated," and "threatened." In each case the sensation of being crowded challenges his need for fluid motion, graceful action. The external circumstances of the apartment loom toward him, littering his sense of freedom with broken toys, dirty Old-fashioned glasses, and lethargic Janice: "He had missed Janice's crowding presence, the kid and his shrill needs, his own walls. He had wondered what he was doing. But now these reflexes, shallowly scratched, are spent, and deeper instincts flood forward, telling him he is right. He feels freedom like oxygen everywhere around him . . ." (195). If he denies that oxygen, if he gives up his instinctive need of freedom for the socially-dictated role in the apartment, he knows the net will engulf him: "He feels the faded night he left behind in this place as a net of telephone calls and hasty trips, trails of tears and strings of words, white worried threads shuttled through the night and now faded but still existent, an invisible net overlaying the steep streets and in whose center he lies secure in his locked hollow hutch" (186).

Coming alive as he plays basketball with the kids, Rabbit connects with his old momentum. Winded, overweight, but momentarily happy, he longs to flow with the rhythm of the game. But the boys see only a tall man, and they play grudgingly. There is no way that Harry can let them know who he once was and what he once felt: "They've not forgotten him: worse, they never heard of him" (153). He is not trying to show off, nor is he trying to live in the past, but he does want to know why his life is stalled at only age twenty-six. For years the motion of his life has been upward, as if aspirations were a natural continuum, a never-ending urging toward accomplishment, but now Rabbit feels discarded, and the only accomplishment expected of him is to sell MagiPeelers. It is not enough:

Rabbit knows the way. You climb up through the little grades and then get to the top and everybody cheers; with the sweat in your eyebrows you can't see very well and the noise swirls around you and lifts you up, and then you're out, not forgotten at first, just out, and it feels good and cool and free. You're out, and sort of melt, and keep lifting. . . . (153)

But no one keeps lifting forever; society demands that he "settle down." Resisting this downward motion more by intuition than analysis, he is the only character still trying to ascend.

Elated by the pick-up game, convinced that "things start anew" in March, Rabbit throws away his cigarettes and runs "up" the alley toward home. He is quickly brought down to earth when he goes to his apartment that varies in "color from bruise to dung" and offers him a "sunless vestibule" and a wife who "just yesterday, it seems to him" . . . has "stopped being pretty" (154–155). Updike calls attention to the contrast between Rabbit's fastidious need for neatness and Janice's uncaring disorder. There is irony in the account of their different responses to the kiddy television show, the Mouseketeers. Janice just stares; watching the tube is something to do while smoking a cigarette with her Old-fashioned. Rabbit, on the other hand, takes the Mouseketeer's advice seriously: "Know Thyself, a wise old Greek once said. . . . It means, be what you are. . . . God doesn't want a tree to be a waterfall, or a flower to be a stone" (157). No matter how much Harry's response to the advice indicates his inability to think, he still believes the Mouseketeer's message, even to the extent of repeating it later when the Reverend Eccles tries to make him feel guilty for abandoning Janice. The key to the advice is not that it comes from television but that the Mouseketeer mentions God. The only believer in God's grace, Rabbit now knows that if God does not want a waterfall to be a tree, He also does not want Harry to exchange upward motion for downward plunge, to give up his individuality to a socially- defined role.

So he runs. Janice has left their son Nelson in one place and the car in another, and she asks Harry to pick up both as well as a package of cigarettes. Clearly, the dilemma is unimportant, but to Rabbit it "clings to his back like a tightening net" (161). Updike ironically defines Harry's problem: Should he first pick up the car or Nelson? Yet this decision *is* major to Rabbit. He does not think but feels, and he senses that when he leaves the apartment to run the errands, he slides downhill, the direction counter to his need for aspiration: "His progress is always down. . . . He tries to think of something pleasant. He imagines himself about to shoot a long one-hander; but he feels he's on a cliff, there is an abyss he will fall into when the ball leaves his hands" (164, 171).

Rather than fall, he leaves his son at his parents' house, retrieves the car, and drives south toward a naive vision of freedom in the guise of barefoot girls and orange groves. Updike emphasizes the offhandedness of Rabbit's decision to run when he shows Harry drifting onto highway 23, which, he assumes, must be a good route since he scored 23 points in his first varsity basketball game. Although this choice is made early in the novel, the reader understands that Harry Angstrom is a simple man with a limited value system, a decent but flawed adult who finds the little complexities of life—a boring job, a dreary wife, a dingy apartment—too much to handle. His problems are not those of poverty, politics, and the nuances of keeping up with the Joneses; rather, they are how to sell junk he does not believe in while returning home each night to a marriage that drains his spirit, that insists on finality instead of fluidity. Only late in the novel, as he sets out on his last but undetermined run, does he glimpse the difference between the right way of social expectation and the good way of individual need: "On this small fulcrum he tries to balance the rest, weighing opposites against each other: Janice and Ruth, Eccles and his mother, the right way and the good way, the way to the delicatessen— gaudy with stacked fruit lit by a naked bulb—and the other way, down Summer Street to where the city ends" (433–434). He aspires while the others accept.

Rabbit needs advice, but no one knows what to tell him. All he hears are clichés and catch-phrases, comments that matter less to him than the Mouseketeer's proverb. The nameless service-station attendant reminds him, for example, that society is goal-oriented: "The only way to get somewhere, you know, is to figure out where you're going before you go there" (175). Rabbit does not agree. The advice may work for a nine-to-five man, but Rabbit must break free of the mold. He intuitively understands that he needs to find not the right way but the good way. The alternative is to accept a lifetime of dirty dishes, a dumpy wife, a dull job.

One does not admire his decision to run from his problems, but one wonders what else he should do. No thinker, he feels that his present life is blocking him from the motions of grace. The only fluidity he can recall is basketball and the years when he knew he was great, so just before he returns to Mt. Judge and Brewer he metaphorically attempts to escape the net by compressing his problems into a ball:

The names melt away and he sees the map whole, a net, all those red lines and blue lines and stars, a net he is somewhere caught in. He claws at it and tears it; with a gasp of exasperation he rips away a great triangular piece and tears the large remnant in half and, more calmly, lays these three pieces on top of each other and tears them in half, and then those six pieces and so on until he has a wad he can squeeze in his hand like a ball. He rolls down the window and throws the ball out. . . . (182)

The metaphor will not work; the problems remain. Returning to his old coach Tothero, he hears only empty advice designed to make him feel guilty. Tothero wants him to "come to grips," to become a winner "in the greater game of life." But Harry cannot even persuade Janice to clean up the apartment.

The first movement of the novel ends when Rabbit drives back to his hometown, and it illustrates his general dilemma until he breaks for his final run. Relationships with his new mistress Ruth and new friend the Reverend Eccles shape the rest of *Rabbit, Run* as Harry tries to reconcile the conflicting demands of physical love and spiritual faith. Indeed, on their first date, Ruth calls him a "Christian gentleman." She is ironic, but the narrator is serious, for in loving Ruth, Rabbit longs to reach not just her body, the "machine," "but her, her" (221). It is to Ruth that he confesses his belief in God, and it is with Ruth that he walks through a park where the tennis court nets are down before climbing up Mt. Judge toward his vision of "upward space": "His day has been bothered by God: Ruth mocking, Eccles blinking—why did they teach you such things if no one believed them? It seems plain, standing here, that if there is this floor there is a ceiling, that the true space in which we live is upward space" (253). This vision is one of the most important clues to Harry's character. It is rivaled only by his acceptance of God's love in the funeral scene, and it shows how he translates Pascal's "motions of Grace" away from "the hardness of the heart" toward aspiration and belief. No wonder he fears the downward slide, the abyss. When, he tells both Ruth and Eccles, one has been good at something, truly good as he has been at basketball, then living a second-rate life is not enough. Even Ruth admits that he has not given up, that "in your stupid way you're still fighting" (233).

Yet Ruth eventually wants him to surrender. At first offering a way out of the net, she later demands commitment when she finds herself pregnant. Like nearly all of Rabbit's friends, she tries to make him feel guilty so that she may forgive him, but she does not manipulate guilt so well as Eccles does. Eccles is Conner's cousin (*The Poorhouse Fair*), a humanist who inadvertently crowds Rabbit with the social obligations of family and job. Eccles and Rabbit do not debate the issues of humanism versus genuine belief as do Conner and Hook, and thus they are not spokesmen for opposed positions. Indeed, Rabbit can speak for nothing; he senses instead of communicates. Rather than articulate ideas, the minister and his wayward charge live their convictions, and it is clear from the way they live that only Harry believes in the abstractions that organized religion professes to exemplify. Although no charlatan, Eccles is a candidate for Hook's accusation—not goodness but "busy-ness." He innocently interferes in other lives because he cannot fathom Rabbit's pursuit of "it." Thinking to free Harry from fear, he tightens the net of humanism that would trap Rabbit by emphasizing guilt.

Eccles would not understand Updike's comment on the relation between faith and doubt: "I've touched a kind of bottom when I've felt that existence itself was an affront to be forgiven. I've felt in myself and in those around me a failure of nerve—a sense of doubt as to the worth of any action. At such times one has nothing but the ancient assertions of Christianity to give one the will to act, even if the act is only the bringing in of the milk bottles off the front porch."[25] Unattractive as Rabbit's running may be to those who live by the social contract, it nevertheless illustrates the man with the nerve to act.[26] Yet Eccles does not act so much as meddle. More a social worker than a man of faith, he burns with anger when his dour Lutheran colleague Kruppenbach lashes out at his humanism: "If Gott wants to end misery He'll declare the Kingdom now. . . . I say you don't know what your role is or you'd be home locked in prayer. *There* is your role: to make yourself an exemplar of faith. *There* is where comfort comes from: faith, not what little finagling a body can do here and there, stirring the bucket. . . . Make no mistake. There is nothing but Christ for us. All the rest, all this decency and busyness, is nothing" (306). In insisting on something—God—as a counterbalance to nothingness— the void—Kruppenbach recalls Karl Barth and his elevation of faith over works. The echo of Hook's retort to Conner is also clear. Even Rabbit says that he gives people faith, and Eccles agrees.

Eccles will always be puzzled by Harry's sense of God's love. The minister realizes that Rabbit is a life-giver, that he wants something better than the mediocre life everyone expects him to accept without resistance, but when Rabbit confesses that he feels something out there is looking for him, Eccles responds with irony. He sees that Harry is a man who does not know what he wants and does not like what he has, but rather than guide Rabbit toward the motions of grace, he urges him toward the apartment. A humanist who believes that all involved should share the guilt, the minister is more interested in Harry's reconciliation with his wife than in his reconciliation with the something Rabbit calls "it."

Eccles is a genuinely concerned man, a person who honestly wants to help, but he relies on busyness instead of belief. In the long run he cannot accept Rabbit's upward spaces, his unseen worlds: "With my Church, I believe that we are all responsible beings, responsible for ourselves and for each other" (290). In short, he speaks for the community, for the humanistic world from which, Updike knows, many of his readers come. Thus one of Updike's challenges is to generate sympathy for the wandering Rabbit, because Harry's rejection of the standard values of work and family distances him from the reader. Rabbit's conversations with Eccles narrow that distance. Unable to explain what he means, he can at least express what he feels: "I don't know what she feels. I haven't known for years. All I know is what's inside *me*. That's all I have" (247). Eccles underestimates Rabbit's fear, his bewilderment, his longing to be a winner again, and the irony is that, for all his inarticulateness, Harry finally breaks through to the minister rather than the other way around.

In one of the most crucial scenes, Eccles again turns on Harry while they are playing golf and tries to make him feel guilty. Calling him "monstrously selfish" and a coward, the same epithets unsympathetic readers hurl at Rabbit, the minister yells that Harry cares nothing for right and wrong, cares only for his own selfish instincts. He even makes fun of Rabbit's intuitive sense of "it," asking if "it" is blue or red or covered with polka dots. But Rabbit has the final word when he hits a perfect tee shot:

The sound has a hollowness, a singleness he hasn't heard before. His arms force his head up and his ball is hung way out. . . . It recedes along a line straight as a ruler-edge. Stricken; sphere, star, speck. It hesitates, and Rabbit thinks it will die, but he's fooled, for the ball makes [t]his hesitation the ground of a final leap: with a kind of visible sob takes a last bite of space before vanishing in falling, "That's *it!*" he cries and, turning to Eccles with a smile of aggrandizement, repeats, "That's it." (272)

From this point on, the reader and Eccles should understand even if they do not approve. Rabbit craves fluidity, freedom, in short the motions of grace as exemplified not only by Pascal but also by the tee shot. It makes no difference that he cannot define "it"; he knows that "it" is there. Approval or disapproval of his run is insignificant beside the larger point of acknowledging the complexity of his predicament.

Rabbit's belief in "it," in God, in the unseen world is so great that he fears God will punish him by letting Janice die as she gives birth to their second child. Guilt propels him back to his wife. Even though he tells her that all she does is drink and watch television, he is eager to begin again with a clean apartment and a new baby. Convinced that life can be as neat and ordered as the flower beds he tends for Mrs. Smith, and aware that his two months with Ruth are a mess, he is ready to give in to external circumstances. Yet note the following exchange between Rabbit and Janice after he declares his love for her in the hospital:

> "I love you," she says. "Do you have a quarter?"
> "I guess. I'll look. What do you want it for?"
> "If you put a quarter in that"—she points toward a small television set on a high stand, so patients can see it over the foot of their beds—"it'll play for an hour. There's a silly program on at two that Mother and I got to watching when I was home." (349)

Further comment is unneeded except to point out that juxtaposed with Janice's dismal request is Mrs. Smith's declaration a few pages later that Rabbit has the "strange gift" of life (356). Janice, apparently, cares more for the concrete quarter than for the abstract gift.

No wonder Harry feels discouraged after saying farewell to Mrs. Smith. Aware of his obligation to stay with Janice and the children, he suspects that "his life has left irrevocably," that "fullness" ends when nature exacts her ransom of children: "Then she is through with us, and we become, first inside, and then outside, junk. Flower stalks" (357). Commitment to family means dismissal of self. The hardness of the heart defeats the motions of grace.

For a while Harry accepts the loss, plays the role of the adjusted husband. He cares for the family and attends Eccles' church. He feels lucky and forgiven, as if guilt has been absorbed by the community ready to welcome him back to the fold. He even gives thanks: "His feeling that there is an unseen world is instinctive, and more of his actions than anyone suspects constitute transactions with it" (366). But he makes the mistake of sexually forcing himself on Janice too soon following the baby's birth, and guilt and frustration return. He runs. Few will disagree with Janice's rebuff, for Harry is obviously in the wrong. But marital tension masks religious questing in *Rabbit, Run*. Updike tempers the reader's sympathy for Janice when he shows her wandering through the apartment, baffled at Harry's absence, dreaming away her problems by imagining that everything will be all right and simple and clean, just as it is in the movies. Lacking all understanding of her husband's desperation, she joins Eccles in wishing that Rabbit would abandon his aspiration toward upward spaces and accept the downward motion of the social routine: "She feels the workday approaching like an army of light, feels the dark ridged houses beneath her as potentially stirring, waking, opening like castles to send forth their men, and regrets that her own husband is unable to settle into the rhythm of which one more beat is about to sound. Why him? What was so precious about him?" (384). She is not intelligent enough to answer her question, and Rabbit lacks the words to say it for her. Only he knows how precious he is to himself. No one else even cares.

Janice lacks his faith except perhaps in the stunningly horrifying scene when, drunk, she accidently drowns the baby and calls on God for help.

Blame is not an issue. Although many readers want to pinpoint culpability and thus force Updike into taking sides, the tragedy is more a combination of Janice's weakness and Rabbit's rebellion than an invitation to pile on guilt. There is no answer to the clash between the social contract and individual need. One admires Rabbit's longing while detesting his actions. All he can do is run, which he does for the last time following the funeral.

Not faith in God but reliance on humanism sets the tone at the cemetery. The mourners gather round. They touch and embrace and whisper forgiveness: "All under him Harry feels these humans knit together" (419). But when Eccles begins the ceremony, when he intones the words of resurrection and eternal life, only Harry "feels their possibility." He is the sole believer at the funeral, and he "vibrates with excitement and strength; he is sure his girl has ascended to heaven" (421). Buoyed by a faith that Eccles does not have, forgiven by a God that the mourners do not acknowledge, Rabbit feels unified with all the world as his baby leaps to heaven: "*Casting every care on thee*. . . . The sky greets him. A strange strength sinks down into him. It is as if he has been crawling in a cave and now at last beyond the dark recession of crowding rocks he has seen a patch of light; he turns, and Janice's face, dumb with grief, blocks the light. 'Don't look at *me*,' he says. 'I didn't kill her' " (422). He wants to forgive as he has been forgiven, to express his vision of the upward spaces, to begin again, but his unintentionally calloused words shock the mourners, who are unable to see the truth of his belief.

So he runs for the final time, "uphill exultantly," away from the hardness of the heart and with the assurance of grace. His direction at the end of the novel is the same as it is at the beginning: "If he walks far enough uphill he will in time reach the scenic drive that runs along the ridge. Only by going downhill can he be returned to the others. . . . He scrambles back uphill. . . . Janice and Eccles and his mother and his sins seem a thousand miles behind" (424, 426). He alone has been able to accept the grace of the baby's rebirth in heaven, and now he wants that grace for himself.

Ruth, pregnant by Harry, offers no haven. Calling him "Mr. Death" and setting the trap of either marriage to her or marriage to Janice, she all but turns him out when he answers her questions about their future together with a series of "I don't know's." Updike stresses Rabbit's panic at the end, his genuine fear. Seeking consolation, he looks toward the windows of a church, but they are dark. The metaphor of the net comes again to his mind as he tries to avoid capture by the external circumstances: "Goodness lies inside, there is nothing outside, those things he was trying to balance have no weight. He feels his inside as very real suddenly, a pure blank space in the middle of a dense net. *I don't know,* he kept telling Ruth; he doesn't know, what to do, where to go, what will happen . . ." (434).

We don't know either. The beautifully written final lines suggest the open-endedness of his search, but the key word *illusion* also indicates deception. Rabbit has nothing left but motion itself: "Although this block of brick three-stories is just like the one he left, something in it makes him happy; the steps and window sills seem to twitch and shift in the corner of his eye, alive. This illusion trips him. His hands lift of their own and he feels the wind on his ears even before, his heels hitting heavily on the pavement at first but with an effortless gathering out of a kind of sweet panic growing lighter and quicker and quieter, he runs. Ah: runs. Runs" (434-435). Like many American literary heroes before him, he lights out for the territory, and like most of them he finds that the open spaces recede the closer he approaches. Rabbit has failed his family and friends just as they have let him down.

The "yes-but" quality that Updike finds in his own fiction determines the tone of the ending of *Rabbit, Run.* One might say "yes" to the lure of motion, but then one must say "no" to the social contract—often at catastrophic cost. The conflict between internal yearning and external circumstances could paralyze a thinking man, but Rabbit rarely thinks. Relying on feeling and an instinct for joy, he maintains his motion through the net. One suspects that Updike's sympathy—but not his unqualified approval—goes with him, for a single word unifies the novel from the title through the final period: the imperative "run." And that's just what Rabbit does.

## NOTES

1. For earlier considerations of this theme in the Updike canon, see the poem "Ex-Basketball Player," *The Carpentered Hen* (New York: Harper, 1958); and the short story "Ace in the Hole," *The Same Door* (New York: Knopf, 1959).
2. Stanley Edgar Hyman, "The Artist as a Young Man," *New Leader,* 19 March 1962, pp. 22-23.
3. John Updike, *The Poorhouse Fair/Rabbit, Run* (New York: Modern Library, 1965), p. 366. Further references will be noted in the text.
4. "Desperate Weakling," *Time,* 7 November 1960, p. 108.
5. John Updike, "Saint of the Mundane," *New York Review of Books,* 18 May 1978, pp. 3-4, 6.
6. John Updike, "A Special Message to Subscribers," *Rabbit, Run* (Franklin Center, Pennsylvania: Franklin Library, 1977).
7. The publishing history of *Rabbit, Run* is not complicated, but I should explain why I shall be quoting from the 1965 Modern Library edition instead of the first edition. *Rabbit, Run* was first published by Knopf in 1960; the first English edition was published by Deutsch in 1961. Updike then revised parts of the

novel, and the first revised edition appeared in 1964 in an English (Harmonds-worth) paperback series, Penguin Books. The first American edition, revised, was published with *The Poorhouse Fair* (also revised) by Modern Library in 1965. Although a signed edition was published by the Franklin Library in 1977, no additional revisions were made in it. Thus the 1965 Modern Library edition of *Rabbit, Run* is the first American edition that contains Updike's latest intentions. See also Randall H. Waldron's essay, published while this book was in page proof, "Rabbit Revised," *American Literature*, 56 (March 1984), 51–67. Waldron shows that in addition to the major revisions in the Penquin edition of *Rabbit, Run* and carried over to the Modern Library edition, Updike gave the novel a "fine tuning" by supplying minor changes for a 1970 reprinting published by Kropf.

8. See Updike, "A Special Message to Subscribers" as well as "Interview with John Updike," in *First Person: Conversations on Writers and Writing*, ed. Frank Gado (Schenectady, N.Y.: Union College Press, 1973), especially pp. 94-97. Warner Brothers did release a film version of *Rabbit, Run* starring James Caan, but few viewers were pleased with it.

9. Charles Thomas Samuels, "The Art of Fiction XLIII: John Updike," *Paris Review*, 12(Winter 1968), p. 111.

10. Samuels, "The Art of Fiction XLIII: John Updike," p. 106.

11. "Interview with John Updike," p. 80; and Jane Howard, "Can a Nice Novelist Finish First?," *Life*, 4 November 1966, p. 74D.

12. Samuels, "The Art of Fiction XLIII: John Updike," p. 100.

13. "Interview with John Updike," p. 92.

14. "Interview with John Updike," pp. 98-99.

15. "Desperate Weakling," p. 108; and George Steiner, "In a Rut," *The Reporter*, 8 December 1960, p. 82.

16. Howard, "Can a Nice Novelist Finish First?," p. 82.

17. J. M. Edelstein, "Down with the Poor in Spirit," *New Republic*, 21 November 1960, p. 18.

18. John Thompson, "Other People's Affairs," *Partisan Review*, 28(January-February 1961), p. 120.

19. "A Novelist Gets Tough," *Newsweek*, 7 November 1960, p. 122. See also Milton Rugoff, "American Tragedy: 1960," New York *Herald Tribune Book Review*, 6 November 1960, p. 7, who praises the novel as an American tragedy about a man who must escape his life without distinction, or strangle.

20. David Boroff, "You Cannot Really Flee," New York *Times Book Review*, 6 November 1960, p. 4.

21. Richard Lyons, "A High E. Q.," *Minnesota Review*, 1(Spring 1961), pp. 385-389.

22. Richard Foster, "What Is Fiction For?," *Hudson Review*, 14(Spring 1961), p. 149.

23. The British response to *Rabbit, Run* is just as mixed as the American. Frank McGuinness dismisses the novel as the same "slush" served up by John O'Hara and Erskine Caldwell: "A wearying round of introspective brooding and interminable sex." Olivia Manning says little more than that *Rabbit, Run* is "pretty much the up-to-the-minute American novel." The unsigned review in the London *Times Literary Supplement* praises the small-town tragedy as "convincing, vivid and awful." See Frank McGuinness, "In Extremis," *New States-*

*man,* 29 September 1961, p. 439; Olivia Manning, "Faces of Violence," *The Spectator,* 15 September 1961, p. 361; and "Enemies of Promise," London *Times Literary Supplement,* 29 September 1961, p. 648.

24. For good discussions of the notion of grace in *Rabbit, Run,* see Clinton S. Burhans, Jr., "Things Falling Apart: Structure and Theme in *Rabbit, Run,*" *Studies in the Novel,* 5(Fall 1973), pp. 336-351; and Paul Borgman, "The Tragic Hero of Updike's *Rabbit, Run,*" *Renascence,* 29(Winter 1977), pp. 106-112.

25. Howard, "Can a Nice Novelist Finish First?," p. 80.

26. For other discussions of religion in *Rabbit, Run,* see Robert Detweiler, "John Updike and the Indictment of Culture- Protestantism," *Four Spiritual Crises in Mid-Century American Fiction* (University of Florida Monographs, Fall 1963; rpt. Freeport, N.Y.: Books for Libraries Press, 1970); Gerry Brenner, "*Rabbit, Run:* John Updike's Criticism of the 'Return to Nature,' " *Twentieth Century Literature,* 12(April 1966), pp. 3-14; and Elmer F. Suderman, "The Right Way and the Good Way in *Rabbit, Run,*" *University Review,* 36(1968), pp. 13-21.

# Rabbit Redux

*"I feel so guilty."*
*"Relax. Not everything is
your fault."*
                    —*Rabbit Redux*

Harry Angstrom's run toward upward spaces and unseen worlds in *Rabbit, Run* slows to bewildered stasis in *Rabbit Redux* (1971). Dashing from personal sluggishness in the first novel, he shrinks from social upheaval in the second. The politics of national unrest rather than the pursuit of grace animates *Redux*. The time is 1969, and Harry is thirty-six years old. Hovering all around him, from the televisions in the local bars to the stories in the local press, is the adventure of the moon shot, the controlling metaphor of the novel. But rather than a celebration of American technology and human daring, the moon shot suggests to Harry and Updike a probe into emptiness, a spectacular show of nothingness. As the astronauts soar up, Rabbit's life sinks down. His family falls apart in this novel. The dark side of the moon sheds its gloom on Brewer and Mt. Judge, Pennsylvania, where Harry still lives and works.

It is a wonder that he stays there. If the lunar spaces suggest a boundless wasteland, then downtown Brewer is desolation and its suburbs are plastic. Sludge chokes the rivers, burger joints peddle "Luna specials" complete with an American flag stuck on top, and young punks litter the street corners while looking for dope and kicks. More than any other Updike novel, *Rabbit Redux* shows the author's concern with social disturbance in the guise of the Vietnam War, the black protest movement, and the drug culture. The title of the novel means "Rabbit led back," but one glances around Brewer and asks why he bothers. The anger and frustration of middle America clash with the anger and needs of the black outsider, and Rabbit feels caught in the trap. How can he care about the astronauts' heroics when political events invade private lives? The more he is personally threatened, the louder he defends the war or accuses blacks; but once he finds himself an outcast in his own town, he calms down.

Harry feels paralyzed by the contrast between the little demands of the day and the looming crises of the nation. This conflict gives *Redux* its sense of counterpoint. On the one hand Rabbit wonders whether to purchase a Roto-Shine Magnetic Shoe Polisher or a Quikease Electric Massage for his dying mother, and on the other hand he struggles to defend the right of the United States to bomb in Southeast Asia. Through it all, he tries to cling to his dignity, to show that the nervous tics that once gave him his nickname are not a sign of aimlessness but a groping toward responsibility. Yet it is hard to act responsibly when one's life is disintegrating. *Rabbit Redux* is filled with disease and death as if Harry's personal predicament were a metaphor for the social collapse of traditional American values in the 1960s.

If Harry is a seeker in *Rabbit, Run,* an uncertain but determined stumbler after unseen worlds and the fluidity of "it," he is lethargic to the point of uncaring in *Redux.* His life bounded by his job as a linotypist at the Verity Press and his boring routine at home, he seems to move only when he takes the bus or drives in to Brewer for a tasteless dinner with Janice and Nelson. Finding him in the front yard, for example, Janice says that it is "funny" to see him outdoors. The man who once had the gift of life and the ability to give others faith now ignores every hint that his wife is having an affair. Although adultery may gall, Harry does not respond. He is too bewildered by changes that loom beyond his control: The moon shot alters his universe, the blacks alter his society, and the adultery alters his home. Updike juxtaposes the crises. While Janice dreams of her lover, "the papers and television are full of the colored riots in York, snipers wounding innocent firemen, simple men on the street, what is the world coming to? The astronauts are nearing the moon's gravitational influence."[1] Janice wants him to protest her betrayal. She even hopes that he will run again, for running would at least offer the relief of motion, but when she readies herself for a showdown, she finds Harry asleep. And when she finally does confess, even to the point of bragging that she does "things" for Charlie Stavros that she never does for him, Harry is not aroused.

Updike's comments on Rabbit and his predicament are revealing. In a well-known "interview" between Updike and his own character Henry Bech (*Bech: A Book,* 1970) in which Bech names *The Poorhouse Fair* as "surely his masterpiece," calls *Rabbit Redux* "Rabbit Rerun," and admits that he has not read past the first pages, Bech quotes Updike's response to a question about whether, in his later work, he hopes to "sing" America: "He said he was pro-American in the sense that he was married to America and did not wish a divorce;" that "by registration he was a Democrat and by disposition an apologist for the spirit of anarchy—our animal or divine margin of resistance to the social contract."[2] Rabbit finds himself in a similar crisis between standing up for America and sheltering the angry dispossessed, between sticking a decal of the American flag to his car window and giving a black fugitive from the law a ride out of town.

A decade earlier, in *Rabbit, Run*, it is Harry fleeing town. He obviously does not get very far. Ten years after the mock interview with Henry Bech, Updike again discussed his sense of Rabbit Angstrom. Noting that there is a lot to say about people who are not "especially beautiful or bright or urban," he describes his relationship with his most famous character:

He is very human in that he's a compound of physical urgencies and spiritual illusions. In this, he resembles not only me but, I suspect, many men. Also, I think, like me, he's kind of good-natured and accepting of what happens to him as though it were a sort of letter from above. . . . A wish to do no harm, as long as it doesn't cost him a great deal to avoid harm, is part of his character. A certain hardness of heart is also true of him; he is kind of callous at times. Yet he also has a great willingness to learn. He, like me, has been taught a lot not only by individual instructors, but by the times. It's been an era of increasing openness, of reconciliation to our bodies.[3]

Although these remarks were made on the occasion of the publication of the third Rabbit novel, *Rabbit Is Rich* (1981), they sketch the Harry Angstrom of *Redux*. Rabbit is caught between old restrictions and new temptations, between the inhibitions of the social contract and the freedoms of a permissive society. He longs for safety but yearns for joy, and the tension caused by the conflict nourishes guilt. Not so much running as stumbling in *Redux*, Rabbit cannot break through the difficult to achieve the beautiful. The net is not so pervasive as it is in *Rabbit, Run*, but it still hovers in the background. Updike comments:

There are prices paid for our strayings from the social net. . . . We're tightly enough packed that if one thing moves or falls out of place, there's a jostling felt all down the line, and someone suffers even if it's not you. You can perceive that your own wealth and happiness are in some sense carved from the hides of people who are less wealthy and happy, that your own sexual happiness is often carved from the hides of people who wind up as losers. So there's a temptation in front of my characters to remain absolutely quiet and not to be guilty of anything—shame or aggression.[4]

Rabbit is quieter in this novel. He listens, watches, and tries to roll with the punches, but not every commentator likes the change. One of the most puzzling reactions is Guy Davenport's. Admitting that Updike's fiction is always substantial and good to read, he argues that Updike's "amazing competence" denies the reader a chance to appreciate the "awkwardness of struggle . . . the exuberant botches . . . the shameless fun" of Fitzgerald or Faulkner or Dickens. This baffling comment suggests that Updike deserves censure because he avoids narrative disasters.[5] Similarly, Brom Weber applauds Updike's characterization of the black rebel Skeeter, a man who slips from the politics of rational protest to the apocalypse of maniacal anarchy, but Weber dismisses *Rabbit Redux* because Updike abandons speculation about spiritual crises to detail the nothingness at man's center.[6] Charles Thomas Samuels, usually a supporter of Updike's work, presents a more developed case for negative judgment. Picking up the tired cry that Updike should take a stand when he dissects the country's social conscience, as if he were a politician, Samuels insists that the author remains "too mute" about the problems of character motivation in *Rabbit Redux:* "Hence the refusal to determine the moral significance of the terrible events is Updike's and not the hero's . . . refusing to sort out the motives or to explain the discontent, he leaves us as baffled and dispirited as the age itself."[7] Samuels wants Updike not to be himself but to write like the Saul Bellow of *Mr. Sammler's Planet.*[8] Finally, in what amounts to a fullscale attack on *Redux*, Eugene Lyons dismisses the novel because Updike tries too hard to deliver a message about the United States in the 1960s and thus loses the objectivity that makes *Rabbit, Run* effective: ". . . to read the novel is to be taken on a guided tour of virtually every negative cliché that can be applied to America today."[9] Lyons documents his argument, but he takes the questionable stance of attributing Harry's and Skeeter's outbursts to Updike. Updike may feel an affinity with Rabbit, but one doubts if he uses the aging runner as a spokesman. There is unintentional irony in these evaluations, because before *Rabbit Redux* Updike was criticized for expending his magnificent prose on subjects too small for his talent. Now that a change occurs, the detractors who urged it do not like what they read.

Ecstatic praise far outweighs these negative comments. Writing what amounts to an overview of the Updike canon for the New York *Times,* Richard Locke comes right out and declares that "*Rabbit Redux* is a great achievement, by far the most audacious and successful book Updike has written."[10] Brendan Gill concurs, arguing that because *Redux* has a more complex plot than *Rabbit, Run*, "it is in every respect uncannily superior to its distinguished predecessor and deserves to achieve even greater critical and popular acclaim."[11] Noting such unqualified opinions, one might wonder if the enthusiasm of the first reading has colored the appraisals of a few commentators noted for their balanced judgment, but an examination of the response to *Rabbit Redux* reveals that critic after critic joins the celebration. John Heidenry, for example, puts the novel up against American fiction of the 1960s and declares that it is the "best American novel in a decade." Updike may not yet be creating masterpieces, says Heidenry, but he is "content to write only more brilliantly than anyone else." If the title is corny, if the ending is unsatisfactory, if Harry Angstrom is of a "limited aesthetic grade," the fact remains that Updike, better than any contemporary, justifies his art in every line.[12] R. Z. Sheppard takes a similar tack, rebutting the reviewers who claim that Updike tries too hard to probe society, and insisting that "*Redux* is superior to recent novels that trudge after social significance like recruits in new boots. Updike, after all, owns a rare verbal genius, a gifted intelligence and a sense of tragedy made bearable by wit."[13] And, finally, in a surprise move so unexpected as to prompt a doubletake, *Commentary* published a positive review.[14] Lauding the portrait of Skeeter as free of "authorial attitudinizing" and the ending as indefinite and hesitant, Robert Alter notes that *Redux* "says something that sounds right about where we are now."[15]

Where we are, according to the world of *Rabbit Redux*, is in a mess. Harry has returned to hearth and home, but he still feels crowded, hemmed in by an overprotective love of parents and son. His need to soar, rootless and free, is now just an "old premonition." But while Rabbit seems sadly stuck in place, as if middle age has bewildered his vision as well as becalmed his feet, the United States is rising above earth-bound problems when its astronauts lift toward the moon.

*Rabbit Redux* is divided into four sections, and for the epigraph to every part Updike quotes a snatch of dialogue by either American or Soviet space explorers. In each case the epigraph looks forward to the moon flight and backward to Harry's trap, for Updike makes sure that the quotations suggest both rocket technology and sex. Part of the epigraph, for example, to the first chapter reads: "I am heading straight for the socket." / "Easy, not so rough." But Harry is uninterested in both connotations of the word *socket*. All but impotent since Janice accidentally drowns their baby in *Rabbit, Run*, he unconsciously equates sex with death. Rather than illustrate an exuberant bursting through the socket toward unexplored worlds, the moonshot depresses Rabbit as a rush into nothingness. Hovering behind all the mundane crises of *Redux* is the ironic soaring of the rocket.[16]

Juxtaposed with the astronauts' adventure is the showing of Stanley Kubrick's famous movie "2001: A Space Odyssey." The film is beyond the comprehension of Janice and Harry, who wonder if the first thirty minutes will bore them. Even Janice's lover, Charlie Stavros, dislikes it because, as he says, he does not find technology sexy. Indeed, no one in the novel does, for *Rabbit Redux* suggests that impersonal technology is at odds with the personal handcraft and fine workmanship that once gave Americans a sense of themselves. Rabbit, for example, still works with his hands in the printing shop, but his job is about to be phased out by computer typesetting.

Thus what most of the world interpreted as an illustration of man's need to know becomes in *Redux* a metaphor for aspiration that is mechanical rather than spiritual and that ends not with transcendence but with the exploration of space, emptiness, and a dead bulk which can only reflect light. The men in the bar, Harry and Pop Angstrom among them, who watch the reports of the blast-off feel no surge. Lethargic and all but spiritless, Rabbit drinks two daiquiris in order to warm himself to the point where he ceases to feel cold, where his heart may begin to "lift off." But it does not lift far. Harry is convinced that intelligence has brought the United States only the atom bomb and the aluminum beer can, and he reveals his longing for the pre-1960 America, for the relative peace of Eisenhower and airplanes, when he laments that the voyage of Armstrong and the *Eagle* lacks the thrill of Columbus and the *Santa Maria*: "They keep mentioning Columbus but as far as Rabbit can see it's the exact opposite: Columbus flew blind and hit something, these guys see exactly where they're aiming and it's a big round nothing"(22).

This nothing permeates Harry's life, eats away at his spirit to the point where he barely resembles the younger searcher in *Rabbit, Run* who will not be beaten down by anyone's death but his own. While personal annihilation does not loom before him, the demise of middle America as he knows it does. Blacks have taken to the streets, Janice has taken a lover, and all Harry can do is take his dying mother a Quikease Electric Massager with Scalp Comb for her sixty-fifth birthday as the *Eagle* lands on the moon. Neil Armstrong touches the nothingness of the dead rock, and Harry touches the flesh of his mother's arm: It feels like "well-cooked chicken." Burger Bliss joins the bandwagon with a Luna Special, and the man who used to sell "Shredded Ralston between episodes of Tom Mix" peddles the moon shot with his news reports. Although Rabbit would not ask this question, he senses it: What ever happened to poetry, to unseen worlds, to the resounding "it" of the perfectly hit tee shot?[17] The opening movement of *Rabbit Redux* ends with the bungled televised monitoring of the first walk on the moon, and it coincides with Harry's first night in ten years without his wife. Armstrong, Aldrin, and Collins leave for the moon while Janice leaves for her lover.

Only Harry, it seems, has no place to go except to dreary Brewer, a city where men do not tan but turn yellow with sweat, and where the "great American glare" mocks Brewer's claim to fame that a "crucial electronic switching sequence" for the rocket is made there. The downtown area is awful enough, but even worse is Rabbit's neighborhood. It is not that the housing development is dangerous and decrepit but that it is plastic. Sterile, baked, and sad, his street is framed above by a "barren sky raked by slender aerials" and below by a "desolate smell from underground" (60). Harry compares the open neighborhood he had as a child with the closed one he has as an adult, and he senses that he is a stranger in a complex of transients. People all but unseen are always arriving and leaving in vans. He has been in the area all his life, but now no one knows his name. He might as well be living on the moon.

Wondering if the moon shot tries to pull America up while the blacks try to yank it back down, he looks at a country stranded in limbo, dying from its heart outward: "the sad narrow places that come and go called Go-Go or Boutique and the funeral parlors with imitation granite faces and the surplus outlets and a shoe parlor that sells hot roasted peanuts and Afro newspapers printed in Philly crying MBOYA MARTYRED" (14). For the first movement of the novel, Harry blames the blacks. Fascinated and repulsed, he resents their noisiness and their Afros, rejects their color and their speech. Characterizing blacks as potential snipers hugging roof tops, he puts a flag decal on the back window of his car to show that he will fight to save his own. They have already taken over basketball, the sport which used to make him shine as if lit by light from a star, and he fears that they will soon take over his country. Why can't blacks be like Tonto, he wonders, a man of another color who is always on "the side of right"? Harry cannot even talk with them because it makes him "feel itchy, up behind the eyeballs, maybe because theirs look so semi-liquid and yellow in the white and sore. Their whole beings seem lubricated on pain" (103).

Rabbit may be right, but the pain does not engage his empathy until later. Puzzled by the challenge to his traditional society in the late 1960s, he does not yet see the relationship between the blacks' sense of alienation and his own. His response is increasing lethargy while theirs is antic motion, and the contrast all but paralyzes him. It is not that Rabbit is a racist but that he distrusts mobility by those who do not accept the system. He has forgotten his own need of years ago to violate the social contract, but we remember.

At age thirty-six, Harry Angstrom is "soft, somehow pale and sour" with a thick waist, a stoop, and a "weakness verging on anonymity" (4). Few call him "Rabbit" anymore, but he still notices real flowers in the restaurant. His father is worn and tired and empty, a "man with no excess left to him," and his mother is dying of Parkinson's disease. Besides his scrapbooks with their cracked glue and forgotten headlines that proclaim he was once great, all Harry has left are family and job. But the former is disintegrating from inertia, and the latter is being phased out by technology. Janice may want to weep for how hard he has worked since his decade-long return from the lure of unseen spaces, but a few tears do not keep her from a run of her own. The point is that Updike uses Harry's perception of his personal decline as a metaphor for the sudden changes in society and space. Rabbit sinks while the rocket soars, but both seem headed for emptiness.[18] Although he still prays, especially when riding a bus, he worries about his house burning down or a madman moving in. Both happen.

Nothing better illustrates his bewilderment than his attitudes toward sex and Vietnam. In both cases Rabbit has unexpectedly turned conservative. Updike skillfully develops the metaphors, for later Rabbit's growing understanding of black pain, while not a major theme in *Redux*, is mirrored in his changing sense of sex and war. But for the moment, Harry is baffled to the point of impotence and clichés. One can only admire Updike's daring to reflect the general cataclysms of the late 1960s through the eyes of a man who is less intelligent than the author and most of his readers. Rarely a thinker, ignorant of ideas, Rabbit has always relied on intuition and feel, but even these have left him now, especially in sexual matters.

"Things don't mix," he says, and his feeling of being at loose ends applies to Janice and himself. The man who used to mix a lust for life with an appetite for sex now turns his back on both. The primary reason is not the accretions of age but the burdens of memory: He has assumed Janice's guilt over the drowning of their baby ten years ago. In *Rabbit, Run* he says to the shocked mourners, "Don't look at me. I didn't kill her," but in *Rabbit Redux* he cannot let go. Sex equals death:

Since he refused to get her pregnant again the murder and guilt have become all his. At first he tried to explain how it was, that sex with her had become too dark, too *serious*, too kindred to death, to trust anything that might come out of it. Then he stopped explaining and she seemed to forget: like a cat who sniffs around in corners mewing for the drowned kittens a day or two and then back to lapping milk and napping in the wash basket. Women and nature forget. (36–37)

But Rabbit does not, cannot, forget. The yawning recesses of the womb recall the grave. His mother's illness provides the counterpoint, for Harry feels trapped by the dying of parents, the death of babies, and the impotence in between. Living in a world of plastic, of modern gadgets that cannot be fixed, of McDonald's and Mobil, he encounters row after row of emptiness when he enters a drugstore to buy the massager for his mother. Updike is masterful here, cataloguing America's sordid plenty.[19] Stuck between women and death, between Snow Queen Blond shampoo-in hair color and Nudit for the legs, Harry is back in the land of MagiPeelers.

His sense of helplessness spills over to his attitude toward the Vietnam War. Harry is a stand-up-for-America guy, a man who shrugs off his wife's charge of fascism and all but says love it or leave it. Inarticulate as he is ("It's our flag, isn't it?"), he feels driven to defend the traditional American values of hard work, no handouts, and the side of right. He believes in the flag as more than symbol, as more than a piece of cloth, but just as Janice's brush with death a decade ago now taints him, so the hippies and blacks who reject the war foul more than the country. They heap dirt on the good guys too: "He has gotten loud again; it makes him rigid, the thoughts of the treachery and ingratitude befouling the flag, befouling him" (45). He believes that the only way he can cleanse himself is to offer to fight, either Charlie Stavros who steals his wife and sides with blacks, or the North Vietnamese.[20] Harry finally does not care about astronauts on the moon or napalm on the Cong. He cares only for his dream of America, but even that is slipping from him in a bombardment of impotence, revolution, and war: "America is beyond power, it acts as in a dream, as a face of God. Wherever America is, there is freedom, and wherever America is not, madness rules with chains, darkness strangles millions. Beneath her patient bombers, paradise is possible" (47). This is not Updike thinking but Rabbit, and his thoughts reflect his frustration as well as his fear. Everything is running down. Completely missing the point, Janice asks Harry if he wants their son to die in Vietnam. Rabbit retaliates, "Kid, I don't want you to die anyplace. Your mother's the girl that's good at death" (48). His accusation is gratuitous, needlessly cruel, and thus lacking the honesty of his baffled charge at the baby's funeral in *Rabbit, Run*. Harry and his country sink together.

But not Janice. Rabbit may continue to call her a dumb mutt, but she is also a new woman, blooming, quick with the latest slang like "bread" and "uptight," hip and ready. Although she is still a terrible cook and a daytime tippler, Rabbit suspects that she has changed to the point where he wonders if he detects another's voice in hers. He does, but he refuses to take the hint. The 1960s have saved Janice so that she may be herself, but Harry longs for the previous decade.

Updike offers more of Janice's point of view in *Redux*, and the result is increased sympathy for her predicament. Her confidence contrasts positively with Rabbit's bewilderment, and the reader realizes that the two have reversed roles. Now the runner in search of love and life, she shrinks from Rabbit's clinging: "She sees her flying athlete grounded, cuckolded. She sees a large white man a knife would slice like lard. The angelic cold strength of his leaving her, the anticlimax of his coming back and clinging: something in the combination that she cannot forgive, that justifies her" (34–35). The sad fact is that Rabbit is no longer the man she needs. Where he equates sex with death, she rushes toward ecstasy. Having a lover renews her, makes her past seem like a flat, fuzzy movie. Adultery has given her a voice, a sense of self, and she uses it to confront an unexpectedly passive husband who wants to live by traditional rules that no one pays homage to anymore.

Still, for all of Janice's renewal and her warm sense of being filled, she longs to love Harry and Nelson if they will accept her offering and let her grow. It is important to realize that Janice is not a radical feminist or a trendy bra-burner. She, too, wants a home and family but no longer at the expense of denying the self: "How sad it was with Harry now, they had become locked rooms to each other, they could hear each other cry but couldn't get in, not just the baby though that was terrible, the most terrible thing ever, but even that had faded . . ." (54). But when she confesses her betrayal, she realizes that adultery promises not a garden of bliss but a moonscape of emptiness. She is ready to snuggle back to Harry if he will only care enough to ask, but he is too complacent. Janice cannot know, for Harry cannot express it, that he fails to act for fear of failing her. Sex reminds him of baby Becky, and Becky reminds him of death. When Rabbit and Janice do make love, he frightened by her new-found knowledge and she ecstatic with her released joy, the silent television in the background shows the news of space modules and race riots. Emptiness seeps into the living room where they lie exhausted on the floor, and Harry all but gives up: He tells Janice to keep Charlie Stavros. Growth, he reasons, is no more than betrayal.

Updike knows that many readers already familiar with Harry Angstrom from the earlier novel will naturally sympathize with Rabbit in the standoff with Janice, so he develops her point of view in *Redux* in order to maintain a balance of sympathy. Rabbit's rebellion in the first novel has the positive factor of spiritual quest. The motions of grace direct his run, and we urge him forward even as we lament the backward glance. Such is not the case in *Redux*. His rebellion in the second novel has the negative factor of stagnation; it is a kind of rebellion in reverse. Updike, the reader, Harry, and most of all Janice understand his predicament, but for the moment no one knows how to prompt him to action. It is to Janice's credit that she has grown enough in the intervening decade to see that Harry is all but dying, that his surge toward life, the force which will not let him be beaten down in *Rabbit, Run,* is faltering.

Rabbit's problem is that he cannot take the first step toward recovery by himself. He understands that "there is no arriving somewhere without leaving somewhere," but he refuses to look beyond Brewer. The ball park is about as far as he dare wander. Yet even a sports arena, always a hallowed sanctum in Rabbit's mythology, carries the curse of emptiness. More than any other clue, Harry's sad disappointment with sports reveals his puzzled disillusionment with the nation: "Rabbit yearns to protect the game from the crowd; the poetry of space and inaction is too fine, too slowly spun for them. And for the players themselves, they seem expert listlessly, each intent on a private dream of making it, making it into the big leagues and the big money, the own-your-own-bowling-alley money;

they seem specialists like any other, not men playing a game because all men are boys time is trying to outsmart. A gallant pretense has been abandoned, a delicate balance is being crushed" (83–84).

Updike never overplays his hand toward didacticism, and he knows better than to confuse his own sentiments with his character's, but he does show in *Redux* that the balance being crushed in the late 1960s is not only that of sport but also those of earth and space, nation and populace, home and city, man and wife, and life and freedom. Rabbit senses all of these, but he can articulate only the magic of sports. Where athletics used to make him soar, propel him toward the joys of grace and rhythm, now they refuse to yield their secrets. He longs to believe what he once knew—"Where any game is being played a hedge exists against fury"—but he is now afraid to join the team. The order guaranteed by that hedge is diminished. Returning from the ball park, he finds Janice gone. Ten years ago he would have fought for his sense of self and started after her, but today he admits that he is a C-minus human being. Confidence leaks away. His scrapbooks cannot bring it back.

Part two, titled "Jill," introduces the first of two people who radically change his life. Janice moves out and Jill moves in, and Harry is yanked into new worlds and strange sex as suggested by the epigraph attributed to astronaut Neil Armstrong: "It's different but it's very pretty out here." Now speaking in the clichés of psychologists and television talk shows, and thus using such terms as "valid identity" and "motivate," Janice in her conversations parallels the nonsense of the Houston Space Command Center with its "Roger, copy" and "gravity align looking good." Jill, the teenaged runaway rich girl, is not immune either, for she preaches to Rabbit about the lack of "reflective content" in his life. The irony is, however, that for all their pleasure in believing they are hip, both Janice and Charlie Stavros want Janice to return home. Stavros, for example, will not marry her, and he comes to Rabbit looking for a way out. He finds Janice too confining, too demanding in her need to play "Helen of Troy," and Janice is furious because Rabbit does not run after her: "You might at least have fought a *little*" (217).

All through *Redux*, Updike contrasts old values with new, pre-1960 America with post, and he sets up Rabbit to shoulder the burden of the change. Value judgments are not necessarily an issue, but Harry's sense of loss is. Many of the columns he sets for the local newspaper are about Brewer's history, and thus he is always reminded how the traditional values of family and country are slipping away: horse-drawn trolley cars, tasteful buildings, permanent homes. Bewildered but not yet bitter, he wonders, "How can the planet keep turning and not get so bored it explodes?" (193). Even his mother, dying herself and dreaming of death, urges him to run, to say "yes" to life, to formalize his break with Janice and

Brewer, but he knows now, as he does not know in *Rabbit, Run,* that "freedom means murder. Rebirth means death" (198). If he says "yes" to the needs of the self, he must say "no" to the demands of society. To do so is to cause grievous pain, and he has already had enough of that.

The problem is that Harry exchanges one kind of injury for another when he offers Jill refuge from the netherworld of drugs and hustlers. A friend tells him that Jill will "hurt herself and anybody standing near," but his lethargy is so pervasive that he refuses to listen (121). Seventeen, dressed in soiled white, and still young enough to look happy when handed a lemonade, Jill is more sexually experienced than Rabbit has ever thought of being, ready to sleep with him immediately just to pay for the hamburger he buys her.

But though a drug addict and a runaway, Jill is no militant hippie rejecting the boundaries of country and home. Although she clearly wants changes in society so that blacks are accepted and the war stopped, she just as obviously longs for the traditions of security and love. The point is that both Jill and Harry are baffled by the breakup of the family. They meet in suspicion but turn toward love. She adopts the roles of mistress and homemaker while he plays the parts of lover and provider. As Jill says, Harry needs more help than she does, for she, at least, has seen God when high on dope. Unlike Rabbit, she still believes in upward spaces and what she calls "ecstasy" as a way out of the ego. She is Updike's flower child, his portrait of the 1960s student rebel who wants to give all she has to life but who seems destined to die.[21] When Harry cranks up his pro-war rhetoric, Jill reminds him that "God is in the tiger as well as in the lamb" (162). She is pliable, gentle, loving, and doomed. Accepting her implied offer to open him to the moment, Rabbit senses that she will receive only pain in return: "How sad, how strange. We make companions out of air and hurt them, so they will defy us, completing creation" (164).

Harry's verbal abuse of Jill is not pretty, especially since he admits that she has renewed his taste for living, but he does not know how to respond to people like Jill who apparently feel no fear. She may confess that she is in love with death in the guise of a former boyfriend who hooks her on heroin, but she also makes Rabbit realize that he has withdrawn from life and love because he does not think enough of himself. A "moonchild," she knows that Harry is earthbound. Updike stresses the final sterility of their mutual dependence on each other when he juxtaposes their love-making with the ever-present television reports of race riots and Vietnam. Each needs more than the makeshift home they set up. Jill hurries toward death while Rabbit creeps back toward Janice.

Updike's choice for the epigraph to part three, titled "Skeeter," is perfect, for it forewarns of the change of tone that the novel delivers.

Quoting a background voice from a Soviet spacecraft, he writes: "We've been raped, we've been raped!" There is no literal rape in part three, but Skeeter, a black madman, takes over Rabbit's house, and the dwelling eventually burns to the ground. Whatever forcible invasion takes place is the penetration of Harry's mind. Listening to Skeeter spout the rhetoric of revolution, Rabbit understands that *alienation*, a word he would never use, is not confined to his own sense of isolation. He is not converted from prejudice, but he finds himself less sure of his position.

Skeeter is one of Updike's most unusual characters, a black Vietnam veteran and dope pusher who wants to mow down the system. Critical opinion of Updike's success in sketching this harbinger of hate is divided. Eugene Lyons, who dislikes the entire novel, argues that Skeeter's elocution is too pompous and that Updike gives way to the lure of sentimentality when he associates the black radical with Christ: "Seldom, if ever, has any white writer been paralyzed into sentimental and self-contradictory blather quite so foolish in attempting to deal with a black character."[22] Others disagree, especially Robert Alter and Bernard Oldsey. Alter admits that Updike may strain the idea of black otherness, but he then agrees that the strategy works because the black man's sheer extremeness dazzles the passive Angstrom into attentiveness.[23] Oldsey goes even further and states that Skeeter is "perhaps the best fictional representation of a black by a white novelist, particularly in respect to his speech patterns and his burning drive."[24]

The question of the success of Updike's characterization of an alienated black man is not especially relevant, for what finally matters is not our individual judgments but Rabbit's fascination as the world out there walks through his front door. Although this is not the place to pursue comparisons, I suspect that the critical debate about Skeeter may be a carry-over from similar disputes in print about the authenticity of blacks in two widely read novels contemporaneous with *Redux*, William Styron's *The Confessions of Nat Turner* (1967) and Saul Bellow's *Mr. Sammler's Planet* (1970). From the calmer perspective of time, one wonders if the hue and cry were raised not because the black characters in the three novels are unsuccessful but because white authors in the midst of the black activist decade dared to create them.

Responding to Skeeter is not an either-or proposition. Updike, many readers, and characters both black and white in *Redux* react to his verbal prancing with fascination and revulsion. Buchanan, Harry's black co-worker, criticizes Skeeter's self-serving politics: "These young ones like Skeeter, they say All power to the people, you look around for the people, the only people around is *them*" (131). And Babe, a black piano player, says that he hates too much. Intelligent but full of clichés, able to act but drawn to violence, Skeeter is uncaring and finally unlikeable. Although he is often ironic, he admits that he is known for his lack of "sympathetic qualities" and that he is "one *baad* nigger." Even Harry can see that Skeeter's individuality is lost behind a series of roles, that he speaks in "many voices . . . and none of them exactly his" (206).

Updike has caught the speech tones and jazzed-up jargon of late 1960s blacks who toy with revolution. Listening to this radical is like tuning in a tape of the televised evening news during those directionless years: "We are fifty miles from the Mason-Dixon line where we sit, but way up in Detroit they are shooting nigger boys like catfish in a barrel. The news is, the cotton is in. Lynching season is on. In these Benighted States, everybody's done become a cracker" (207). Harry initially believes that this enraged little man is evil, like a "pit of scummed stench impossible to see the bottom of," yet he seems more upset when Skeeter mocks his belief in God and then proclaims himself the black Jesus. But passive Harry lets Skeeter hide in his house because Jill asks him to and because, he thinks, Janice may come home to rescue her husband and son from the danger. Even Jill, a pushover for everyone, confesses that Skeeter is "horrible. He really is. He feels all scaly, he's so bitter" (214).

The problem is that Jill, Harry, and perhaps Skeeter himself do not know why he has exchanged meaningful action for bitter denunciation. Is he furious because of what he has seen in Vietnam, or because he is a black man in a white society, or because he is unemployed in the land of plenty, or because he cannot adjust to the system, or because of all the above? His combination of jive talk and radical rhetoric baffles and intrigues Harry. It is as if the civil rights marchers he watches on television were suddenly in his own kitchen. But while magnetized, Angstrom realizes that living with Jill and Skeeter pulls him out of his depth toward a world of disorder and dirt. All his life he has relied on simplicity and light, cleanliness and order. When they have not been forthcoming, he has struck out on his own, running uphill toward openness. But not now. His house has degenerated from a home to a "refugee camp," and he is more an outsider in his dingy bedroom than the transients. Worse, after listening to Skeeter and Jill, he increasingly suspects that he is a stranger in his own land. When Skeeter gives him a lesson in American history complete with hip language and a simplistic grasp of cause and effect, Harry understands the lecture to say that all blacks are beautiful and all whites belong to "AMURRI-KA." All he can do is ask if anyone wants a beer. Skeeter's anger is the active side of Rabbit's passive prejudice. When Jill, for example, warns Harry to kick the radical out of the house, she sees that Harry is just as lethargic about the black madman as he is about his runaway wife. The result of his unwillingness to find his old stride is fire and Jill's death, but as always he survives to scamper away toward tomorrow. In the meantime his confusion muddles his sense of the present. Not sure whether a televised funeral is Everett Dirksen's or Ho Chi Minh's, or whether the attacking jets on the news reports are Israeli or Egyptian, he bounces back and forth between the safety zones of house and job. Hovering in the background all along is the threat of his mother's death, which he sees as the promise of his own.

Skeeter is a brilliant creation, a forerunner of the more poetic but still angry Ellelloû, but the entire section goes on too long. The reader loses what sympathy he may have had for this abused but crazed man when Skeeter deliberately hooks Jill on hard drugs after she has suffered to clear herself. His vengeance is gratuitous. Nor are the novel's suggestions that blacks *have* been crucified and that Skeeter has earned his claim to be a black Jesus supported by such quotes as the following when Rabbit looks at the black man's chest: "His skinny chest, naked, is stunning in its articulation: every muscle sharp in its attachment to the bone, the whole torso carved in a jungle wood darker than shadow and more dense than ivory. Rabbit has never seen such a chest except on a crucifix" (279). The same doubt lingers around the policeman's bulletin for the fugitive Skeeter: ". . . hair Afro, name Skeeter, that is Sally, Katherine, double Easter—" (329). One misses the saving tone of irony.

Watching Skeeter pull down everything he touches, Harry feels panicked by his hope for "catastrophe and deliverance" (252). He gets both. In some ways he has earned the disaster, for he stands by while Skeeter hooks Jill, and he ignores his neighbors' threats against his refugee camp. His solution is to rumple Nelson's hair and then plod to the kitchen for another beer. Jill is correct: It is too late for him to try to love her, for love requires action, something he has all but abandoned. Faced with such direct accusations, he slumps under the "puzzling heavy truth" (301). Harry is on his way from the heights of winning to the pit where losers congregate while life passes by. The hero of the scrapbooks and the perfect tee shot has all but come to nothing along with the yellowed clippings and the cracked glue. Jill dies when Harry's neighbors, furious at seeing Skeeter and her make love in the living room, set fire to the house.

A touch of irony pierces Rabbit's grief. Fleeing the net in *Rabbit, Run*, a metaphor that Updike brilliantly establishes throughout the novel, Harry now longs for the protective clinging of the "net of law" in *Redux*. It slips from him when his house burns, but losing the house frees him to pick up the pieces. Skeeter remains disturbingly bitter at the end. Nonchalant about Jill's death, he accepts Rabbit's offer of a ride out of town and then spits in Harry's outstretched hand. Rabbit may choose to view the spit as a blessing, but we know better. Skeeter is death.

The final section, titled "Mim" after Rabbit's high-class, call-girl sister, begins with another epigraph of sex and space as Updike quotes astronaut

Aldrin directing Neil Armstrong toward the lock. The domestic particulars of the novel are resolved in this section, but Updike resists the opportunity to provide perfect bliss. At the end he leaves Janice and Harry together in a motel, halfway between home and love nest. With gentle irony he lets them do nothing but sleep. Both have traveled a tiring road back.

Harry survives the ignominy of having to set type for the newspaper story that describes the burning of his own house, but the injury is intensified when his linotype position is phased out as obsolete. Wife, house, job: He loses all three. When his boss apologizes for the way everything moves faster "nowadays," Rabbit can only reply with the sad truth, "Except me." He longs for the world of "blameless activity," where motion is grace and all men are scorers, but he has no place to go except to his parents' home. Thirty-six years have circled him back to the beginning. The occasional shift to past tense in these pages emphasizes Rabbit's sense of loss, his feeling of stasis, his premonition of ending.

Updike's fiction shows that salvation wears a mask of many colors, from dead pigeons to crows in the woods, that the joys of blessings reveal themselves in unexpected ways. The humanistic abstractions of a Reverend Eccles will not work with Rabbit, but practical action by a tough-minded sister might. Mim comes home to see her dying mother but leaves after saving her baffled brother.

Mim is the only character who has taken total advantage of the wide-open 1960s. Rather than interpret every event as a catalyst for a cause, she rolls with the punches, prospers from the absurdities, refuses to give in to the emptiness. Mim grows while the others, except for Janice, barely survive, and she treats the chaos of the Angstrom household with the bemused irony that it deserves. A west-coast call girl who is confident and successful, she dazzles her eyes with "Egyptian" makeup and wears the modish clothes we all remember: bell-bottoms and short skirts and oddly shaped shoes and panty hose without panties. With her big-city gestures and tough-minded colloquialisms, Mim strides through the hallways bringing energy and color to the dreary Angstrom lives. She sees through the smoke and cuts through the lethargy to the central fact left untouched in Harry's dilemma: Janice wants to return home.

Despite the upheavals, Harry has not learned much beyond some experiences in sexual freedom, and he insists to Mim that his days with Jill and Skeeter still "feel" right to him, that he has been a Good Samaritan for giving them shelter. But Mim knows that Harry is soft and thus weak, and she warns him that the desert creeping over the western states has its sights set on Brewer. The blasted surface of the moonscape will soon be everywhere, fouling inner as well as outer spaces. Janice, Mim argues to Harry's amazement, is much tougher than Rabbit. Her contribution to the rehabilitation of the Angstrom home, her "service" as she calls it, is to separate Janice and Charlie. All she has to do is seduce Stavros, which she accomplishes with professional ease.

Mim is a flashy manager of people in the amateur world of Brewer. Making the family laugh, drawing out Nelson, bringing her mother downstairs, she opens up the house. Someone has to act, since Harry just sits around without even a job to move him in the mornings, a muddler with no idea about how to get out of his mess. Only Mim knows enough to tell him, "Everybody else has a life they try to fence in with some rules. You just do what you feel like and then when it blows up or runs down you sit there and pout" (370).

How right she is. Rabbit keeps looking for the securities of yesterday while his present crumbles before him. *Rabbit Redux* is the novel in which Harry Angstrom finally says good-bye to his past. The little details of the quotidian that once shaped his life even after graduation from high school are meaningless to him now as he drifts rather than runs into middle age. Without these details he has no bearings. Without bearings he all but gives way. The typical American literary hero ignores time to try to escape in space, but in *Rabbit Redux* time has caught up with Harry Angstrom. The pathos associated with the final grounding of Hawkeye, Huck Finn, Gatsby, and Ike McCaslin is a natural reaction to America's literary escapists. Harry Angstrom is about to join the queue. Time always overtakes space no matter how far the hero flees:

These mundane surfaces had given witness to his life; this chalice had held his blood; here the universe had centered, each downtwirling maple seed of more account than galaxies. No more. Jackson Road seems an ordinary street anywhere. Millions of such American streets hold millions of lives, and let them sift through, and neither notice nor mourn, and fall into decay, and do not even mourn their own passing but instead grimace at the wrecking ball with the same gaunt façades that have outweathered all their winters. (373–374).

With little remaining but memory, he finds an old basketball to shoot to a rusted rim on a crooked backboard in the rain. Wearing an old jock jacket will not help, and no one shoots set shots anymore.

All he has left are Janice and Nelson, the wreckage of the order he needs, so he and Janice return to each other: "Her trip drowns babies; his burns girls. They were made for each other" (395). The pastures and brooks he imagines at the end of the road turn into hamburger joints and motels, and Harry accepts the truth that has seared him in the past: inner needs may propel him, but there is no place to go. Mim's desert is moving east, and the lifeless moon hovers overhead. Janice's accusation hits home, "When're you going to grow up, even a little bit?" (399). He does not know. All he can do is start over. His first tentative step is to take Janice to the "Safe Haven Motel" where they can burrow into bed not for sex but for rest. Harry speaks first:

> "I feel so guilty."
> "About what?"
> "About everything."
> "Relax. Not everything is your fault."
> "I can't accept that." (406)

But he does. Updike's final words address the reader and suggest the equilibrium achieved, the truce declared: "He. She. Sleeps. O.K.?"

For the moment there is nothing else beyond this tenuous reconciliation. The final "O.K." hints that theirs is the sleep not of transcendence but of acceptance.[25] Run to ground, Rabbit abandons the quest for upward spaces to huddle with the person who first drove him to run. He has indeed been led back.

## NOTES

1. John Updike, *Rabbit Redux* (New York: Knopf, 1971), p. 57. Further references will be noted in the text.
2. Henry Bech (John Updike), "Henry Bech Redux," New York *Times Book Review*, 14 November 1971, p. 3. Bech-Updike also comments indirectly on the lack of protection Rabbit has from the threat of mortality when the uniform edition of Updike's books is described as "shingles, with the which this shivering poor fellow hopes to keep his own skin dry in the soaking downpour of mortality."
3. Michiko Kakutane, "Turning Sex and Guilt into an American Epic," *Saturday Review*, (October 1981), p. 15.
4. Kakutane, p. 22. Updike also suggests another parallel between himself and Rabbit when he comments in this interview on the relationship between sports and writing: "Certainly writing is, among other things, a kind of athletic achievement—just the mental quickness, the ability to combine thoughts simultaneously."
5. Guy Davenport, "Even as the Heathen Rage," *National Review*, 31 December 1971, p. 1474.
6. Brom Weber, review of *Rabbit Redux*, *Saturday Review*, 27 November 1971, pp. 54–55.
7. Charles Thomas Samuels, "Updike on the Present," *New Republic*, 20 November 1971, pp. 29–30.
8. For a reply to Samuels' censure see Alice and Kenneth Hamilton, "John Updike's Prescription for Survival," *Christian Century*, 5 July 1972, pp. 740–744. One should remember, however, that the Hamiltons always applaud Updike's work. They do not, on the other hand, try to counter Marvin Mudrick's charge that *Rabbit Redux* begins with an impassioned defense of Rabbit but ends with features of "urban apocalypse" that remind him of Joyce Carol Oates. See "Fiction and Truth," *Hudson Review,* 25 (Spring 1972), pp. 151–152.

9. Eugene Lyons, "John Updike: The Beginning and the End," *Critique*, 14, 2(1972), pp. 44–59.

10. Richard Locke, review of *Rabbit Redux*, New York *Times Book Review*, 14 November 1971, pp. 1 ff.

11. Brendon Gill, "A Special Case," *New Yorker*, 8 January 1972, pp. 83–84.

12. John Heidenry, "The Best American Novel in a Decade," *Commonweal*, 7 January 1972, pp. 332–333. Bernard Oldsey agrees, saying that "it is doubtful that he has an equal in this country." See "Rabbit Run to Earth," *Nation*, 10 January 1972, pp. 54–55.

13. R. Z. Sheppard, "Cabbage Moon," *Time*, 15 November 1971, p. 89. Even the short notices of *Redux* reveal the highest praise. Bruce D. Allen calls it "reckless and contrived and probably his best," and the *Virginia Quarterly Review* says that Updike dramatizes our follies and moral poverty "brilliantly." See Bruce D. Allen, "Of a Linotype Operator at the Edge of Obsolescence," *Library Journal*, 1 November 1971, p. 3640; and "Notes on Recent Books," *Virginia Quarterly Review*, 48(Spring 1972), p. xlviii.

14. Robert Alter, "Updike, Malamud, and the Fire This Time," *Commentary*, (October 1972), pp. 68–74.

15. The British reaction to *Rabbit Redux* is generally favorable and may be summarized by William Trevor's comment: "Updike's Rabbit saga may not yet be complete, but so far it suggests that if the novel is dying it's managing to do so while still in remarkably good health." See "All Right, Sort of," *New Statesman*, 7 April 1972, pp. 462–463.

16. For an interesting discussion of Updike's use of the moonshot in light of how Norman Mailer and Saul Bellow treat it, see George Held, "Men on the Moon: American Novelists Explore Lunar Space," *Michigan Quarterly Review*, 18(Spring 1979), especially pp. 333–341.

17. For Updike's spoof of a later moon shot and its connection with golf, see "The First Lunar Invitational" in *Picked-Up Pieces* (New York: Knopf, 1975), pp. 92–94.

18. Although I imply no connection, I find it interesting that Updike's combination of the rocket and emptiness looks forward to a splendid fictional account of the same relationship, Thomas Pynchon's *Gravity's Rainbow* (New York: Viking, 1973).

19. Those who have read *The Coup* know that Rabbit may turn an aisle and bump into Ellelloû in the same drugstore.

20. For a variation on this topic in the Updike canon, see his short story "Marching Through Boston," *Museums and Women* (New York: Knopf, 1972).

21. For another look at Updike's pictures of flower children, see "The Hillies," *Museums and Women* (New York: Knopf, 1972).

22. Lyons, pp. 57–58.

23. Alter, p. 73.

24. Bernard Oldsey, "Rabbit Run to Earth," *Nation*, 10 January 1972, p. 55.

25. Ten years after the publication of *Rabbit Redux*, Updike authorized a special signed edition of the novel for the Franklin Library. In a short "special message to subscribers," he writes, "The question that ends the book is not meant to have an easy answer." He also all but identifies Harry with America itself: "America and Harry suffered, marvelled, listened, and endured. Not without

cost, of course." See John Updike, "A Special Message to Subscribers," in *Rabbit Redux* (Franklin Center, Pennsylvania: The Franklin Library, 1981).

# Rabbit Is Rich

*"So who says he's running out
of gas?"*

—*Rabbit Is Rich*

When Rabbit Angstrom and Janice scamper back to each other at the end of *Rabbit Redux* to fall asleep in a motel room, Harry seems momentarily freed from the need to scurry from family and friends, crammed ash trays and stagnation, in search of grace and fluidity. Grace in all its guises still eludes him in *Rabbit Is Rich* (1981), and fluidity is lost in an expanding waistline and bank account, but Rabbit is alive and well and moderately wealthy. The Rabbit novels are John Updike's Barchester chronicles, for, like Anthony Trollope, Updike uses his fiction to choreograph the social dance of an age. Each Rabbit novel records the tone of a decade. *Rabbit Is Rich* is about the late 1970s, and the rainbow Harry chases in the 1950s and 1960s has shrunk as the American dream goes sour with the bad taste of advancing age and aimless youth.

Farmland turns to shopping malls, overflowing garbage cans stink beside unsuccessful plywood restaurants, and people reel from a combination of less energy and higher prices. Now forty-six years old and gaining, Rabbit does not blame anyone for Skylab's falling or Exxon's greed, but death beckons from the horizon and he is afraid of running out of gas. When he looks over his shoulder at the glory of early fame too easily won on the basketball court nearly three decades earlier, and thinks of himself as "King of the lot" and "star and spearpoint" of the flourishing Toyota dealership his family owns, we know that he has not changed too much from the man in the earlier novels whose value system is defined in terms of athletics.

But he has changed somewhat: Golf has replaced basketball, and he rumbles rather than runs with a forty-two-inch waist and a tendency to avoid mirrors when he used to love reflections of himself. Still, Rabbit is rich in the ironic sense of being able to afford cashews instead of peanuts, country clubs instead of bowling alleys. Life is sweet. For the first time in twenty-five years he is happy to be alive, even content with his marriage to Janice. Despite Janice, golf, and money, however, Rabbit needs to run, not so fast and not so far, but somewhere. He muses on the "entire squeezed and cut-down shape of his life," and he realizes that middle age is upon him, a time when dreams decline to an awareness of limits, and stomachs take on a noticeable sag.[1] The strained jollity of the country club set, the kind of crowd that "will do a marriage in if you let it," makes him uneasy, but his flight in this novel is not so urgent as it is in *Rabbit, Run* and thus not so poignant (67).

Later, Rabbit "glimpses the truth that to be rich is to be robbed, to be rich is to be poor" (375). In part he means spiritually poor, though he would not say it that way, so he and Janice break with his mother-in-law and buy their own home. Perhaps his rainbow is in the suburbs. He still longs for a world without ruts, but God at times is no more than a raisin under a car seat. In *Rabbit, Run*, Harry runs toward transcendence, toward what he calls "it," but now he has only a vacation in the Caribbean to rejuvenate him. There, engaged in wife-swapping where he once pursued life's rhythm, he even misses his dream girl when his second choice leads him away by the hand.

But no matter; he has his own life to live. At age forty-six, ten years after Jill dies and Janice returns, Rabbit is not so tied to the news of the day as he is in *Rabbit Redux*. Accounts of space flights and race riots all but surround him in the earlier novel. From the newspaper items he sets as a linotypist to the nightly blarings of the televised news, the despair of his life is linked to the disintegration of his country. Public matters invade domestic affairs, and inarticulate Rabbit finds himself forced to discuss such controversies as Vietnam and civil rights about which he knows little but worries much. In *Rabbit Redux* he is ripped from the self and hurled to the world. He does not belong there, and he knows it. Ever the man with the singular vision, with the sole response of what *feels* right to him, Rabbit can only be more baffled when made to think about the needs and accomplishments of those beyond his immediate circle. How, he wonders, can he react to the spectacular demands of astronauts and blacks when he cannot meet the mundane requirements of family and friends? The conflict between the headline events of the day and the dailiness of his own predicament all but paralyzes him. The novel ends the only way it can: the newspapers are unread, the television is off, and Rabbit is asleep.

In *Rabbit Is Rich*, however, the relationship between headlines and Harry has been reversed, and Rabbit awakens from his sleep in the Safe Haven Motel to focus once more on the needs of the self. He thinks more in this novel. Religious speculation (*Rabbit, Run*) and political concerns

(*Rabbit Redux*) give way to interior monologues about economic practicalities. Newsworthy events abound, especially OPEC's prices and the decline of the dollar, but Harry now discusses them only insofar as they affect his ability to peddle Toyotas or to speculate in gold. It is not that he is back on the road toward the motions of grace as he is in *Rabbit, Run*, but that he is comfortable enough in *Rabbit Is Rich* to put the headlines behind him. Not Skeeter's diatribes but *Consumer Reports* guides his response to the world.

The return from the world to the self has also affected his attitude toward sex. In *Redux* he is indifferent to the point of impotence because he peers at the dark enclosure of the womb and sees the grave. Janice may be more than willing and utterly uninhibited, but Harry associates her with the baby's drowning in *Rabbit, Run* and shoulders the guilt she has outgrown. Only Jill reawakens his sexual life in *Redux*, but then she dies too. No wonder all he can do at the end of the novel is sleep despite an eager, naked wife in his motel bed.

In *Rabbit Is Rich* impotence and indifference are gone. Slim and tan and never looking better, Janice leads Rabbit to a sex life that is often imaginative and usually fun. After two and a half decades of marriage, they admit an attraction to each other. But while the mystery of sex is ever present once Harry manages to divorce it from death, the frantic anguish associated with sex in *Rabbit, Run* seems lost forever. The contrast is one of Updike's ironies, for *Rabbit Is Rich* has more sexually explicit scenes than any of his other novels to date. Indeed, Rabbit cannot glance at attractive women without imagining how they would look stripped of this dress or posed in that position. Yet while not so lusty as in the past, sex for Harry is now a gift to be enjoyed rather than a wonder to be examined. His equation of sex with the lure of upward spaces and unseen worlds gives an affirmative quality to his affairs in *Rabbit, Run*, but it also causes pain to himself and others when he watches the real always stumble short of the ideal. No matter how far he runs, or how many women he pursues, the "it" of the perfect tee shot remains out there, beyond him.

Such anguish is not a factor in *Rabbit Is Rich*, and Harry is all the happier for its absence. His failure to get desirable Cindy Murkett into bed after viewing photographs of her in athletic positions and seeing her breasts swing in a loosely cut bathing suit brings disappointment but not despair. Rabbit may admit to Janice that it is "frightening" when he does not long for a platinum-haired woman who sells them gold coins, but his sex life is not winding down too quickly. He enjoys more with less. Unconsciously mimicking *McTeague*, Janice is eager when he covers her body with coins. Rabbit looks her over and sees that he is rich.

As he did upon the publication of *Redux*, Updike consented to an interview with his character Henry Bech when *Rabbit Is Rich* was finished.

His most interesting response to Bech suggests that Harry Angstrom is more typical than many readers may want to admit: "I distrust books involving spectacular people, or spectacular events. Let *People* and *The National Enquirer* pander to our taste for the extraordinary; let literature concern itself, as the Gospels do, with the inner lives of hidden men. The collective consciousness that once found itself in the noble must now rest content with the typical."[2] As he explains elsewhere, the less-than-spectacular quality of Rabbit's life is one reason why he continues the tale every decade: "I left some dangling threads in that book [*Redux*], possibly to be picked up later. But the real shape of *Rabbit Is Rich* didn't occur to me until the gas crunch of June 1979." Harry's economic predicament during that summer is as representative as that of any motorist who has had to wait in line at the local Exxon station while the price per gallon goes up by the hour. Rabbit's reflection of middle America's problems is why he may be with Updike for a while: "I don't know what the decade will bring me. I hope to be alive and writing still, and if I am, I expect Rabbit will be alive too, in his corner of Pennsylvania."[3] If Harry remains near his stomping ground of Brewer, Pennsylvania, he is likely to enjoy what Updike calls "the relative happiness and freedom from tension that you might find in your 40s." But this contentment does not mean that Rabbit's shaky repose is Updike's personal goal: "There's a moment in the organism when its thrust outward into the world and the call to mate and the need to make your mark no longer clamor at you, but the body hasn't quite begun to collapse, so in a strange way it's a kind of happy moment. But while being at peace is probably a pretty good condition for a car salesman, I'm not sure it's a good condition for a writer."[4]

Most of the commentators who reviewed *Rabbit Is Rich* greeted the novel with the pleasure one reserves for meeting an old friend who is not lethargically at peace. But not James Wolcott. Denying the humor in Rabbit's latest round of befuddlement, Wolcott argues that the novel is "grumpy and despairing, swollen with forlorn rue." The old runner who has been shackled by circumstance in the earlier novels is now "lashed to the mast of Updike's theme. . . . impaled on the pike of Updike's grim sense of purpose" that entropy dooms everything: "it's a stoically grim affair."[5] Wolcott develops his case at length, but nearly everyone else disagrees. Roger Sale, for example, dislikes *Redux* but praises the sequel as "the first book in which Updike has fulfilled the fabulous promise he offered with 'Rabbit, Run' and 'The Centaur' 20 years ago."[6] Thomas R. Edwards agrees in almost the same terms. He, too, feels uneasy about *Redux*, but he finds *Rabbit Is Rich* "a strong, secure novel, one of Updike's wisest and funniest. . . . Here a remarkable literary talent, far from running out of gas, rides smoothly and efficiently in overdrive, getting maximum mileage from minimal apparent effort."[7] In a splendid essay, V.

S. Pritchett praises the Rabbit novels as "a monumental portrayal of provincial and domestic manners. He is both poet and historian, so various in observation and so truthful, so inventive and adept, that he leaves one brooding on his scene and remembering his epithets."[8] Finally, Paul Gray lauds the book as "a superlative comic novel that is also an American romance," and Eliot Fremont-Smith welcomes the "renewal of affection," the "return of grace" that *Rabbit Is Rich* offers.[9]

Affection and ease accompany Harry with nearly every stride of his jog into middle age. The frantic scurrying of *Rabbit, Run* and the lethargic stasis of *Rabbit Redux* are gone, and Harry moves through *Rabbit Is Rich* in a leisurely fashion as Updike lingers over descriptions of Angstrom's ride home after work and his small talk after golf. Yet Harry is still not an ideal person, as the two epigraphs suggest. Playing with the echoes of Babbitt and Rabbit, Updike quotes from Sinclair Lewis and Wallace Stevens. The passage from Lewis is George Babbitt's definition of the Ideal Citizen: "At night he lights up a good cigar, and climbs into the little old 'bus, and maybe cusses the carburetor, and shoots out home. He mows the lawn, or sneaks in some practice putting, and then he's ready for dinner." The passage from Stevens is three lines of "A Rabbit as King of the Ghosts":

> The difficulty to think at the end of day,
> When the shapeless shadow covers the sun
> And nothing is left except light on your fur . . .

George F. Babbitt, of course, personifies Lewis' satire of middle America. He is the naive yet vaguely unfulfilled man who exchanges ideas for cigars, experience for routine, and then settles down to some putting practice and a good meal. Stevens' poem comically exposes a rabbit who, disappointed with his status in the unyielding light of reality, engages the imagination to create a perfect world where he is puffed up to heroic stature. Harry Angstrom touches both extremes but rests more comfortably between them. He may not cuss the carburetor of his fancy Toyota before shooting on home, but he is nicely settled between Janice's lousy dinners and his own lousy golf. Like Stevens' rabbit, the world is there for him if only he can imagine dominion over it. But Harry has trouble dominating even his own house.

Updike's Rabbit is continually pulled down by the pressures of reality. The potential promise of the moon shot in *Redux*, for all its ironic exploration of nothingness, is gone. No one is soaring toward the moon in *Rich*; each person is just trying to hang on. Brewer has deteriorated even more since *Redux*. Although the city fathers have tried to rescue the downtown area with pedestrian malls and trees, "Everywhere in this city, once the fourth largest in Pennsylvania but now slipped to seventh, structures speak of expended energy. . . . These acres of dead railroad track and car shops and stockpiled wheels and empty boxcars stick in the heart of the city like a great rusting dagger" (32–33). The dagger does not pierce Rabbit because he has found a measure of comfort in middle age, but he looks at this world from the security of forty thousand a year and all he sees is everything running down.

The first word of the novel is "running," but it no longer pertains to anguished searches for unseen worlds. Rather, the word refers to a planet that is literally and figuratively running out of gas. OPEC limits production while Exxon smiles and collects, and the joyride of the past slows to a crawl. Later in the novel Rabbit worries about running down himself, but for the moment the combination of outrageous prices for gasoline and American gas guzzlers has made him comfortable with his Toyotas. Entropy threatens but Harry seems untouched. Such scientific notions are beyond him anyway. Questing in the first novel, mired in the second, he is secure and almost smug in the third. Life can be good in the middle forties with golf partners ready on Saturday and a wife who has never looked better: "Middle age is a wonderful country, all the things you thought would never happen are happening. When he was fifteen, forty-six would have seemed the end of the rainbow, he'd never get there, if a meaning of life was to show up you'd think it would have by now. Yet at moments it seems it has, there are just no words for it, it is not something you dig for but sits on the top of the table like an unopened dewy beer can" (231). The trick is to stretch toward the table and open the can, but Harry's inner drive has slowed down more than he likes to admit.

The roar of athletic glory only pricks the memory now, but Rabbit has not yet entirely forgotten. His press clippings yellowing on the walls of his office, he can glance at them when necessary. The key point is, however, that he no longer feels crowded by younger athletes elbowing their way through the locker room, and he is grateful to some of the dead, such as Janice's father, for owning the Toyota dealership and then dying and willing him space. As he looks around the showroom and over to Parts and Service, he knows that he is "a center of sorts, where he had been a forward" (6). He does not like the clothes salesman pointing to his waist, and he resents the slack cords blooming beneath his chin and down his neck, but "life is sweet. That's what old people used to say and when he was young he wondered how they could mean it" (6). No wonder he can hire Charlie Stavros, Janice's former lover, as a salesman. Their bitter debates about Vietnam a decade ago have given way to serene disagreement about whether President Carter and big oil are responsible for the energy crisis, but they are selling too many Toyotas to whip up much emotion with their opinions. Still, behind all the profits and the security and the fun, behind all the glow of middle age and the sense that life is sweet, lurks the leer of death. Rabbit is more than halfway home, and he knows it. At the beginning of the novel he does not want to face the leer directly, but he senses its grin behind the bedroom wall. The dark specter is a factor throughout *Rabbit Is Rich:* "The dead, Jesus. They were multiplying, and they look up begging you to join them, promising it is all right, it is very soft down here. . . . The obituary page every day shows another stalk of a harvest endlessly rich, the faces of old teachers, customers, local celebrities like himself flashing for a moment and then going down" (9–10).

Janice has no sympathy with such gloom. She may be Rabbit's victim at times, but she is a survivor, stronger than her husband, able to consolidate her strength with that of other women and grow. Making Harry proud by playing tennis four times a week at the country club, she tans as easily as she exudes confidence. Rabbit admires her manner and admits that "the decade past has taught her more than it has taught him" (138). Her refusal to move out of her mother's house rankles a bit, but even with Mom watching "M.A.S.H." in the next bedroom, her interest in sex is open and free. With her tubes tied to avoid the side effects of the pill, Janice is animated and aggressive in bed. Updike treats their tumbles through the sheets comically, especially in the scene in which a slightly high Janice tries to seduce a slightly drowsy Rabbit while he reads *Consumer Reports.* The unstoppable lover of *Rabbit, Run* has gotten older. Without some hint of adventure, thinks Harry, sex is often just another duty.

Sadly, for those who remember his earlier rebellion, Rabbit wants to pull over, if only to let a teenaged girl in a yellow LeMans pass him on the road. Even before his son Nelson returns home to precipitate the crisis in the novel, he worries about the sheer destructiveness of the younger set: "Was he that way at that age? You want to make a mark. The world seems indestructible and won't let you out. Let 'em by" (35). But while he feels relatively uncrowded in his life, he senses a trap in his home. The galling point is that it is not his home. Twenty years ago he would have run from the hemmed-in feeling, from the diminishing spaces of crammed rooms and dirty dishes, but all he does now is jog after dinner. Such limited running does not lead to air and light: "there isn't a corner of the Springer house where Harry feels able to breathe absolutely his own air, feels the light can get to him easily" (38). His intuition is the same as two decades ago, but the result today is frustration instead of fear.

In his more desperate moments, he tries to blame Janice for what he sees as the cut-down quality of his life. Yet unlike the Rabbit of old, he does not want out; he wants in, a house of his own, before he runs out of gas. How can he grow, he muses, when he lives with his mother-in-law in a house that his unlikeable son wants to invade, while just down the street resides a "crew of butch women" who seem to do nothing except hammer and saw? Skylab may be falling, but Harry has other concerns: "Our lives fade behind us before we die" (47). Each day he is a little more cognizant and a little less fearful of death, and he realizes that Janice must wonder if he still equates the recesses of the womb with the depths of the grave. It is not that he finds her unappealing or that the old equation of sex and death interferes. The problem, as Updike comically describes it, is a matter of confidence: "He blames it on money, on having enough at last, which has made him satisfied all over; also the money itself, relaxed in the bank, gets smaller all the time, and this is on his mind, what to do about it, along with everything else: the Phils, and the dead, and golf" (49). Harry's problems in middle age are not theological, political, or even economic. They are personal, so personal that at any given moment a losing streak by the Philadelphia Phillies seems as significant as his sporadic sex drive. Indeed, at one point Rabbit wonders if he gets a greater thrill from tumbling with Janice or from maneuvering a soft chip shot toward the pin. Golf, he decides, is like "life itself in that its performance cannot be forced and its underlying principle shies from being permanently named" (50). At the country club he feels nourished by space and cherished by friends. People there at least know his name.

Readers of *Rabbit Is Rich*, then, join Harry in wondering if his instinctive surge for life has burned out. He is too young to call it quits, but he may be too old to keep it up. The prospect is both sad and frightening, for his interior life shrinks as his external circumstances expand. Harry is no psychologist, but he thinks enough in this novel to realize that he does little about his interior losses except recognize a daily diminishment: "In his inner life too Rabbit dodges among more blanks than there used to be, patches of burnt-out gray cells where there used to be lust and keen dreaming and wide-eyed dread . . ." (13). These blanks in his otherwise comfortable circumstances are why he wonders if the twenty-year-old woman in the Toyota lot is his illegitimate daughter by Ruth, the woman he shacks up with in *Rabbit, Run* when he leaves Janice and who still lives near Brewer. Rabbit senses his need for a quest, and he hopes that the young woman with the skimpy clothes and the soft body will provide it. An illegitimate daughter in exchange for a dead one would be a blessing from immortality. Yet as with the quester in a medieval romance, not consummation but pilgrimage is all. Harry needs the chase, not the certainty, and thus he wanders rather than hurries toward Ruth and the answer: "Harry wants to ask, but doesn't, lest he frighten her, and destroy for himself the vibration of excitement, of possibility untested" (22). Middle-aged rabbits run slower.

But he has not quit his scampering altogether. George Babbitt has his fairy child; Rabbit Angstrom has his Cindy. Young and married and able to wear slinky bathing suits at the country club without ruining the effect with self-consciousness, Cindy Murkett has "an exciting sexually neutral look" (57). Harry's quest for unseen worlds has ironically narrowed to his need to see Cindy's body, but one wishes him luck anyway. Updike describes Rabbit's dream woman perfectly by providing a few key details. For example, when Janice walks to the clubhouse in her modest bathing suit, she covers herself with a towel. When Cindy does the same thing in her more revealing suit, she never thinks of hiding. Modesty is not the issue; confidence is, and Cindy has it. Harry's desire is apparently obvious to everyone, but no one cares enough to speak up except Janice. After twenty-five years of marriage, years in which both have sidestepped toward other lovers, she recognizes his gleaming eye and calls his number: "You *always* want what you don't have instead of what you *do*" (72). Janice speaks this truth when Rabbit mistakenly mentions his longing for the daughter, but the effect is the same. What makes Harry "Rabbit" is his refusal to be pinned down.

Janice is correct, of course, insofar as she can determine her husband's mysterious inner needs; but we understand, even if she does not, that at least in *Rabbit Is Rich* Harry can define roughly what he wants. In the earlier novels he cannot describe the object of his frantic quest except to point to the perfect tee shot and shout "That's it!" But the years and the pounds and the comfort of money have combined to readjust his sights closer to earth: A home of his own, a life without Nelson, a real live daughter, and one hour in bed with confident Cindy.

Cindy Murkett is twenty-nine, married to a suave gentleman older than Harry, and the mother of two children. A non-practicing Roman Catholic who does not take the sacraments but who nevertheless believes, she defends Pope John Paul II's visit to the United States. Everything else about her is up-to-date: her clothes, her house, her aura, and most of all her joyful willingness to pose in various sexual positions while her husband shoots away with his Polaroid SX-70 Land Camera. As Rabbit says while comically feasting on the photographs and lamenting the absence of his forgotten eye glasses, he now knows what the S and X stand for.

Harry's discovery of these snapshots while guiltily rummaging through Cindy's bedroom drawer was excerpted for publication in *Playboy* (September 1981), but in the context of the novel the episode suggests more than the thrill of coming across revealing pictures. Unobtainable Cindy represents mystery to Rabbit, evidence for himself as well as the reader that his longing for the unknown has not totally bogged down in expanding waistlines and safe routine. His grown son a disappointment and his rejuvenated wife too available, he longs for a new experience to season his middle years. Alluring Cindy provides the spice, all the more zesty because he cannot have her beyond his memory of the x-rated photographs. In this scene he is part voyeur and part quester. One wishes him well, but the combination says a good deal about the decline of his spiritual aspirations.

Yet desire is the opposite of death. As Rabbit himself muses, "So who says he's running out of gas?" (55). A trip to the Caribbean with the Murketts and the Harrisons recharges his idea of God: "God, having shrunk in Harry's middle years to the size of a raisin lost under the car seat, is suddenly great again, everywhere like a radiant wind" (390). Part of his sense of renewal comes from his soaring into space as the airplane lifts him toward sun and sand, and part is his still lingering hope that Cindy will slink into his bed once the freedom of the islands stirs the blood and lulls the brain. Blood stirs, and husbands and wives exchange for one night, but Harry does not get Cindy, just as he does not reach the upward spaces except with a tee shot or a plane ride. Updike knows his man. To grant him the rainbow would be to halt the run. Even at age forty-six, Rabbit has a lot of running left.

The irony is that he has to hurry back to Nelson's wife, who has been deserted by her husband in her last hours of pregnancy. Twenty-two years old, Nelson is short and grubby and still not graduated from Kent State.[10] Harry does not like him or his various girl friends, and his sense of middle-aged comfort is threatened when he learns that his son wants to return home with one of his girls. Rabbit calls him a "shiftless arrogant goof-off" and, sad to say, he is correct. Even Janice's mother, who defends and loves Nelson, admits that the boy has not turned out the way she and her dead husband had hoped.

What Harry really hates is Nelson's lack of coordination, the same flaw he detects in Janice. It is not that everyone must be an athlete but that coordination suggests balance, order, connection. There is something metaphysical about glide, about rhythm, that enables one to roll with experience, but Rabbit knows that Nelson will always be at odds as if the soundtrack of his life were warped. Some readers may think that Nelson makes all the old mistakes that Rabbit has already muddled through, but to do so is to ignore the absence of grace in the son while underestimating the drive in the father. Updike takes a gamble with Nelson, just as he did with Skeeter in *Redux*. Both represent outsiders to Rabbit's world, young men so radically different from Harry as to encourage the temptation to see Harry through their eyes. The gamble is complicated in *Rabbit Is Rich* because one expects the son to follow the father's footsteps: Big rabbits, after all, beget little rabbits. Updike wisely refuses the bait. Taking the son through many of the physical misadventures suffered by the father, Updike denies him the spiritual qualities that make such bumbling simultaneously reprehensible and appealing.

The question, then, may be one of reader sympathy for the son when it has been long established for the father. Eliot Fremont-Smith finds Nelson a flaw in the novel: "Rabbit's son Nelson is too much a nerd; he seems more programmed by Updike's loyalty to Rabbit than by Rabbit's genes or will." Thomas R. Edwards agrees: "Nelson seems to me the one failure in *Rabbit Is Rich*, an irate caricature of the 'Me Generation' where there might better be a difficult, confused, vulnerable human presence."[11] It seems to me, however, that not failure of characterization but intensity of characterization is the crux. Like the Skeeter section in *Redux*, the focus on Nelson holds too long. Updike tells the reader more about him than he wants to know, and the additional information does not extend the character so much as pile similar details upon those already established. The result is that the reader gets impatient when Nelson hurls another insult or wrecks another car. Without inner strength to deepen his character, Nelson plows through a series of repetitions finally more frustrating to the reader than to himself.

Yet Updike needs Nelson in *Rabbit Is Rich*. The persistent contrast between the son's sour whining and the father's joyous pursuit stresses the uniqueness of Rabbit's lifelong run. Although one will not know for certain until Updike completes the Rabbit chronicles, the sustained emphasis on Nelson in this installment suggests that there will never be another Rabbit Angstrom. Such titles as *The Son of Rabbit* or *The Return of the Rabbit* seem impossible when one watches Nelson mimic Harry's stumble without the grace. No one is going to say about Nelson that he has the gift of life or that he gives people faith. He is too complaining, too irresponsible with cars and bodies, too uncoordinated. He has no sense of magic, no need for quest. He slouches, he always shows a troubled expression, and he looks less like a rabbit than like a mean dog. Harry clumsily loves him but wants him out of the way. His presence in the house increases Rabbit's fear of being crowded and intensifies his desperation for a home of his own. How can a father deal with a son who thinks that golf is stupid? The question is comic to us but serious to Harry. He does not, after all, think in such trendy terms as "parenting" and "maturation." Nelson has no manners, no consideration for others, and, like all losers, he believes that everyone picks on him. Not Harry but Updike may dislike him too much.

Nelson accuses his father of thinking that cars are magical and then turns around and requests a job at the Toyota agency. The situation is ironic, for he is a taker, a young man with his hand out and with no idea how to offer something in exchange. Given his inability to smile and his perpetual whine, it is idiotic for him to want to join Harry in sales, but the situation is complicated when Janice and her mother argue that the family owes him the same chance it once gave Rabbit. Yet when he wrecks

Harry's car, he does not care beyond embarrassment because, he says, there are no injuries. What can one say except to admit that this is only one way of looking at the problem? Desiring company in his misery, he criticizes his father for being happy.

Harry sees his son as looking "humpbacked and mean, a rat going out to be drowned" (122). Nelson is too old to come sneaking home, and the reader suspects long before Rabbit that the son returns because the girl friend at Kent State is pregnant. Too selfish to commit himself and too scared to act, Nelson rushes to Brewer to hide as if time will solve the problem. The son runs from while the father runs toward. The contrast is significant even if both discover that flight in space does not mean escape from time. The nine months of the pregnancy are always there.

Nelson gets his chance to sell cars when he works at the agency during Rabbit and Janice's vacation. Using the firm's money to buy old convertibles, he deserves Harry's outburst when he promises that the cars will sell: "You'll promise me nothing. You'll promise me to keep your nose out of my car business and get your ass back to Ohio. I hate to be the one telling you this, Nelson, but you're a disaster" (169). The cars do sell, but Nelson realizes that other people have realms of experience he cannot reach and that he does not know how to break out of his alienation. One of his girl friends is correct when she tells him that he lacks a "capacity for responsibility."

The primary responsibility that he cannot handle at the moment is Prudence, a redhead with an awkward beauty and a resigned face showing flashing green eyes. When she arrives at the Angstrom house pregnant and lonely, Harry surges to protect her. Her pregnancy promises him a stay against the insistent crowding of the dead. With the question of the other daughter by Ruth up in the air, Rabbit believes that he may still be a life giver through his son and future daughter-in-law. Pru's presence makes Nelson more docile, but he is as selfish and ungracious as ever when he says in front of her that he will go through with the marriage because he has said he will. We know that he will never serve as Rabbit's immortality after he tells Pru that the dead are dead and that religion is "stuff." Nelson makes fun of the young minister who offers premarital counseling, but Harry's reaction is more to the point: "Laugh at ministers all you want, they have the words we need to hear, the ones the dead have spoken" (243).

Yet when Nelson and Pru marry in a ceremony and reception that allow Updike to show his comic touch, Rabbit glances back at the wedding that trapped him with Janice twenty-five years ago, foresees a similar predicament for his son, and wants to shout out "Run!" But nothing happens. Nelson walks the aisle while Harry weeps. Updike's long account of the ceremony and celebration captures the mixture of tackiness and tenderness with a perfect ear that overhears all the little stabs at conversation which people use to fill in the lull between sips of champagne.

The switch to Nelson's point of view for parts of the novel after the wedding does not swing reader sympathy to his side. Ever selfish and pouting, he is upset that Pru, seven months pregnant and tired, does not want to go out for a beer at night. His musing in these sections convinces him that Harry is the killer of Becky in *Rabbit, Run* and of Jill in *Rabbit Redux* and that the solution to the Iranian hostage crisis is to drop a "little tactical H-bomb." One of the highlights of this segment is the contrast between Janice and Harry's evening at the Murketts', when Rabbit finds the photographs, and Pru and Nelson's evening at a friend's, when he mixes beer and desire. Conversation at both is mundane, the kind one expects when people gather for drinks and small talk. The primary difference is another slap at Nelson, for while Harry's group tries to be jolly and even plans a trip to the Caribbean, Nelson sits in a corner with his beer and pouts because pregnant Pru dances herself into a good time. He feels a spark of joy only when he talks to the sexy young woman who may or may not be Rabbit's fugitive daughter, but his desire for her is drowned in yet another beer: "He doesn't mind any of it very much, he's just tired of being young" (322). That may be so, but he is too surly to grow up. Any challenge defeats him immediately, so his runs are always backward, toward what he perceives as home, instead of toward the upward sweep of unseen worlds. He longs for revenge for his failures but has no idea how to achieve it beyond petty spite. When, for example, he meets the mysterious young woman at the party, he betrays Pru by mocking her pregnancy. Pru tells him what we know and what he needs to learn, that he is a spoiled bully. When he cries and then bumps her so that she tumbles down the long stairs, Updike carries the shocked reader back to the moment when Janice accidentally drowns the baby. But this time, to Rabbit's good fortune especially, the baby does not die.

The specter of death plus a sense of the world running out of gas would be enough to stun a less optimistic man: "The world keeps ending but new people too dumb to know it keep showing up as if the fun's just started" (88). What Harry does not want to contemplate is his own ending. Money allows him to accept his now limited inner spaces so that his need to wander is partly thwarted, and he hopes that the beginning of his comfort signals the beginning of his life: "He sees his life as just beginning, on clear ground at last, now that he has a margin of resources, and the stifled terror that always made him restless has dulled down. He wants less. Freedom, that he always thought was outward motion, turns out to be this inner dwindling" (97). This is why Pru's baby is so important to him, for a birth might expand his shrinking inner spaces. It is sad to see his drive dwindle, because the refusal to say "no" to the demands of the spirit has always given Rabbit a glow that carries his readers and him over his bumbling disasters. He cannot be frantic forever, but while the pursuit of "it" may degenerate to a peek at Cindy's breasts, it soars with the promise of Pru's baby. Harry is not about to give up, the way Nelson seems to have done, for death may linger just on the other side of the Toyota lot.

In *Rabbit, Run* Harry prays when faced with such a dark perspective, but now "a stony truce seems to prevail between himself and God" (140). The Caribbean interlude momentarily eases the truce, but death rather than grace looms ahead of him. Although his final run is still a long way down the corridor, he finds himself thinking about all the dead who have passed through his life, even when he walks along a fairway playing golf. Thus he decides at the end of the novel to renew the search for what may be his illegitimate daughter. Proving her identity may grant him an inch of immortality, the abstraction he has yearned for since the first novel in the series. His closest contact with the motions of grace that used to animate him comes when the girl's boyfriend buys an orange Corolla. Rabbit accepts the sale as a sign: "God has kissed him out of space" (273). All he has to do is find the orange car to discover both the girl and Ruth. He succeeds easily but not with the longed-for results. Fat enough to look like a billowing sail, Ruth smashes his illusion of immortality: The alluring young woman is not his.

Sad, but no matter; Updike is not about to let Rabbit Angstrom drift away. His quest for the possible daughter thwarted, he falls back on his demand for a new home and his joy in a new baby. Janice's mother and Nelson object to his plans for a house, especially Nelson, who believes that his parents should remain in place to take care of him, but Harry knows that without space and privacy his life will shrink further. Updike's simile is perfect when Rabbit asserts himself and moves. Surveying the new house, "he thinks in this room he might begin to read books, instead of just magazines and newspapers, and begin to learn about history, say. You have to step down into the den, one step down from the hardwood floor of the living room, and this small difference in plane hints to him of many reforms and consolidations now possible in his life, like new shoots on a tree cropped back" (453). One doubts that he will give up *Consumer Reports* for history books, but Rabbit's private den sits next to the living room and he sees new promise in a life that has been wilting too long. He is finally king of his own burrow: No mother-in-law, no Skeeter, no Jill, no Nelson, no trap.

All he needs now is Pru's baby to take the place of the daughter he cannot have and the son he does not like. The baby, a girl, fills the void with real flesh, sparkling life, and at age forty-six Rabbit Angstrom, former rebel, looks around and finds himself a grandfather. The description of the baby hauntingly recalls his thoughts two decades ago when he looked at baby Becky: "Oblong cocooned little visitor . . . the tiny stitchless seam of the closed eyelid aslant, lips bubbled forward beneath the whorled nose as if in delicate disdain, she knows she's good. You can feel in the curve of the cranium she's feminine, that shows from the first day" (467).

But life and death are one, a truth Rabbit glimpses as he examines Pru's baby and glances at his own mortality. The more he ages, the more he loses what he calls "witnesses": "The more dead you know it seems the more living there are you don't know. . . . maybe God is in the universe the way salt is in the ocean, giving it a taste" (462–63). Thus while Pru's daughter promises Rabbit a future, she does so in a dual sense. His blood now surges through an inheritor's heart, but the longer it circulates there, the thinner it becomes for himself. He looks at the baby and sees both tomorrow and extinction: "Fortune's hostage, heart's desire, a grand-daughter. His. Another nail in his coffin. His" (467). These are the last words in the novel, and they promise the death of one of the most fascinating characters in contemporary American literature. But not yet. It is to Rabbit's credit that he understands the dilemma and does not run. Long years remain if Updike chooses to give them to him in future novels, but for the moment Harry "Rabbit" Angstrom sits still, a newborn baby in his arms, and contemplates the truth that the dead now crowd him more closely than the living have ever done.[12]

Updike's Rabbit chronicles reflect the post-1950 United States with a combination of realistic and metaphorical accuracy not seen in other contemporary American fiction. The point is the combination of realism and metaphor as well as the accuracy, for Updike's gifted sense of figurative language lifts his Rabbit novels beyond the socially accurate but resolutely unpoetic fiction of, say, William Dean Howells and John O'Hara from earlier eras. Updike's sentences matter as much as his details, and the result is narrative that one admires for its art as well as its precision.

Just as important is the character of Harry Angstrom. Returning to Harry each decade, Updike invites the reader to shake hands with an old friend and, by contrasting his situation with Rabbit's, to gauge his sense of how his own aging body and shrinking possibilities relate to the constantly changing course of the country. Rabbit's urge to say "yes" to life, his inarticulate yet intuitive feeling that around the next corner or down the next fairway or in the next baby exists a possibility for grace despite the hardness of the heart, makes him a character worthy of joining the long line of fictional American questers from Natty Bumppo to Augie March. The list is a kind of honor roll of American culture. Some readers will try to deny membership to Harry, pointing to the grievous consequences of his obvious faults. But he belongs there in spite of their objections because he believes in the possibility of new territories, the glow of affirmation, and the renewal of love. Despite national bungling or personal disaster, Harry Angstrom will not give up. And that is why Rabbit should keep on running.

## NOTES

1. John Updike, *Rabbit Is Rich* (New York: Knopf, 1981), p. 42. Further references will be noted in the text. The novel won the Pulitzer Prize, the American Book Award, and the National Book Critics Circle Award for 1981-82.
2. "Updike on Updike," New York *Times Book Review*, 27 September 1981, p. 35.
3. "Books," *Time*, 5 October 1981, pp. 90, 92.
4. Michiko Kakutani, "Turning Sex and Guilt into an American Epic," *Saturday Review*, (October 1981), pp. 15, 20.
5. James Wolcott, "Running on Empty," *Esquire*, (October 1981), pp. 20, 22-23.
6. Roger Sale, "Rabbit Returns," New York *Times Book Review*, 27 September 1981, pp. 1, 32-34.
7. Thomas R. Edwards, "Updike's Rabbit Trilogy," *Atlantic*, (October 1981), pp. 94, 96, 100-101.
8. V. S. Pritchett, "Updike," *New Yorker*, 9 November 1981, pp. 201-206.
9. Paul Gray, "A Crisis of Confidence," *Time*, 5 October 1981, p. 90; Eliot Fremont-Smith, "Rabbit Ruts," *Village Voice*, 30 September—6 October 1981, pp. 35, 55.
10. On 27 June 1982, the New York *Times* reported a splendid literary hoax: "Nelson Springer Angstrom never showed up to claim his diploma during the 1981–82 commencement at Kent State University, although his name, which appeared in the graduation program of the College of Arts and Sciences, was read aloud during the ceremony." The *Times* also noted that several years before completing *Rabbit Is Rich* Updike asked an administrator at Kent State if it would be appropriate to send Nelson to that university. For the complete story, see Edwin McDowell, "About Books and Authors," New York *Times Book Review*, 27 June 1982, p. 26.
11. See Fremont-Smith, p. 55, and Edwards, p. 101. See also a British reaction in Carol Rumens, "The Tackier Textures of Success," London *Times Literary Supplement*, 15 January 1982, p. 48. Rumens wonders if the compromises Rabbit faces in middle age dull the sense of excitement: "Lust, keen dreaming and wide-eyed dread were the very qualities which made the two earlier novels as engaging as this one, over all, is not." But she also praises Updike's eye for life's textures: "Few other writers have a more thrilling sense of the tacky, cluttered beauty of urban surfaces."
12. Updike did not deliver his prepared speech when he accepted the American Book Award for *Rabbit Is Rich*, but he did permit its publication. In the speech he tells of the many readers who wrote to point out that Janice could not be driving a Maverick convertible since the Ford Motor Company does not make one, and he promises to correct the error for the paperback edition. On a more

serious note, he comments on the author's need to believe in himself: "But the essential support and encouragement of course come from within, arising out of the mad notion that your society needs to know what only you can tell it." See "What Updike Was Going to Say," *Publishers Weekly,* 14 May 1982, p. 118.

# HOME

*The Centaur* (1963)
*Of the Farm* (1965)

# The Centaur

*"What is a hero?"*
—*The Centaur*

A first reading of *The Centaur* (1963) is not likely to invite comparisons with *Rabbit, Run*. Harry Angstrom is a rabbit while George Caldwell is a horse, and the one scampers while the other plods. Even more obvious is the direction of their lives, for as Rabbit darts away from family toward the unreachable recesses of "it," Caldwell struggles through the snow to return home with a bag of groceries and a bruised spirit. Yet Updike has a comparison in mind, a pair of novels in which each story indirectly illuminates the other.

As the jacket copy for *The Centaur* makes clear, *Rabbit, Run* was in the background when Updike wrote the novel: "*The Centaur*—originally conceived as a contrasting companion to Mr. Updike's previous novel *Rabbit, Run*—retells the myth of Chiron. . . ." More significant is one of Angstrom's last thoughts as he begins his final run. Wondering if immortality in the mundane world is limited to "the vertical order of parenthood, a kind of thin tube upright in time in which our solitude is somewhat diluted," he turns from the apartment and lights out for the beyond.[1] To hold on to the possibility, however remote, that his search for expanded boundaries will survive, Harry abandons the "order of parenthood" and rejects the domestic responsibilities which would bind him to a spirit-numbing daily routine that stifles all aspiration, smothers the will to believe. George Caldwell, the centaur, takes up the burden that Harry, the rabbit, casts down. He suffers rather than runs, sacrifices rather than quests, for the sake of parenthood and his son Peter (Prometheus). Spiritual sureties fade, and 1936 Buicks become hearse-like, but Caldwell dismisses immortality to face the quotidian in order that Peter may fly toward the future.

Peter runs from the farm and Olinger High School to a loft in New York with a black mistress and a roomful of his second-rate abstract expressionist paintings, but the novel suggests that he has yet to soar. As narrator, the question that he asks from the perspective of maturity is whether the centaur's sacrifice is worth the cost. His story is a loving portrait of the father as a tired man. Telling the tale to his silent mistress, Peter creates a hymn of praise to Caldwell, a narration that explains as much to the narrator as to the listener the glory of the intelligent, eternally curious, always stumbling man who, in sprinkling happiness on Peter's youth, enters the realm of myth. Only in telling the tale does the son understand the sacrifice of the father's life for the promise of his own future. He must narrate the story to peer into the recesses of his paternity: "I am glad I have met you, glad, proud, glad; I miss only, and then only a little, in the late afternoon, the sudden white laughter that like heat lightning bursts in an atmosphere where souls are trying to serve the impossible. My father for all his mourning moved in the atmosphere of such laughter. He would have puzzled you. He puzzled me. His upper half was hidden from me, I knew best his legs."[2]

Peter's act of narration is cathartic. His primary problem in the present time of the novel is not how to paint better paintings but how to shape his tale. The challenge is, of course, Updike's; and he suggests that the pyrotechnical displays in *The Centaur*, the mixture of lyricism, myth, elegy, pastoral, newspaper obituary, and even tenses, illustrate his understanding of the complexities involved when one begins to tell a story. He explains:

I have read old sagas—*Beowulf*, the *Mabinogion*—trying to find the story in its most rudimentary form, searching for what a story *is*—Why did these people enjoy hearing them? Are they a kind of disguised history? Or, more likely I guess, are they ways of relieving anxiety, of transferring it outwards upon an invented tale and purging it through catharsis? In any case, I feel the need for this kind of recourse to the springs of narrative, and maybe my little buried allusions are admissions of it.[3]

As all readers know, the allusions in *The Centaur* are not buried. The point is that the way the novel is constructed says a good deal about the subject at hand. The narrative intricacies of *The Centaur* reveal both George Caldwell's complicated personality and Peter Caldwell's complicated response to it. The eye-catching technical display is not meant merely to dazzle the reader, as some critics have complained, but to offer a framework that the narrator considers equal to the task of revealing the heroic properties in the life of an otherwise forgotten man. Updike continues: "The author's deepest pride, as I have experienced it, is not in his incidental wisdom but in his ability to keep an organized mass of images moving forward, to feel life engendering itself under his hands. . . . My work is meditation, not pontification."[4]

This quality of meditation is one reason why *The Centaur* seems strange to readers who expect the conventional props of developing action and a clear-cut relationship between narrator and reader. Indeed, a survey of the criticism suggests that many readers fail to make the connection between Peter and the narrator, the man struggling to "keep an organized mass of images moving forward." Thus Peter's role as a painter is crucial, not to make him the butt of his own joke that his work is second-rate, but to qualify him as a man at home with the commingling of created images and remembered myth. His grandfather, a minister, lives within the framework of religion; his father, a teacher, understands the framework of science; Peter, a painter, tangles with the framework of art. His story, then, is about story-telling as well as about nostalgia and myth. How the tale is told is as important to *The Centaur* as what the tale tells, and one of the truths it tells Peter is that the abstract quality of his painting and the erotic intensity of his love for the mistress do not equal the mythic properties of his story or the transcendent level of his love for the father. James M. Mellard is correct: "The Greek myths allow Peter to discover the one *mythos* which is appropriate for him. That is *art* as an eschatology, as a way of expressing and containing those furtherest things that trouble man."[5]

Updike is well aware of the difficulties his novel poses for readers unprepared for Peter's image-moving process. When *The Centaur* was voted the National Book Award for 1963, Updike briefly addressed the issue of its strangeness in an acceptance speech delivered in March 1964. Urging the quality of accuracy in fiction, a plea that might strike some as ironic when halfway through *The Centaur*, he praises "lifelikeness" as a "virtue seldom extolled these days." Yet he also understands that his elaboration of the Chiron-Prometheus myth may appear to many readers as anything but lifelike: "It may seem too daring of me to touch on this when my book appeared, to many, a bewildering, arbitrary, and forced mixture of uncongenial elements, of mythology and remembrance, of the drably natural and the bookishly supernatural. I can only plead that the shape of the book formally approximates, for me, the mixed and somewhat antic experience it was trying to convey. The book as well as the hero is a centaur." He goes on to define fiction as an approach to actuality and to advise observance of the intricacy of the mundane: "Fiction is a tissue of literal lies that refreshes and informs our sense of actuality. Reality is—chemically, atomically, biologically—a fabric of microscopic accuracies. Language approximates phenomena through a series of hesitations and qualifications; I miss, in much contemporary writing, this sense of self-qualification, the kind of timid reverence toward what exists that Cézanne shows when he grapples for the shape and shade of a fruit through a mist of delicate stabs. The intensity of the grapple is the surest pleasure a writer receives."[6]

This sense of the book itself as centaur, of the intense grapple illustrated by the hybrid of the "drably natural and the bookishly supernatural," is one reason why Updike tends to point to *The Centaur* when asked to name his favorite among his books: "Well, it seems in memory my gayest and truest book; I pick it up, and read a few pages, in which Caldwell is insisting on flattering a moth-eaten bum, who is really the god Dionysius, and I begin laughing."[7] Part of his joy with the novel stems from its connection with his own youth. Aware of the tendency among some critics to dismiss *The Centaur* and many of his short stories as little more than sugarcoated glimpses of the past, Updike defends the glance over the shoulder as an honored tradition in American literature: "I'm still running on energy laid down in childhood. Writing is a way of keeping up with that childhood. . . . I really don't think I'm alone among writers in caring about what they experienced in the first eighteen years of their life. Hemingway cherished the Michigan stories out of proportion, I would think, to their merit. Look at Twain. Look at Joyce. Nothing that happens to us after twenty is as free from self-consciousness, because by then we have the vocation to write."[8]

One key to *The Centaur*, however, is not the reverie of childhood but homage to the parent. Part of Updike's call for accuracy, for lifelikeness, is his belief in the mystery of the quotidian, in the always surprising variety of the everyday. But sensitivity to mundane nuances does not mean viewing the world through rose-colored lenses. A child of the Great Depression, Updike is aware of what he calls "the despair of the daily": "One suspects . . . that it's good to be alive, that there is much more beauty around us than we ever notice, that existence is charged with goodness. Yet even though one isn't willing to die, life still, day by day, often seems monotonous and long."[9] Updike's father, Wesley Updike, lived the long monotony. Forced into high school teaching by the economic realities of the depression, he nevertheless held his family together in spite of his despair of the daily and his conviction that he was unsuited for the special demands that public schools place on their teachers. One result was that the son watched the father resolve to live even though he sensed the shrinking of his spirit and the deterioration of his body. Time and again in his descriptions of *The Centaur*, Updike mentions his father's suffering during the years that frame the novel: "The main motive force behind *The Centaur* would be some wish to make a record of my father. There was the whole sense of having for fifteen years watched a normal, good-doing Protestant man suffering in a kind of comic but real way."[10] And, "*The Centaur* was to some extent motivated by the idea that my father was an economic victim, and more specifically, that public high school was a kind of baby-sitting service in which people at their most vital were caged with these underpaid keepers of which he was one; so there was some social idea that went with my psychological impression of him as a suffering man."[11] This combination of heroism and suffering, of resolving to live instead of longing to die, illustrates what Updike calls the "yes, but" quality of his fiction: "Yes, in *The Centaur,* to self-sacrifice and duty, but—what of a man's private agony and dwindling?"[12]

Updike realized that one way to tell his father's tale was to view it from the perspective of classical myth, especially the Chiron version of the Hercules saga which he describes as "one of the few classic instances of self-sacrifice, and the name oddly close to Christ." He goes on to explain that he wanted to publicize the Chiron myth and to show how that old story could not only operate as "a correlative of the enlarging effect of Peter's nostalgia" but also dramatize Caldwell's "sense of exclusion and mysteriousness around him."[13] The drabness of Caldwell's life contrasts with the ideality of the myth, and the happy result is a glimpse of heroism in a flawed man.

Several readers have pointed out that myths other than the tale of Chiron's sacrifice inform Updike's third novel. Calling *The Centaur* Updike's best, Larry Taylor argues that Caldwell's story combines pastoral elegy and epic. Updike uses the four short chapters (numbers three, five, eight, and nine) that gloss the legend of Chiron to illustrate the conventions of the pastoral elegy in such a way that changes in tone and imagery prepare the reader to accept modern Olinger as ancient Olympus. The novel is often comic but rarely satiric because the formal lyricism of these four chapters keeps the story in touch with the seriousness of the elegy. *The Centaur* is a hymn to a hero; the satirical laughter of traditional mock-epic literature is not an issue.[14] Taylor shows how Theocritus' *Idyls* and Milton's *Lycidas* echo around Updike's retelling of the moving Chiron myth: "To this extent, the language of the four touchstone chapters is highly important. The chapters become the formal structural clues for reading the whole book. Idyl, hymn, obituary, love lyric, lament, epitaph—these recognizable forms within the pastoral elegy form give the novel its coherence, its dignity, its eloquence as a universal statement."[15] Taylor also translates the Greek sentences that Updike positions between Chiron's final word "*Now*" and Peter the narrator's comment, "Chiron accepted death":

And having received an incurable wound, he went off to the cave. And he willingly went there to die; and although he was immortal and thus not able to die, when Prometheus exchanged fates with him, in order that Chiron might die in his stead, then the Centaur died.[16]

By using the original Greek, Updike reminds the reader at the very end of the novel that the deeds of sacrificial heroes serve as the foundation of all tales.[17]

As might be expected, however, debate continues as to how successfully Updike handles the various myths. He defends *The Centaur* vigorously, and he does not shy away from naming critics who miss the point. John Aldridge is one such critic: "I think Aldridge is a man with quite coarse critical perception and he was quite crass about that book. . . . There are enough books written with submerged myths; I wrote one in which the myth was overt. It jangled—the way life sometimes does. It was about a man who sees myths everywhere—that was the point. I tried to create the effect of sense eroding away; that was something that felt right to me. A much more kindly critic than Aldridge, Arthur Mizener, also complained that its Greek gods and goddesses didn't have the luminous power of, say, the gods in the *Cantos*. Well, I wasn't trying to do what Pound had done in the *Cantos*. I was really quite pleased with that book." [18] But despite Updike's pleasure, uneasiness between the novel and some readers persists. John B. Vickery, in a perceptive essay on *The Centaur*, correctly suggests that the continuing discussion about the mythic materials worries many readers to the point where distress often leads to dismissal.[19]

Such an attitude is unfortunate, and it indicates more about the reader's expectations than the author's abilities. Updike's insistence on the correspondences between the minor characters and their mythic counterparts as listed in the index to *The Centaur* may be, in Richard Locke's word, "embarrassing," but the major myths are convincing.[20] Even readers who query the efficacy of the index and the appropriateness of Peter's role as Prometheus often applaud the brilliant first chapter with its astonishing mixture of myth and realism, and the portrait of George Caldwell with its combined tones of frustration and love.

Norman Podhoretz disagrees, of course. He worries about the way Updike describes pain, he makes the mistake of assuming that Caldwell commits suicide (How well *did* he read the novel he so eagerly attacks?), he fails to understand that Caldwell's "death" is the sacrifice of his spirit to the disillusionments of teaching, and he dislikes mythic trappings assigned to a man stuck squarely in the mundane.[21] Since Podhoretz always criticizes Updike, his negative opinions are expected and thus disarmed. Such is not the case with Richard Gilman and George Steiner. Their reactions all but summarize general reservations about the novel. Gilman dismisses the mythic overtones as harmless, but he criticizes the prose as pretentious and thus standing in the way of a genuine engagement with the existence of death and the value of life. Steiner wonders about the apparent split between the technical virtuosity and the significance of the tale, and although he concedes that "on Mr. Updike's ability to grow ride some of the best hopes of present American fiction," he decides that the "allegoric scaffold" of *The Centaur* "obtrudes with arty deliberation."[22]

The problem is that Updike's deliberate originality is an easy target for those who wish to attack it. Anything so strikingly new invites contrast with the safety of the well-established, and thus insight and imagination may be misread as frivolity and fancy. Renata Adler's commentary illustrates a more balanced approach. In an essay that lauds *The Centaur* as a "fine, rich work," Adler simultaneously admits that the novel has its faults and reminds us that *Ulysses* does, too. The point is not the questionable index or the occasional lists of plants and objects but the accuracy of Updike's observations and the brilliance of his prose: "the Greek legend acquires at his hands new poetry, and the American father and son can stand, as modest contemporary archetypes, on their own."[23]

The dichotomy between myth and man, legend and the mundane, begins in *The Centaur* with the epigraph from Karl Barth's *Dogmatics in Outline:* "Heaven is the creation inconceivable to man, earth the creation conceivable to him. He himself is the creature on the boundary between heaven and earth."[24] The mythic frame of the novel reflects the divisions between soul and body, heaven and earth, immortality and the ordinary, and Olympus and Olinger. Unable to be sure of one, humanity creates the other in order to consider both. That is, man makes metaphors to explain his predicament, and the hero straddles the extremes. Caldwell's fundamental nature of immortal centaur mixed with mortal man illustrates his situation on a border trying to reconcile the conceivable and the inconceivable, but he finds that struggle does not necessarily result in unity. Gods forever shift their shapes while man plods on toward the demands of the next day. The novel suggests that reconciliation of the conceivable and the inconceivable may take place only in art, in the pages of *The Centaur* itself. In this sense, then, Peter is also on the boundary. Memory and desire, frustration and devotion, youth and age swirl about him. He turns to lyricism and myth to plumb the depths of the relationship between yesterday and today, between childhood and maturity. As he tells the story, what he finds is love.

Readers of the Updike canon know that he has written about the father figure in shorter, more conventional ways. One thinks immediately of "Tomorrow and Tomorrow and So Forth" (*The Same Door*, 1959), "Home" (*Pigeon Feathers*, 1962), and "Leaving Church Early" (*Tossing and Turning*, 1977), but none has the imaginative richness of *The Centaur*. The paradox of the blameless, immortal Chiron, noblest of the centaurs, wounded, longing for death, and thus willing to exhange a life of never-ending pain for the ease of mortality to atone for Prometheus' theft of fire, results in another paradox at the end of the novel that confuses some readers:

Caldwell himself does not die. Abandoning his need for a better life, a life free from the spirit-numbing demands of teaching in a public high school, he returns through the snow to the hallways for his son's sake.

The first two sentences of the novel place both Caldwell and the reader on the border between the conceivable and the inconceivable: "Caldwell turned and as he turned his ankle received an arrow. The class burst into laughter" (3). The reader immediately assumes that the arrow is a metaphor for the students' jeering, but Updike insists that we remain on the boundary with Caldwell when he describes the teacher's agonized retreat to Hummel's garage where the master mechanic removes the arrow with the aid of an acetylene torch. Myth and reality merge, and the reader is prepared for such lyrical descriptions as this later account of pain: "Truly, the pain is unprecedented: an entire tree rich with bloom, each bloom showering into the livid blue air a coruscation of lucid limegreen sparks" (217). In Caldwell's mythic vision, as seen from Peter's point of view, anything is material for metaphor.

Hummel's garage is a case in point. A refuge for teachers and a fix-it shop for students whose jalopies need repair, the garage exudes an aura of otherworldly gloom. The wounded Caldwell looks about him and sees "overturned fragments of automobiles, fragile and phantasmal, fenders like corpses of turtles, bristling engines like disembodied hearts. Hisses and angry thumps lived in the mottled air" (7–8). No wonder that Caldwell defines Hummel as Hephaestus and his wife Vera as Venus. But where he looks for gods in the garage, Vera sees her husband as a "despicable, sad, grimy, grizzled, crippled, cuckolded tinker" (26).

The age has something to do with the decline of myth. The year is 1947, a time when car buyers prefer Detroit's junk to Hummel's craft, and all Caldwell can do is commiserate with the mechanic and hobble back to the school. Yet cynicism is not his style. Recalling a golden age when school children were obedient, teachers respected, and cars not mass produced, he remains a modest man of gratitude and love. His compassionate view of life is part of his dignity, and his mixture of generosity and fear is revealed when he returns to his classroom to find the principal Zimmerman (Zeus) waiting for him. Confronted with Zimmerman's sarcastic graciousness, Caldwell nevertheless teaches his students with patience, self-effacement, and wit.

Caldwell's science lesson is a spectacular example of how Updike keeps the reader perched between the conceivable and the inconceivable. With Zimmerman watching from the back of the room, and with his counterpart Zeus leering at the rise and fall of the girls' breasts, Caldwell limps to the front and launches into a commentary about the galaxy and the archer Sagittarius, which, of course, Chiron becomes. Discipline is a disaster.

Boys ogle, paper airplanes fly, eager girls give the wrong answers, and Caldwell lectures with humility and knowledge:

"Do these figures mean anything to you?"
Deifendorf said, "No."
Caldwell disarmed his impudence by agreeing. He had been teaching long enough to keep a step or two ahead of the bastards occasionally. "They don't to me either. They remind me of death." (37–38)

His fate as a sacrifice to the ignorant hordes is foreshadowed by his explanation of the volvox whose cells are potentially immortal but which die voluntarily for the good of the whole. It is a story he loathes to tell, for the lesson leads to the emergence of man from the primeval void. With man comes mortality.

Perusing Caldwell's commentary, the reader is all but lulled by the contrast between the students' highjinks and the teacher's seriousness. Verisimilitude seems apparent, and the reader recalls similar hours in high school classrooms. But the inconceivable suddenly breaks through the lecture, and all are caught up in the combination of myth and mundane. One of the boys tumbles a clot of living trilobites onto the floor. Ranging from a few inches to a foot in length, "they scuttered among the scrolling iron desk-legs, their brainless heads and swishing glabellae brushing the ankles of girls who squealed and kicked up their feet so high that white thighs and gray underpants flashed." The illustrations in Caldwell's lecture have come to life, but Updike's imagination is not done. As the terrified trilobites curl into balls that the boys bombard with heavy textbooks, "one of the girls, a huge purple parrot feathered with mud, swiftly ducked her head and plucked a small one up. Its little biramous legs fluttered in upside-down protest. She crunched it in her painted beak and methodically chewed" (43). Olympus crosses the border to Olinger, and the gods once more shift their shape. Watching the mayhem, the humble centaur decides there is nothing to do but ride the lecture until the bell.

Ride it he does, to the astonishment of the reader but to the expectation of students and family. Caldwell calls the school his "hate factory," but his wife Cassie replies that the kids love him. Indeed they do. Blessed—or cursed—with a genuine curiosity that makes simple replies to casual questions impossible for him, poor to the point where he buys cast-off clothes that humiliate Peter, and all but incapable of meeting the demands of time, Caldwell stumbles through the three days of the novel fearful of Zimmerman's wrath and his own death.

Peter may fret about appearances, but his father worries more about the clock. Caldwell's dissecton of the old saw, "time and tide wait for no man," illustrates his precarious sense of time's progression in any direction other than death. Living in a house with two clocks keeping different time is bad enough. One clock is ancient and is associated with Peter's grandfather, Pop Kramer (the god Kronos, time) who understands the intricacies of eternity. But Caldwell observes the ticking of the unreliable, more modern clock that he buys on sale and that persists in indicating that he is consistently late. Comically, but earnestly, he wastes earthly time to speculate on the meaning of the old saying in light of eternal time while his wife and son scurry around the crowded kitchen frantically trying to get him to leave for school on time. With the minutes ticking away that he needs to drive to Olinger High School before the tardy bell wracks him with guilt, Caldwell stops everything and wonders why, if man is the "last best thing in His Creation," humanity is inferior to time and tide. He receives no answer, of course. Eyes on the eternal, feet in the kitchen of the mundane, he is fearful of one and exasperated by the other. The scene ends humorously as both his family and the reader throw up their hands in frustration at his final question before dashing out the door: "Hey what time is it?"

No one else has his obsession with unanswerable questions, unsolvable problems. It is not that the others are dull but that they reserve such discussions for appropriate moments. When, for example, Caldwell tries to talk about predestination with the Reverend March while the minister flirts with Vera during a basketball game, all March can think is that the teacher must be a maniac. Searches for truth inevitably disrupt the easy swing of normal affairs, but Caldwell walks beyond the normal. Contradictory, bumbling, embarrassingly earnest and good, he is a hero in a world where Olympus degenerates to Olinger and where eternity falls back into time.

Caldwell's good-natured but harried stumble through the world is shown in the way he talks to strangers. He is so eager that he befuddles them: "My father brought to conversations a cavernous capacity for caring that dismayed strangers. They found themselves involved, willy-nilly, in a futile but urgent search for the truth" (82–83). Such behavior not only humiliates but also angers Peter, as when Caldwell allows his gloves to be stolen or ruins Peter's opportunity to see an exhibition of Vermeer's paintings during a rare visit to New York. Caldwell talks too much, but the gods watch over their own.

Peter wonders if they care as much for him. In his father's eyes he is Prometheus because he has the fire of life in him and because his psoriasis recalls the wounds made by the mythical vulture. Peter's flaking skin may be the sign of God's touch, which, while embarrassing at times, is nevertheless a source of pride. Lacking his father's zest for life, he sees the world as full of "oppressive detail of pain and inconsequence," and he understands that his mother, in forcing them to move to the farm, dooms them to electricity but no plumbing, heat downstairs but not up. From the perspective of today, as he tells the tale, Peter realizes that his mother is Ceres, a goddess of the earth, just as his father is intellectual man, and that she is thus part of another opposition which he as artist must reconcile if he hopes to write the novel. He also sees now that even while a teenager he was aware of his mother's complex nature: ". . . I thought guiltily of my mother, helpless at her distance to control me or protect me, my mother with her farm, her father, her dissatisfaction, her exhausting alternations of recklessness and prudence, wit and obtuseness, transparence and opacity, my mother with her wide tense face and strange innocent scent of earth and cereal . . ." (138).

To capture these complexities is one of the reasons Peter turns to art, for he is very much aware of what time can do to memory. Art can stabilize time and transform it into the eternal. Peter's need to freeze the moment is one rationale for the tale: "It was this firmness, I think, this potential fixing of a few passing seconds, that attracted me, at the age of five, to art. For it is at about that age, isn't it, that it sinks in upon us that things do, if not die, certainly change, wiggle, slide, retreat, and, like the dabs of sunlight on the bricks under a grape arbor on a breezy June day, shuffle out of all identity?" (62). One of Caldwell's lessons to his son is the threat of death, a permanence that Peter shrinks from in the hope that a world that permits the banal conversation of his father will not admit the awful inertness of death. Thus Peter's goal when a teenager is to escape to the city where his skin is smooth, where his clothes are beautiful, and where Vermeer's paintings guarantee his freedom, his introduction to "the tracery of the cracks whereby time had inserted itself like a mystery within a mystery . . ." (85).

Equally puzzling to Peter is the way his father's mythic stature with the students rubs off on him and thereby grants him status, identity—life. The teenagers mock and love Caldwell at the same time, and Peter understands that he himself becomes the "petty receptacle of a myth" when his friends gather round to tell him still another outrageous story of life in his father's class. Yet the mythic reputation conferred on Caldwell and spilling over to the son does not lessen Peter's uncertainty about the possibilities of immortality. His father's unceasing concern with death challenges his own belief that gods should live forever. Not yet an artist and thus unable to sneak up on the eternal with paint or words, Peter can only simultaneously hate the afterglow of Caldwell's status and bask in its shine, wondering all the while that "if the blue dome beyond the town was an illusion, how much more, then, of an illusion might be what is beyond that?" (124). Doc Appleton's metaphor for George's illness—that Caldwell believes in the soul and thus mistreats his body as if it were a horse—increases Peter's puzzlement before the paradox of mortality and myth. Unable as a teenager to straddle the border between the conceivable and the inconceivable, he must learn that life cannot exist without death and that perfect health is an inhuman condition.

Doc Appleton shrewdly diagnoses that Caldwell's condition is not that of a teacher but of a learner. Peter later realizes that his father's eagerness to learn, "even by the last flash of light before annihilation," opens him to life in such a way that the students respond to his enthusiasm with love (274). But Caldwell is not sure of this affection. Rather than see vitality in the faces of the children he teaches, continuity in their blurred presences from year to year, he glances around the room and glimpses finality: "You fall through those kids' heads without a trace" (92). As "Chiron," Caldwell has a duty to bring men out of darkness, and as Chiron he will succeed when Zeus lifts him to the constellation Sagittarius. But as "Caldwell," the teacher will die in spirit to achieve immortality finally in Peter's art. Only the mythical students of Olympus care about his caring, as Updike illustrates when he interposes the short chapters in the mode of pastoral elegy. So long as he is George Caldwell, the louty and careless students of Olinger High School spurn his gift while sapping his strength. Yet in the fickle way of selfish adolescents, they occasionally respond. Even Peter admits that love joins mockery in the myth. As it turns out, Deifendorf, the most loutish student of all, follows Caldwell into teaching. This unexpected metamorphosis confirms the centaur's power.

Mythic vigor does not, however, guarantee strength in the mundane world. Caldwell's daily life is a shambles, much to Peter's embarrassment and his own despair. He cannot even climb into his 1936 Buick without wondering whether it will crank on a cold day. Black and hearse-like and smelling of death, it suggests his crippled life as the wounded centaur. It is not that the battery needs replacing or that the ignition refuses to spark but that riding denies walking. Wheels replace feet, garages resemble morgues, and all Caldwell can do is explain to his exasperated son, "My ideal is to walk to my own funeral. Once you've sold out your legs, you've sold out your life" (150). Stuck in the town with his broken-down car, he finds that his reputation with the recalcitrant students rescues him from the dark and cold and leads Peter and him to shelter in a hotel even though he has no money. This scene is simultaneously moving and funny, a metaphor for George Caldwell's life. When Peter asks, "Why *don't* we have any money?" his father answers, "I've been asking myself that for fifty years. The worst of it is, when I write them a check it'll bounce because I have twenty-two cents in the bank" (163). This centaur is a kind of anti-Ulysses, unable to get his son home. As the long day and dismal night draw to a close, Peter is confident that he will one day step beyond his father and triumph in the city of the future.

Updike sketches Peter with irony and affection. The brightest student in the school, and well aware of his reputation, Peter is nevertheless an awkward-looking adolescent who is tolerated because he is Caldwell's son. Just beginning, for example, his first gropings toward sexual experience, he fancies himself an expert of sorts. Updike, the reader—and Peter himself as an adult—grin when the teenager gets frustrated at his father's overreaction to a probable liaison between the principal Zimmerman and a female member of the school board: "Peter is exasperated at his father's inability to see the obvious, that women who run for the school board are beyond sex, that sex is for adolescents. He does not know how to put this to his father delicately" (208).

Now living with his mistress and all but trapped in the egotism of second-rate abstract-expressionist paintings, Peter experiments with various narrative modes to create a delicate, first-rate homage to his father. Immediately following the beautifully written account of a day and a night in the life of the centaur, Peter inserts an obituary for his father written in the formal tone of the small-town newspaper. The death notice is a modern expression of communal grief, full of clichés but heartfelt. Caldwell literally does not die, and the obituary touches only the surface of the man, but the account of his teaching is a clue to the way his rebellious students remember him: "A thorough mastery of his subjects, an inexhaustible sympathy for the scholastic underdog, a unique ability to make unexpected connections . . . a by no means negligible gift for dramatization. . . . What endures, perhaps, most indelibly in the minds of his ex-students (of whom this present writer counts himself one) was his more-than-human selflessness . . ." (174).

The more Peter tells his tale, the more he realizes that Caldwell's selflessness is an unconscious offering to him. Convinced of the validity of the truism that "things never fail to fail," Caldwell knows that his own father's query at death is worth the asking: "Eternally forgotten?" No wonder he feels like a "burnt-out candle." But Peter's narration lights the spark of memory because he understands that his father, stuck between gravity and giddiness, between anger and self-deprecation, worries more about his son's future than his own present. The spider in Caldwell's intestines may spring, and the hollow in his tooth may throb, but his physical pain mirrors more important spiritual concerns. Time and tide are rushing by him, and he wonders if he should let them go. Yet every time he thinks of giving up, he sees Peter. His death would not only hamper the son in the routine of the mundane but it might also blunt the son's freedom to soar. He knows that Peter needs not the assignments of today but the promises of tomorrow. Sensing, even as a teenager, his father's enduring tentacle of hope, Peter is embarrassed when, in silly debates, the centaur denies the existence of God. He realizes that Caldwell is "overworked, worried, conscientious, and anxious," but to doubt the Creator is to spurn the father (210). This he cannot do.

Similarly, Caldwell cannot give up the throbbing in his stomach and the ache in his teeth because of his commitment to self-sacrifice. Only death can vanquish pain in its many guises, but, for the moment, in a comic allusion to the myths of Chiron and Sagittarius, he sees his pulled tooth as a kind of star when the dentist holds it above him. Humor keeps him earthbound: "Another day, another molar" (219). Caldwell cannot let go because he argues that the "kid" does not have a "clue." He may be correct, but the irony is that he is just as baffled. The teacher's favorite question is, "What's the answer?" and the answer is that he does not know. "Ignorance is bliss," he tells a fellow instructor, but fifteen years of teaching belie such facile dismissals. For Caldwell is a worried man. He glances around and spots waste, rot, and emptiness; and he suspects that the road to Olinger leads to annihilation.

The centaur needs answers. With a mixture of earnestness and naiveté that makes him look the fool to those who bother to notice, he upsets such people as Reverend March when he walks up to the minister in the middle of a basketball game and says, "I can't make it add up and I'd be grateful for your viewpoint" (252). Listening to Caldwell explain that he cannot understand the concept of infinite mercy except that God must keep His mercy at an infinite distance from man, March initially thinks that the teacher is preposterous and then shouts over the cheers of the fans, "This is burlesque!" But Peter and the reader know that it isn't. "Heavy and giddy with his own death," Caldwell retreats into the crowd (253). All questions are forever open, all answers forever closed.

Unlike his father, Peter exudes both confidence and the lack of it in turn. Where the father worries about eternal bleakness, as if nothingness itself grips him at the core and oozes through to smother the world, the son is simultaneously stunned by the promise of blankness between his girl friend's thighs and fascinated by the suddenness of a snowstorm. "He feels the universe in all its plastic and endlessly variable beauty pinned, stretched, crucified like a butterfly upon a frame of unvarying geometrical truth" (256). Disease and loss plague Caldwell's trek through Olinger, but Peter looks through his psoriasis and sees "a sort of ultimate health." Exasperated by the differences between them, all he can do is accuse his father of being unable to relax since he spies menace in every nuance. Such accusations frighten Peter because he knows that no one else has Caldwell's combination of gullibility and kindness. When the old Buick stalls in the snow and forces them—miserable with frustration and cold— to slosh past a cemetery on a three-mile hike back to Olinger, Caldwell indirectly apologizes by placing his hat on Peter's freezing head. The father believes that the disasters are his fault, but only Peter knows that they are God's.

Yet in another sense they are Caldwell's too. As Peter comes to understand, his father abandons contentment when he gives in to the dream that he will one day leap beyond the hallways of Olinger High School: "The reason, it came to me, was that our family's central member, my father, had never rid himself of the idea that he might soon be moving on. This fear, or hope, dominated our home" (273). Caldwell's dream strands him between the mythic and the mundane. Their house rarely has such luxuries as bananas and never a refrigerator or a bathroom or an adequate furnace, yet such domestic deprivation is part of the centaur's myth.

Peter's childhood escape from these shabby particulars is the local museum that he visits with his mother. The Vermeer paintings may be left behind in New York, but the promise of art is everywhere. Yet even in the museum, amid all the wonder and the beauty and the hope, lurk the dead. Whether it be an exhibition showing a snake swallowing a field mouse or a mummy stuffed with secrets, a sense of ending awes Peter as soon as he enters the doors and thus links his childhood to his father: "So much death; who would dream there could be such a quantity of death?" (267). Today an unsatisfied artist who may not achieve permanence in museums, he admits the inadequacy of his own life when measured against the impact of his grandfather's and father's: "Priest, teacher, artist: the classic degeneration" (269).

There is an element of guilt in Peter's backward glance, for he knows that he is unequal to the freedom willed to him at great cost. Lying beside his mistress, he muses on the "wistful half-Freudian half-Oriental sex-mysticism" of his current daily routine, and he wonders if it is for this that Caldwell gives up his life (270). If he has failed, he looks to the past to understand how his father has succeeded. The contrast between father and son is clarified even more because Peter and the reader know that Caldwell would never be bothered with the nostalgia of the backward look: The challenges of each day fill him to the full. The very act of narration shows Peter that he must not submit to the lure of egotism illustrated by abstract-expressionist paintings and sexual mysticism because the energy that motivates his father and grandfather—a longing for permanence and for insight into the inconceivable—surges through him too.[25] Thus a simple irony of The Centaur is that although his paintings fail to express the unsayable, his tale tells better than he knows. What he calls his "curious sense of past time" irrevocably shapes his present. Telling the story suggests that he is glad for the mold, for in his narrative he is able to idealize the farm and the earth that as a boy he sees too often as only excrement and rot. Art offers the potential for making passing moments permanent. Accepting mortality, Caldwell abandons the myth. Peter recaptures it in narrative art. The movement of the novel points to the timeless ritual of leaving and returning to the earth. Now a city-dweller, Peter returns but this time in memory:

The stone bare wall was a scumble of umber; my father's footsteps thumbs of white in white. I knew what this scene was—a patch of Pennsylvania in 1947—and yet I did not know, was in my softly fevered state mindlessly soaked in a rectangle of colored light. I burned to paint it, just like that, in its puzzle of glory; it came upon me that I must go to Nature disarmed of perspective and stretch myself like a large transparent canvas upon her in the hope that, my submission being perfect, the imprint of a beautiful and useful truth would be taken.(293)

The truth is this novel but with the perspective of myth.

Caldwell and Peter finally return home after an absence of three days because of the balky Buick and the surprise snowstorm, Caldwell with a bag of groceries that includes bananas, Peter with a fever. There, during a telephone call to Doc Appleton, they learn that Caldwell's x-rays for cancer turn out to be negative. The body holds on. Sick in bed, Peter has his surest vision of the future, his dream of how to get out of Olinger.[26] From his sickbed he watches through the window the next morning as his father strides into the snow, white with the color of death, to face once more the long corridors of the high school. From the point of view of maturity, from the angle of vision in which the future has become the present, the adult Peter peers through the window of memory, sees once again his father in the snow, and knows now, as he does not know then, that Caldwell resembles Chiron the centaur: "Alone he walked through the wide width. His hooves clattered, the fourth scraping (bone against bone), on the limestone plateau, sunstruck from above" (293). Literally, Caldwell still lives, but metaphorically he accepts spiritual death when he turns again toward the school.

The heroic vision fades into the snow, and the mature Peter, remembering the scene, is left with a loss of metaphor that sustains him when a child but that now forces him to consider his father on the realistic level and to face Caldwell's sacrifices in light of his own shortcomings. Peter realizes that in shouldering the burdens of the day, Caldwell abandons his search for the inconceivable stationed just on the other side of the border. In other words, he embraces mortality for his son's sake. "*What is a hero?*", Peter asks at the end; and he answers, "A hero is a king sacrificed to Hera." Hera (Juno) was Zeus's wife and sister, the fierce protectress of marriage. In *The Centaur* Hera is Mrs. Herzog, the schoolboard member whom Zimmerman seduces and whom Caldwell sees coming out of the principal's office. She knows that the teacher suspects the truth, and thus he fears for his job. Yet he returns, frightened of reprimand and dismayed by death. A hero may indeed be a king, but he is also George Caldwell. What he has given his son are the pleasures of the past, the example of love, and the mythic vision necessary to probe the inconceivable through the metaphors of art.

## NOTES

1. John Updike, *The Poorhouse Fair/Rabbit, Run* (New York: Modern Library, 1965), p. 433.
2. John Updike, *The Centaur* (New York: Knopf, 1963), p. 269. Further references will be noted in the text.
3. Charles Thomas Samuels, "The Art of Fiction XLIII: John Updike," *Paris Review,* 12(Winter 1968), p. 105.
4. Samuels, pp. 116, 117.
5. James M. Mellard, "The Novel as Lyric Elegy: The Mode of Updike's *The Centaur,*" *Texas Studies in Literature and Language,* 21(Spring 1979), p. 124.
6. John Updike, "Accuracy," *Picked-Up Pieces* (New York: Knopf, 1975), pp. 16-17.
7. Samuels, p. 103.
8. Jane Howard, "Can a Nice Novelist Finish First?," *Life,* 4 November 1966, p. 82; and Samuels, p. 94.
9. Howard, p. 76.
10. Eric Rhode, "Grabbing Dilemmas," *Vogue,* 1 February 1971, p. 184.
11. Richard Burgin, "A Conversation with John Updike," *The John Updike Newsletter,* 10 and 11(Spring and Summer 1979), p. 7.
12. Samuels, p. 100.
13. Samuels, p. 103. Consider also the following comment: "*The Centaur* was a formal experiment and it was done very much with *Ulysses* in the back of my mind. I wanted to somehow bring the myths forward rather than have them lurk in the background, and I'm not sure it worked out the way I planned; but the message, I suppose, was that all our childhoods are mythological to a degree." See Burgin, p. 4.
14. But see Suzanne Uphaus' fine essay that argues that *The Centaur* is a mock epic: "*The Centaur*: Updike's Mock Epic," *Journal of Narrative Technique,* 7(Winter 1971), pp. 24-36.
15. Larry E. Taylor, "*The Centaur:* Epic Paean and Pastoral Lament," in his *Pastoral and Anti-Pastoral Patterns in John Updike's Fiction* (Carbondale: Southern Illinois University Press, 1971); this quotation comes from a reprint of the chapter in *John Updike: A Collection of Critical Essays,* eds. David Thorburn and Howard Eiland (Englewood Cliffs, New Jersey: Prentice-Hall, 1979), p. 123.
16. Taylor, p. 125.
17. James Mellard's essay amplifies some of Taylor's ideas. See also Ronald Wesley Hoag's essay, "A Second Controlling Myth in John Updike's *Centaur,*" *Studies in the Novel,* 11(Winter 1979), pp. 446-453. Hoag suggests that Albert Camus' "The Myth of Sisyphus" is as important as the myth of Chiron, Milton's *Lycidas,* and Theocritus' *Idyls:* "Indeed, *The Centaur* achieves its full connotative power only when read as an extended, fictionalized adaptation of Camus' essay, differing

mainly in its final emphasis on Sisyphean joy over scorn and in its more sanguine attitude toward religious faith."

18. Frank Gado, "Interview with John Updike," in *First Person: Conversations on Writers and Writing* (Schenectady, New York: Union College Press, 1973), p. 106.

19. John B. Vickery, "*The Centaur:* Myth, History, and Narrative," *Modern Fiction Studies,* 20(Spring 1974), pp. 29- 43.

20. Richard Locke, review of *Rabbit Redux,* New York *Times Book Review,* 14 November 1971, p. 13.

21. Norman Podhoretz, "A Dissent on Updike," *Doings and Undoings: The Fifties and After in American Writing* (New York: Farrar, Straus, 1964), pp. 251-257.

22. Richard Gilman, "The Youth of an Author," *New Republic,* 13 April 1963, pp. 25-27; George Steiner, "Half Man, Half Beast," *The Reporter,* 14 March 1963, pp. 53-54.

23. Renata Adler, "Arcadia, Pa.," *New Yorker,* 13 April 1963, pp. 182-188. See also Thomas Curley, "Between Heaven and Earth," *Commonweal,* 29 March 1963, pp. 26-27. Curley writes: "As I read *The Centaur,* slowly and pleasurably, I was never aware of any discrepancy between will and imagination, but rather of a steady urgency to conceive anew; for if man is on the boundary between heaven and earth, he must have commerce with both." One point to make here is that George Caldwell has "commerce" with both the mythic and the mundane. The reaction in British journals is generally laudatory. Richard G. Stern calls *The Centaur* a "good, if smudged book," and he worries not so much about the mythic overtones as about the tendency to linger over little details lovingly described merely for the sake of the description. Robert Taubman praises the novel as a "daring technical success" and says that "in point of finesse it's clearly among the most notable of recent American novels." Finally the anonymous review in the *Times Literary Supplement* recommends the novel with the highest praise, calling it "outstandingly good": "*The Centaur* makes it clear that Mr. Updike is now one of the best, if not the best, of the American prose writers at work today. . . . he has produced an intellectual and emotional creation with a universal application which lifts the book from the national to the international level." See Richard G. Stern, "The Myth in Action," *Spectator,* 27 September 1963, p. 389; Robert Taubman, "God Is Delicate," *New Statesman,* 27 September 1963, pp. 406-407; "A Mythical Animal," London *Times Literary Supplement,* 27 September 1963, p. 728.

24. Updike has long been interested in Karl Barth's theology. See his essays "Faith in Search of Understanding," *Assorted Prose* (New York: Knopf, 1965), pp. 273-282; and "To the Tram Halt Together," *New Yorker,* 12 March 1979, pp. 135-144.

25. See Uphaus, p. 25: "For, in this novel, Updike is demonstrating the artist's need for a framework of belief, a metaphoric vision, whether Christian or classical, while he simultaneously shows the impossibility of resurrecting from the past a mythical framework, a scheme which answers to our spiritual needs."

26. Compare this scene with the later story "The Egg Race," in *Problems* (New York: Knopf, 1979), especially pp. 243-244.

# Of The Farm

*"My wife is a field."*
—*Of the Farm*

Joey Robinson, the thirty-five year-old narrator of *Of the Farm* (1965), is Peter Caldwell with a different name. Like the narrator of *The Centaur,* he momentarily exchanges the distraction of the big city for the enchantment of words and, despite an appalling weakness of character, successfully shows himself to be an artist capable of resurrecting from his past the personality of an extraordinary parent. One can even argue that Mrs. Robinson brings the artist in Joey to life, rather than the opposite, for the complexity of her character and the confusion of Joey's feelings for her, now that he is an adult, urge him to heights of creativity that he might have avoided had she not been a formidable parent. Surely Peter Caldwell experiences a similar inspiration when he puts aside his second-rate paintings to write a first-rate novel about his father.

Although his own father is dead, Joey's memories of him indicate that the myth of the centaur reverberates in this tale too. Even the speech rhythms of George Robinson echo those of George Caldwell: "Whereas my father, who hated to have his picture taken (for thirty years the yearbooks of the high school where he taught had printed the same unflattering photograph of him), was nowhere in sight, which gave his absence vitality. I could see him shying out of camera range, saying, 'Keep my ugly mug out of it.' "[1] Recalling the father's energy and the mother's presence, Joey becomes a kind of Adam figure as he tells his story, naming the highlights of his past, longing to give life to his mother's fields and his wife's body, redeeming his failures through the artistic control of language. Although trying to break free of the spell of the farm, he is keenly aware of the cyclical nature associated with all gardens of life, from the process of the seasons through Peggy's menstrual flow and Mrs. Robinson's impending death to the sermon on Adam and Eve he hears before returning to the city.

Updike candidly acknowledges the connections between his fiction and autobiography and between *The Centaur* and *Of the Farm,* and thus he indirectly supports the suggestion that Joey Robinson has taken up Peter Caldwell's pen:

I suppose there's no avoiding it—my adolescence seemed interesting to me. In a sense my mother and father, considerable actors both, were dramatizing my youth as I was having it so that I arrived as an adult with some burden of material already half-formed. There is, true, a submerged thread connecting certain of the fictions, and I guess the submerged thread is the autobiography. That is, in *Of the Farm,* although the last name is not the name of the people in *The Centaur,* the geography is not appreciably changed, and the man in each case is called George. *Of the Farm* was in part a look at the world of *The Centaur* after the centaur had indeed died.

The irony of naming both fathers George becomes clear when one considers that the name means farmer, from the Greek *geōrgos.*[2] Just as interesting is Updike's distinguishing among the various influences of father, mother, religion, and farm: "My mother was mentor number one in the matter of art, my father in the matter of life and reality. At the age of thirteen I was moved to a farm where I had extra amounts of solitude to entertain. Adversity, in the form of allergies and financial insecurity, visited me in stimulating but not overwhelming amounts . . . . Religion was and is a helpful peripheral presence, giving me hopefulness and a sense of reward beyond the immediate and a suspicion of intrinsic excellence as an ultimate standard."[3] It is fair to say that *The Centaur* and *Of the Farm* are the most autobiographical of Updike's novels and that the latter is, as Charles Thomas Samuels points out, the most subtle: "Though smaller in scope than his masterpiece, *Rabbit, Run,* it is artistically more polished, without taint of obviousness. For Updike's belief that ordinary relationships contain manifold complications, this book provides impressive evidence. In general, Updike's mimetic emphasis makes his fiction peculiarly resistant to summary; *Of the Farm* is the most irreducible of his works."[4]

The subtlety of the novel contrasts strikingly with the undisguised glow of its immediate predecessor, *The Centaur.* A quiet tale, *Of the Farm* resonates with the dilemma that Updike first worked out in his superb short story "Flight" (*Pigeon Feathers,* 1962) in which the adolescent boy must juggle the contradictory demands of both mother and girlfriend before he can combine the definition bestowed by the past with the freedom promised by the future. *Of the Farm* is thus Updike's most Jamesian novel in its psychological intricacies and the use of a narrator (albeit first person) to reflect the clashes of personal relationships.[5] Nothing happens except the fleshing out of characters, especially Joey and his mother, but, reminiscent of the complexities in a James fiction, character is action. The lyrical rhythm of their meetings and partings, their discussions and betrayals, *is* the curve of meaning, the movement of the novel.[6]

The lack of overt action turns off the masses of readers geared for the thrills of a best seller, but *Of the Farm* ranks high among those who care for the Updike canon. Indeed, Updike wonders if it is admired too much: ". . . some books have been blighted by people liking them too well. In a way *Rabbit, Run* is like that, and a little book called *Of the Farm*, which I suspect is harmless enough but people are always picking it as their favorite."[7] Updike made this comment in 1978, a decade and a half after the publication of the two novels he mentions, and it may be that in the intervening years he forgot the negative responses to the novel, some of which will be mentioned later.[8] It may also be that the popularity of *Of the Farm* among Updike's readers stems from its position as one of the final touches to his myth of the ordinary, of which the vicinity of the imaginary town, Olinger, Pennsylvania, is the center. Commenting in 1968 on his visits to his parents in Pennsylvania, he said, "Returning, I feel the larger—dare I say coarser?—scale of the state, the intensity of the green, the something mythic—an intensity, perhaps, of ordinariness—that I have tried to express in the novels and Olinger stories. After 'Of the Farm' I was determined to leave the state fictionally."[9] In this sense, then, *Of the Farm* is Updike's homage to his own past, as if he, too, were Peter Caldwell or Joey Robinson, graced for a moment with the nuances of language and using that moment to redeem an earlier failing through art. Art and redemption seem bound just as past and present are wedded. Updike comments, ". . . in a way the past is all we have. The present is very thin, it's less than a second wide, and the future doesn't exist. I think that *Of the Farm* is about moral readjustment, and the readjustment is somehow in terms of harsh deeds done in the past; the mother and boy need, in a way, to excuse each other, or somehow to give a blessing. It's a little hard for me to see my work from the outside, as it were, but I do notice a recurrence of the concept of a blessing, of approval, or forgiveness, or somehow even encouragement in order to go on."[10] In short, Joey Robinson finds himself between past and present, youth and middle age, farm and city, son and husband, mother and wife; and he discovers "that all the alternatives are unattractive."[11] Reconciliation demands more than he can offer—except in his art.

The critical response to Updike's handling of Joey's dilemmas is almost laughable in its contradictions. An overview of the commentary shows that the opinion of nearly every observer is disputed by another. Roger Sale and Bryant N. Wyatt, for example, fuss about what they consider to be the inconclusiveness of the ending, but Marcus Klein, in a witty essay, calls *Of the Farm* an "elegant little conceit of a novel" and praises Updike's handling of the ending: "Updike seems to be one of the few novelists of this time in this country who know how to bring a novel to an end. The secret of his virtuosity is in the fact that his novels start to end before they begin, and they will not be distracted from the beautiful curve of their resolutions by impertinent actualities."[12] Similarly, D. J. Enright argues that *Of the Farm* is "a sophisticated exercise in naivete," but Anthony Burgess points out its maturity: "It does not dare as much as *The Centaur* but, in the sense that it knows almost perfectly how to encompass a foreknown and limited success, it is far more mature."[13] Finally, Walter Sullivan complains that Updike's difficulties begin when he "attempts to probe beneath the surface," but Joseph Epstein praises Updike for just such probing: "That it hasn't much in the way of scope, however, ought not to be accounted a criticism, for Updike has never been quite so interested in spreading out as in boring in."[14]

The contradictory evaluations illustrate the puzzled critical response that nearly always greets an Updike novel, but the starkness of these particular disagreements may result from the distinctiveness of *Of the Farm* in Updike's writing. Short, introspective, even brooding, the novel is unexpectedly different to those used to the pyrotechnical qualities of *Rabbit, Run* and *The Centaur.* Peter Buitenhuis and Charles Thomas Samuels laud the difference in the highest terms.[15] Writing for the New York *Times*, Buitenhuis calls the novel a small masterpiece, and he observes, "When a book like this comes along, a critic must, before attempting anything else, raise his voice in a halloo of praise. In 'Of the Farm,' his fourth novel, John Updike has achieved a sureness of touch, a suppleness of style and a subtlety of vision that is gained by few writers of fiction." Similarly, Samuels writes, "This small, perfect novella is a multiple achievement, showing a new mastery."[16]

The touch of the master molds the shape of the characters as Updike relocates his vision from the Olympus of *The Centaur's* Olinger to the fields of Mrs. Robinson's farm. The farm has no specific use beyond providing a sanctuary of life and love for Mrs. Robinson and her myths and memories. As Joey's new eleven year-old stepson Richard asks, "What's the point . . . of a farm nobody farms?" (4). Joey is not sure, but his mother knows that to betray the land by selling it to real estate men who would "develop" it—that is, destroy it by building houses and shopping centers on it—is something she shrinks from doing. She can connect the land's weeds and pheasants to God, but her son can barely drive the tractor over the fields. God has little to do with Joey's sense of the farm. It is the domain of past associations for him, but he hopes to find his sustenance in the city of the future. Transcendence of the sort his mother experiences is impossible when one sets foot on the farm only a few weekends a year.

Against Joey's life of "stones and glass and subways," Mrs. Robinson offers a mythic vision of the land as sacred, as a locale in which she can touch both the temporal and the eternal.

All is not pastoral happiness, however, for Mrs. Robinson fears the signs of her impending death and the demise of her dreams that Joey become a poet. Aware that Joey has squandered his gifts on advertising as well as abandoned her own myth for his new wife's myth of sexual possession, she can do little except maneuver her son into betraying Peggy, a tactic she pulls off with alarming ease. Both wife and mother seek to deny the freedom of the other's understanding of Joey, and both must learn that to have freedom is to acknowledge it in others. In this sense, Updike's epigraph for the novel is informative. He quotes from Sartre: "Consequently, when, in all honesty, I've recognized that man is a being in whom existence precedes essence, that he is a free being who, in various circumstances, can want only his freedom, I have at the same time recognized that I can want only the freedom of others." But do Mrs. Robinson and Peggy want it in this novel? *Of the Farm* concerns the nature of freedom and its relation to the obligations naturally assumed when one takes on the burden of family. The novel also poses a corollary question: What happens when a person desires his own freedom but is reluctant to encourage it in others?

The sense of defeat in the novel is generated by the unwillingness of either wife or mother to permit Joey his own concept of freedom—whatever it may be—because both recognize his weakness as an opportunity for domination, the mother by appeals to nature and the past, the wife by appeals to sexuality and the future. The mother seeks openly to control; the wife seeks openly to submit. Yet each tactic is merely a means to the end of wrenching Joey from the other. His story, then, is a tale of loss; of his children through divorce, of his continuity through reaction against his mother's grasping myth, and perhaps of his new wife through weakness. Sadly, Joey Robinson is not a seeker as are George Caldwell, Rabbit Angstrom, Colonel Ellelloû, and John Hook. Caught up in the concerns of the self which are reinforced by his first-person narration, he can give money but not give care, bric-a-brac but not his presence. His sensitivity to natural beauty, as illustrated by his lyrical interior monologues, does not spill over to his dealings with other people, as illustrated by his defensive conversations. He remains stranded on Sartre's border between existence and essence.

To blame Mrs. Robinson for Joey's dilemma is to a large extent fair, for in his youth she wraps him in her dreams of art and nature, while in his adulthood she encloses him in her myths of the past. She gives him existence in birth but warps the essence in life. Yet Joey himself is also partly at fault, for he is too weak to define his own sense of self: Mom or

Peggy or former wife Joan is always around to do it for him. A modern, diminished Faust who has sold out the promise of poetry for the lure of advertising's dollar, he has abandoned his muse and is about to sacrifice his earthy wife.

The dust jacket material, which Updike may have written for the first American edition, points to the conflict: "For three days, a quartet of voices explores the air, relating stories, making confessions, seeking alignments, quarreling and pardoning. They are not entirely alone; ghosts—fathers, lovers, children—press upon them, and an increasingly crowded and greedy America erodes their rural island."[17] The jacket to the first British edition (Andre Deutsch, 1966) follows suit: "No one knows more than John Updike about the mixture of resentment and love, hostility and complicity, which can exist between parent and child, nor about marriage." The hostilities and confessions stem from the first sentence which hints that the farm is other worldly in the sense of being separated from the crowdedness and greed that soil domestic life in late twentieth-century America. There is a retreat of sorts implied in the words that open the novel: "We turned off the Turnpike onto a macadam highway, then off the macadam onto a pink dirt road" (3).

The local mailboxes stand deep in a mixture of honeysuckle and poison ivy, sweetness and gall, and Peggy is immediately apprehensive, as well she might be in this strange land, for Joey's description of the farm reveals a sense of possession that excludes her. He points to "our" farm and "our" meadow, and he does not mean Peggy's. He means his and Mrs. Robinson's, and the psychological battle of ownership unobtrusively begins. Although Joey thinks of himself as a city man, as an educated success who has made good his boyhood vow to escape the farm, he proudly describes the acreage as "probably the biggest piece of open land left this close to Alton" (4). Transplanted to the farm when he was fourteen, he is now in his middle thirties and, perhaps unfortunately, far from free of its influence: "It was true, whenever I returned, after no matter how great a gap of time, to this land, the acres flowed outward from me like a form of boasting. My wife had sensed this and was so newly my wife she thought it worth correcting" (5).

Her instinct is right. The farm confuses Joey. Pleased by the plenty he sees when he returns, he is wracked by the guilt he experiences when he leaves. Having lunged for the city as soon as he could abandon the farm, he has tried over the years to make up for his absence by sending expensive gifts of Mexican pottery and Italian glass which, he now realizes, are only cheap substitutes for his presence. Not his unadorned youth but what he calls "the scintillating dregs of my corruption" greet him when he walks through the door. As he and Peggy understand, Joey's problem when he crosses the threshold is his sense of being enshrined in the farmhouse, as if his mother were attempting to arrange his boyhood as the central exhibit in her monument to the past. Each time he returns he finds more of himself already there: "I was so abundantly memorialized it seemed I must be dead" (15). The reader recognizes, as does Joey, that what Mrs. Robinson covets most of all is Joey himself. Aware that her obsession for mementos had begun before he left the farm for New York, he tells his stepson Richard that the house is too full of him, that it has become his "glade of ghosts." Whenever he turns off the highway to drive up the pink dirt road to the farm, he drowns in a wave of photographs, trophies, medals, and memories.

Yet Joey is full of contradictions, as he undoubtedly knows. His dream of freedom on—not away from—the farm, a freedom he hopes will be blessed by Peggy's smile that can redeem the dismal hours of his lonely youth there, suggests the opposite pulls on his life at the border of middle age. On the one hand he longs to escape what he calls his history of fear and sorrow, but on the other hand he waits for Mrs. Robinson's blessing on at least one of the women he all but parades through her museum for approval. The following comment penetrates to the core of the tension about which Updike builds his most subtle novel: "I think of myself as a weak man; one form my weakness takes is to want other people to know what they can and cannot have. I can tolerate only to a limited degree the pressure of the unspoken. Whereas my mother is infinitely at home in the realm of implication, where everything can be revised" (61). Joey wants everyone to know what he can have, and what he thinks he desires for himself is a break from the farm even while he remains the center of his mother's life. Wanting to be a boy who is cared for like a child, yet longing to be a man who is equal to Peggy's sexual gifts, he both blames his mother for his marital problems and looks to her to solve them. His weakness prevents him from having it both ways, so he lapses into a confused state of passivity that encourages Mrs. Robinson and Peggy to slash at each other on the battlefield of emotions.

Beautifully physical, earthy, sexual, fertile, and most of all aggressive and caring at the same time, Peggy is the "center, the seat" of Joey's life. Mrs. Robinson would like to unseat her. As some men push back their shirt sleeves when sensing a confrontation, Peggy brushes back the hair from her forehead and cheeks, an act that is simultaneously erotic and energetic. She has the strength to criticize Joey, and weak Joey is honest enough to admit his need of correction. He knows, however, that Peggy's aggressiveness will clash with Mrs. Robinson's defensive subtlety, and as they ride up the dirt road he thinks not of the time when his new wife will greet his mother but of the moment when Mrs. Robinson will be "upon us." He had not, after all, wanted his mother to attend the wedding: "Joan in her innocence had once gently suggested that my mother needed a washing machine. She had never been forgiven. My instinct, now, in these last moments before my mother was upon us, was to talk about her aloud, as if to expel what later must be said" (5). But he expels nothing. All he offers to ease Peggy's uncertainty is the comment that he does not expect them to get along. His declaration of love is hasty, his pat on her thigh jerky. Joey fears the impending collision as much as Peggy does.

Updike's handling of Joey's complex motives is one of his most succinct considerations of the pitfalls dotting a middle-age marriage. Sexuality, freedom, and self-definition are all somehow involved. He shows how thirty-five year-old Joey has spun out of one marriage and plunged into another with a woman totally different from his first wife because of her sexual space, her sense of plenty, her promise of openness that allows Joey to justify his desertion of the land. Peggy has become his farm: "Not fat, my wife, as a woman, is wide, with sloping swinging shoulders and a pelvic amplitude that affects me as a kind of radiance and that gives her stride a heartening openness, a sense of space between her thighs" (8). Later he laughs when he sees bikini-clad Peggy hoeing Mrs. Robinson's garden, but he also knows that his mother rejects his substitute of Peggy for the land when he recalls her extravagant gesture of traveling by bus to a judge's hot chambers to witness a wedding she openly disapproves of and to greet the warmth of his joy with the coolness of her eyes. Peggy's strength in the face of such possessiveness is confidence in her physical gifts. As she pointedly tells Joey, "Love my cunt, love me." He does, and as he does he skims, glides, feels free: "And this freedom, once tasted, lightly, illicitly, became as indispensable as oxygen to me, the fuel of a pull more serious than that of gravity" (47). Although Mrs. Robinson's desire for Joey flirts with dormant incest, she cannot match Peggy's "pull" at that level. She possesses, as Updike brilliantly shows, other weapons.

His most complex character, more subtly drawn than Rabbit, more sure of who she is than Caldwell, Mrs. Robinson is the heroine of *Of the Farm*. She is old, strong-willed, and clever in her mastery of insinuation; and now, in the clouds of age, she is permanently enshrouded in her own myth of the farm. The cornerstone of the myth is her conviction that she did not force Joey and his now dead father to leave the town for the country, that Mr. Robinson supported her desire to buy the farm. No one agrees with her version of the story, and looking back Joey realizes that the purchase was "the great effort of her life." A woman who used to outrace her husband from the barn to the house, she now moves slowly because of angina and emphysema. She is aware of her deterioration, and she views Peggy's obviously healthy femininity with irritation. Where Peggy unselfconsciously dons a bikini to open her body to the sun, Mrs. Robinson wears an old gray sweater closed down the front. Joey notices the contrast immediately. He foreshadows his foreboding of what will happen when mother meets wife by describing the fall day as having a "sense of expiration." The nearby creek is "choked" and a bat jerks by "like a speck of pain." Freighted with these barely concealed personal antagonisms, the heavy atmosphere merges with Mrs. Robinson's myth to envelope the three visitors in a special aura that promises the pain of wounds wrenched open by verbal thrusts. Joey describes the danger: "Her spirit had acquired a troubling resonance, a murky subtlety doubly oppressive out of doors—as if in being surrounded by her farm we had been plunged into the very territory of her thoughts" (13).

One of the weapons that support the saga of the past and protect her territory is her manipulation of photographs. Updike understands how mementos judiciously spaced around a parent's house indicate not only preservation of the past but prior ownership of the child. Two women have since married Mrs. Robinson's child, but she signals her need for control by rearranging the formal portrait of Joan, the first wife, which hung in the living room for twelve years, and replacing it following Joey's marriage to Peggy: "My mother had made the appointment without consulting us, and we had both resented it. . . . When the proofs came back, my mother chose for enlargement one that had caught Joan off guard. . . . It was typical of their relations that the photograph turned out to be not what my mother really wanted" (16, 17, 18). In its place now hangs, with all the symbolism the subtle mother can muster, a painting of a "fabulous rural world," a farm. The battle with the first wife concluded in victory, Mrs. Robinson readies for the second. Joey realizes that Joan's grace, reserve, shyness, and dazzling smile must have been a disadvantage when confronting the bluntness of closed sweaters and open fields, so he marries wide, spacious Peggy as a substitute field to plow. His most pressing current question is whether his mother will accept the replacement and leave Peggy free of the implied threat posed by the painting on the wall. The epigraph suggests that to have freedom is to grant freedom, but Mrs. Robinson has not read Sartre. The answer to Joey's question, as the novel reveals, is negative.

The struggle begins in little ways. Mrs. Robinson pours coffee for Richard after Peggy says that he never drinks it. Peggy announces that Richard loves his absent father after she misinterprets Mrs. Robinson's remark that her own father was often a "pretty ugly customer." Mrs. Robinson wants Richard to drive the tractor despite Peggy's emphatic disapproval. Note how the dispute spills over from coffee cups and tractors to a battle for Joey:

"How can Richard manage my people sanctuary if he can't drive a tractor?"
Peggy cut in. "He's not going to manage anything for you. He's not going to be another Joey." It was a reflex, ruthless and needless.

My mother, slashed, her subtlety crushed, said weakly, "Dear Peggy, one Joey is enough for me." (92)

Mrs. Robinson's retort may be weak, but she is determined to have that "one Joey." His own weakness, which he readily admits, gives her every reason to expect success.

Mrs. Robinson's unfortunate tendency to detect motives for the accidental motions of the day exacerbates the tension: "As primitive worshippers invest the indifferent universe with pointed intentions, so my mother superstitiously read into the animate world, including infants and dogs, a richness of motive that could hardly be there—though, like believers everywhere, she had a way of making her environment supply corroboration" (23). This method of dealing with life's vagaries leads her to strike a two year-old child who has accidentally tapped her with a yardstick. Belief in God encourages her to treat all life as equal, be it children, adults, or the pheasants in her fields. It is all part of her mythic definition of life as existence sustained by the land, so that now, as she nears the end of her days, she elevates the years on the farm to saga and legend and then adjusts the past to fit the fiction. Especially sensitive to any hint that she is being replaced, Mrs. Robinson resents people who try too diligently to help her even though she seems too ill to resist: Peggy washes the dishes while she dries. All she has left is the myth.

Updike's observation of the agony of the old is neither sentimental nor condescending. It is also not surprising when one considers that two of his three earlier novels—*The Poorhouse Fair* and *The Centaur*—probe the dilemma of advancing age and diminishing hope. The extent to which he draws on personal experience is finally irrelevant, but it seems clear that growing up on a farm as an only child with grandparents in the house promised an abundance of material that he shapes with sensitivity and tact.[18] As Updike knows, the past looms large to the elderly, and thus he understands how Joey, listening to the mother talk after dinner, realizes the paradox that readjustment of the past is the constant in her life. She becomes a shaper of her own story: "Talk in our house was a continuum sensitive at all points of past and present and tirelessly harking back and readjusting itself, as if seeking some state of equilibrium finally free of irritation. My mother was bothered by my saying, an hour back, of my father, 'He never farmed,' and implying, with this, that the farm had been a burden upon him and had shortened his life. I felt this was true; my mother feared it might be" (29). So she continually retells the tale, revising history, strengthening the rationalization with each revision.

The centerpiece of her myth is that rather than burden her husband with anguish when she insisted on the move to the farm, she permitted his freedom. Her fiction connects with the epigraph of the novel, but even

Joey knows that it is a daring reconstruction of the past. "My mother within the mythology she had made of her life was like a mathematician who, having decreed certain severely limited assumptions, performs feats of warping and circumvention and paradoxical linkage that an outside observer, unrestricted to the plane of their logic, would find irksomely arbitrary" (31). Unfortunately for Peggy, she is the outside observer who is more than irked by the way everything in the myth points to the father's general unhappiness with life on the farm. Yet Mrs. Robinson defends the past, insisting that by not denying his freedom she gave it. This warping of fact, this utterly subjective interpretation of history, surprises Joey, but it first puzzles and then angers Peggy. For what Updike sets up in this novel of personalities is a clash of myths which touch base with the role of woman as defined by tradition. Mrs. Robinson's view of her role is shaped by her saga of the past, and it collides with Peggy's idealization of women as help mates. The mother's feat of warping scrapes a sore point in Peggy "around which revolved her own mythology, of women giving themselves to men, of men in return giving women a reason to live" (31).

Unlike the uneasy relationship that existed between his parents, Joey believes that he finds freedom with Peggy. She is his landscape, a terrain that promises a wealth of views: "Over all, like a sky, withdrawn and cool, hangs—hovers, stands, is—is the sense of her consciousness, of her composure, of a non-committal witnessing that preserves me from claustrophobia through any descent however deep" (47). With Joan he feels smothered, the way he feels when he walks through the door of the farmhouse, but with Peggy space soars before him. Mrs. Robinson dismisses Peggy's belief that psychological differences between the sexes are as significant as physical qualities. Nor can she accept Peggy's explanation that she has divorced her first husband and married Joey because he acts as if he owns her and thus gives her definition. Friction is unavoidable so long as their conversation focuses on women's responsibilities to men in the various guises of fathers, husbands, lovers, and sons.

Joey plays all four roles, and the complexity confuses him. His one hope for clarity is his wife's femininity, displayed as she reveals long legs and hair while "overflowing" a chair. The sight offends the more dominating mother, but Joey gazes at his dozing wife as if she were a prize he has snatched from beyond the confines of the farm to prove to his mother the value of his life there. Yet so long as he feels compelled, however unconsciously, to ask for Mrs. Robinson's approval of his brides, the longer it will take him to break free of her insistence that she grants freedom to her men. When, for example, she offers him the chance to advise her to sell the farm before she dies, he refuses. Memorialized by the myth, he finds identity there. Joey does not like the shape of the past, but he lacks a definition of the future. Too weak to walk free of the saga, he sits still while wife and mother fight out their conflicting versions of women. He is not an attractive character, but self-awareness and first-person narration guarantee sympathy by narrowing the distance between the reader and Joey's point of view.

Updike foreshadows the end when he shows Joey reentering the house after feeding the dogs and going to his mother even while he feels the pull of Peggy's waiting for him upstairs. Note the odor not of honeysuckle or verbena but of dust: "The invisible mementos and objects around me seemed gathered into the intense expectance of the votive implements in a shrine. The smell was, not of my youth, but of dust" (42). Here, amid the musty atmosphere of legend, Mrs. Robinson opens up her attack with a departure from her usual method of insinuation and in a way that the reader does not forget. She tells Joey that Peggy is stupid. When he does nothing but leave the room, the reader knows that Mrs. Robinson will always hold the upper hand.

Joey is a curious mixture of awareness and uncertainty. He admits that it is degrading to submit to his mother's hold, but he does little to break the grip. When he dresses the next morning in his father's dungarees and shaves with his father's razor, the reader can only shake his head and suspect that Joey needs the trappings of the past because that is where his identity lies. His weakness is the mother's accomplice, and both know it, just as both recognize her weapons to be the fiction of the past and her clever way of putting herself on the defensive so that the others politely back down. When, for example, Peggy urges her to eat more pancakes, Mrs. Robinson implies to Joey that she is being "ingeniously" murdered.

Nowhere does Updike better illustrate the difference between mother and son than in the account of the mowing of the field, the central episode in the novel:

My mother's method, when she mowed, was to embrace the field, tracing its borders and then on a slow square spiral closing in until one small central patch was left, a triangle of standing grass or an hourglass that became two triangles before vanishing. Mine was to slice, in one ecstatic straight thrust, up the middle and then to narrow the two halves, whittling now at one and now the other, entertaining myself with flanking maneuvers acres wide and piecemeal mop-ups. I imitated war, she love. (58)

She shows her love of the farm by cutting around a pheasant's nest or a vivid patch of flowers, but the sexual nature of Joey's "one ecstatic thrust" is clear and sends his thoughts to Peggy. He mows the meadow as he would plow his wife: "The tractor body was flecked with foam and I, rocked back and forth on the iron seat shaped like a woman's hips, alone in nature, as hidden under the glaring sky as at midnight, excited by destruction, weightless, discovered in myself a swelling which I idly permitted to stand, thinking of Peggy. My wife is a field" (59).[19] The metaphor is perfect, an illustration of what a psychologist might call substitution, and it suggests Joey's effort to transfer the open meadows of the farm to the closed-in concrete of New York by personifying the land in Peggy.

If he is to avoid Mrs. Robinson's myth of homecoming, then he must escape what he calls "the hook of her death." Signs of the mother's death prick the guilt of desertion in the son, and the reader joins Joey in sympathizing with her sad plea that "people must be told when they're no longer fit to live, they musn't be left to guess at it, because it's something nobody can tell herself" (71-72). Yet Peggy is correct: Mrs. Robinson uses her plea and her temper, turning them off and on like a weapon, taking every throw-away remark as personal. Joey's emotional confusion in the face of conflicting loyalties causes him to retreat to the realm of petty accusation when, taking a cue from his mother's comment that his new wife is stupid, he queries Peggy about her first marriage. That part of her life is none of his business, and Peggy, while not subtle, is surely not stupid. But his weakness gives his mother the lead. As Peggy tells him, "You don't stand up to anything. You let us slug it out and then try to make peace" (93). All he can do is accept the accusation and her subsequent declaration of love, but he returns to the mowing wearing his father's trousers and his mother's hat. His last glimpse of Peggy before parking the tractor reminds him of a concubine in chains and a death mask.

The irony is that not Mrs. Robinson but Peggy tells him what the reader already suspects: "The cute thing about you, Joey, is you're really sort of a bastard" (123). But he is not a villain. A stumbling artist trying to come to terms with the materials of his own story, he offers a faint possibility for the unification of existence and essence when he creates a fairy tale at Richard's bedtime.[20] His make-believe describes a frog who disappears into itself while searching for a treasure in its guts. When spring arrives, the frog open its eyes, turns from the self, and looks out at the world. After Joey finishes the story, he walks downstairs to his wife and mother, expecting "some nostalgic treasure unlocked by the humidity within the stones, plaster, wood, and history of the house," but he notes instead the aroma of Peggy's damp hair. Updike does not insist on the meaning of the episode, and it does raise hopes that Joey will finally place not nostalgic treasure but Peggy at the center of his life. Although some read the novel this way, the hope seems dashed when he betrays his wife to his mother a few moments later.

Adequately fulfilling Peggy's comment that he is a bastard, he sits between the women during their last night at the farm and does nothing except listen while each gently but insistently accuses the other. Personal myths regarding the role of women stand behind the accusations: "Peggy's idea, which now, in the awful fullness of this exchange, she could expand from a suspicion to an accusation, a detailed indictment of a past that had touched her only through my hands, was that my mother had undervalued and destroyed my father, had been inadequately a 'woman' to him, had brought him to a farm which was in fact her giant lover, and had thus warped the sense of the masculine within me, her son" (134). Mrs. Robinson's parry is equally the stuff of legend: "And my mother, on her side, swept forward with a fabulous counter-system of which I was the center, the only child, the obscurely chosen, the poet, raped, ignorantly, from my ideally immaterial and unresisting wife and hurled into the shidepoke sin of adultery and the eternal damnation of my children's fatherlessness" (135). Trapped between the two myths and afraid to break out, Joey tries to convince himself that they are both correct, that all misconceptions have a kernel of truth, that truth is no more than the "solidification of illusions." Ordinarily in an Updike fiction, one might accept Joey's effort to contain the opposites as his recognition of the inevitability of subjectivity when confronting the objective world. One person's truth is another's illusion; compromises are struck and life goes on. But not in *Of the Farm*. Too much evidence of his weakness has piled up. The reader knows that Joey's attempted balancing act comes not from clarity but from fear. Terrified at losing his place in the pastoral myth of the past, he prepares for his betrayal of Peggy later in the evening. He senses that their accusations are no more than a "collision of darknesses," but he sees his mother's darkness as nurturing, his wife's as cold and metallic: "Surely in becoming my wife she had undertaken, with me, the burden of mothering my mother, of accommodating herself to the warps of that enclosing spirit. Her cigarette smoke insulted the room" (135).

One would like to examine the marriage contract that calls for Joey's interpretation of marital accommodation. Dismay crowds out sympathy when he cowers under Mrs. Robinson's attack and confesses that he has made a mistake in divorcing Joan. Responding like a small child to his mother's patient prodding, he agrees that Peggy is stupid, declares his love for Joan, and refuses to defend his wife when, rather fantastically, Mrs. Robinson describes her as fierce, as a woman who will have her dead within a year. His feeble reply that his mother is too egocentric goes unheeded in the face of her sustained attack: "It pleased me to feel myself sinking, smothered, lost, forgotten, obliterated in the depths of the mistake which my mother, as if enrolling my fall in her mythology, enunciated: 'You've taken a vulgar woman to be your wife' " (140-141).

Mrs. Robinson cleverly plays on their shared sense of superiority to Peggy, on their satisfaction in a society of two. Updike illustrates how thoroughly the mother has shaped the son by drawing a brilliantly conceived parallel. The more pointed Mrs. Robinson's jealousy of Peggy becomes, the more obsessed Joey becomes by Peggy's past relationship with her former husband. He is as suspicious of the ex-husband as his mother is of the current wife. Cunningly using her impending death and her son's remorse at losing his children in the divorce, Mrs. Robinson spins out the double strand of jealousy so that Peggy gets tangled in the web of invective. Jealousy leads to accusations that inevitably gouge wounds, and wounds of this sort, wrenched through the emotions by slashing verbal thrusts, do not quickly heal.

Peggy looks at the dilemma on the farm with an outsider's eyes, and even though she has her own myth of the female role, she does not warp accidental situations to fit personal sagas. Joey stares at his spacious wife and feels guilty, but his response to his guilt at betraying her is pathetic, a clue to his failure ever to control the complex demands on his emotions: "I was angry at the ease with which she had accepted my betrayal of Peggy, had absorbed it parasitically, sitting there motionless, devoting her thought, her innermost thought, not to me but to her farm. So I scorned her death" (142). But mothers with this kind of strength are not scorned quite so easily. As Peggy says, in her open manner of directness, Joey should never have left the womb. When he considers sending Richard and her home alone after his mother falls ill, his heart soars in anticipation of their absence and expands to the far limits of the farm. Insulting Peggy to her face, accusing her of wantonness, he resents his inability to visualize wife and farm together, as if his failure were her fault. Not surprisingly, his apology falls flat.

Arching over every nuance of this tension-filled weekend is the central fact of Mrs. Robinson's current life—her death. Updike is too fine a writer to divide the novel along lines of them versus us, and he surely does not want the mother to take on the one-dimensional role of wrathful parent scourging any female who walks up the lane to tempt her son. Reader sympathy is crucial in a novel as subtle as *Of the Farm*. Updike makes certain that Joey senses his mother's predicament in a way that we too may understand it. Joey, for example, exclaims that Mrs. Robinson's love of life is grotesque, but he is mistaken, just as Peggy is wrong to brand the mother's concern for Joey's children as a way of making her feel guilty. Life is short and death is near, and Mrs. Robinson clutches at the past as a way of holding on. The variety of the farm feeds her vision of God's plenty, for life surprises her every day with something new in the fields or in the weather. This is why she sees the city where Joey lives as the death of the poet in him, as a place where air-conditioning makes all the seasons similar.

Uncertainty about the rest of her days unfortunately but understandably encourages her self-centeredness to the extent that when Richard talks about the moon, she takes the topic personally as a desertion of her presence on the earth. Yet in her need for attention as a way of certifying the validity of the rest of her life, she carelessly accuses where accusation is unwarranted, as when she says that Peggy has taken her grandchildren from her. Only in these few situations, where his mother is clearly in the wrong, can Joey stand up for his wife and express what has been hovering beneath the surface all during the unhappy visit: "You ask for advice, for pity. You carry yourself as if you've made a terrible mistake. You pretend you emasculated Daddy and when some innocent soul offers to agree with you you're hurt" (113). The evening rain does not clear the senseless pain of this exchange, and the air of the house "takes" a wound. Thus when Mrs. Robinson deliberately smashes dinner plates to break the silence after supper, she is not so much expressing her willingness to challenge the legend of the past as she is rallying attention back to herslf. Peggy correctly understands that what she calls "so much neuroticism" poisons the weekend, but Mrs. Robinson's fear of living a useless life is more the issue. Unexpected noise guarantees the spotlight. There is little activity more surprising in the Robinson farmhouse than an old lady dashing plates to the floor. When Joey later looks at her sleeping figure following a severe attack of angina, he sees her for what she is—an aged woman, no longer able to outrace anyone, barely able to climb the stairs. His mother has entered, he realizes with a penetrating phrase, "the arctic of the old": "Death seemed something minor, a defect she had overlooked in purchasing these acres, a negligible flaw grown huge" (167).

The specter has grown so large that it reenforces her need for Sunday church service. There, with only Joey for a companion, she listens to a minister years younger than herself. His sermon is the climax of the novel which has all along been a meditation, disguised as a psychological thriller, on the nature of freedom and women. Taking as his text Genesis 2:18—"And the Lord God said, It is not good that the man should be alone; I will make him an help meet for him"—the minister argues the unity of men, women, and the earth. He insists that men and women were placed on the land not to love one another but to work together. As the sermon continues, the minister's discourse about language touches on the role of art. Updike connects tilling the earth with telling the novel. Both are creative acts of faith: "And is it so strange that Adam's first piece of work was to name his mute helpers? Is not language an act of husbandry, a fencing-in of fields? We are all here farmers or the sons and daughters of farmers, so we know how the lowly earthworm aërates the soil. Likewise, language aërates the barren density of brute matter with the penetrations of the mind, of the spirit" (151). This comment is one of Updike's most concise observations about the relationship between religion and art, and it suggests that with all his flaws Joey brushes the eternal through his effort to tell the story of the long weekend on the farm. The eternity of art more than equals the brevity of life. Mrs. Robinson's immortality is to be found not only in her fields but also in Joey's tale.[21]

In this sense, God's creation of women is also a work of art. As the minister explains, women are less than equal to men, a part of the whole; women are finer than men; and women offer the opportunity for faith. But as Joey listens, the opportunity is also for partial confusion, for the sermon suggests both a return to the mother and a cleaving to the wife. On the one hand, Joey hears a justification of sorts for his decision to elevate Mrs. Robinson over Peggy. Note the emphasis on nostalgia in the minister's words: "Man, with Woman's creation, became confused as to where to turn. With one half of his being he turns toward her, his rib, as if into himself, into the visceral and nostalgic warmth wherein his tensions find *re*solution in *dis*solution" (152). On the other hand, Joey hears the suggestion that in committing himself to his wife he ties himself ethically to the earth. We hope that his identification of Peggy as a field leads to a reconciliation of wife and farm in his vision of the future, but the end of the novel dashes that promise. Joey is described in the sermon as man trying to understand the creation of woman, but the minister then points out to the reader, if not to Joey, his crucial flaw: Women appeal to the kindness in men, but Joey has not been kind. Quoting Karl Barth, long one of Updike's favorite theologians, the minister explains, "In designating her with his own generic name, Adam commits an act of faith: 'This is *now* bone of my bones, and flesh of my flesh.' In so declaring, he acknowledges within himself a responsibility to be kind. He ties himself ethically to the earth" (153). Joey's dilemma is clear. If he abandons the farm, he loses the nurturing that his mother represents, her nostalgic warmth. If he abandons Peggy, he loses the sexual freedom that she offers, a step toward the future. His indecision is a negative equilibrium, and one fears that he will give up the latter.[22]

Needless to say, Mrs. Robinson does not like the sermon, for in her massive yet necessary egocentricity she thinks that men who talk about women are merely trying to excuse themselves from women's pain. In the next breath she attacks Joan as too respectable, as not, after all, the right woman for Joey. Having persuaded him first to betray Peggy, she now seeks the same for Joan. At the end, when she calls from the sick bed that she wants Peggy to have a photograph taken during the next visit, we know that Mrs. Robinson is still determined to banish all women from her son's life, that Peggy's portrait may also be eventually replaced by a picture of a rural landscape.

The final sentences circle back to the first as Joey tries to comfort his sick mother by speaking of "our" farm:

"Joey," she said, "when you sell my farm, don't sell it cheap. Get a good price."

We were striking terms, and circumspection was needed. I must answer in our old language, our only language, allusive and teasing, that with conspiratorial tact declared nothing and left the past apparently unrevised. "*Your* farm?" I said. "I've always thought of it as our farm." (174)

It is possible to interpret this ambiguous ending as Samuels does, arguing that Mrs. Robinson accepts Peggy and that Joey's "our" pays her "respect for his freedom by affirming the reality of their bond."[23] If this interpretation is valid, then the mother gives way to the wife, and the son becomes a man. Essence joins existence.

The thought is comforting, but the novel suggests otherwise. Too many wounds have been opened, too many positions declared, for the pain of this weekend to be eased so suddenly. Joey's "our" recalls the first page where he indicates to Peggy "our" barn and "our" meadow. There, as here, the word does not include the wife. Joey's betrayals of Peggy have been too blatant, the mother's accusations of stupidity and vulgarity too sharp, and the symbol of the photographs too pointed for the reader to gloss over in his desire that the three characters be reconciled at the conclusion. As Updike himself notes, the weekend shows Joey that all the alternatives are unattractive. Joey will always be of the farm, trapped between conflicting myths about the role of women, frozen in existence as he gropes toward essence, stuck to the past until others, as Sartre says, desire his freedom in order to guarantee their own. Given such circumstances, reconciliation can come only in art, and that is why Joey Robinson tells this tale.

## NOTES

1. John Updike, *Of the Farm* (New York: Knopf, 1965), p. 15. Further references will be noted in the text. Interestingly, Joey's new wife Peggy is briefly associated with a centaur. Observing her dress of polka-dot bikini top and blue stretch pants, Joey thinks, "Indeed she seemed in this centaurine costume more natural, more practically resolved to give herself—my city wife, my habituée of foyers and automatic elevators—to the farm" (p. 161).
2. Charles Thomas Samuels, "The Art of Fiction XLIII: John Updike," *Paris Review*, 12(Winter 1968), p. 92. I am indebted to my colleague David Cowart for pointing out the echo of Virgil's *Georgics* in the name of these reluctant farmers and in the title *Of the Farm*. One also wonders if Updike nudges the reader to consider Joey and his mother, Mary Robinson, as an ironic parallel to the Christ story. Redemption in the form of a child is not forthcoming from this Mary and Joseph.
3. Quoted in Cynthia Pincus, Leslie Elliott, and Trudy Schlachter, *The Roots of Success* (Englewood Cliffs, New Jersey: Prentice-Hall, 1980), pp. 122-123.
4. Charles Thomas Samuels, *John Updike* (Minneapolis: University of Minnesota

Pamphlets on American Writers, 1969), no. 79; rpt. *John Updike: A Collection of Critical Essays*, eds. David Thorburn and Howard Eiland (Englewood Cliffs, New Jersey: Prentice-Hall, 1979), p. 151.

5. For more commentary on the relationship with Henry James, see James R. Lindroth, review of *Of the Farm*, *America*, 27 November 1965, p. 692: "As in James' *The Turn of the Screw*, those absent roam the house exerting pressure, influencing decisions, determining emotional alignments. . . . In style, Updike leaps over the tradition that extends from Hemingway, Stein, and Twain to realign himself with Henry James. The narrator, like so many of James', is a sensitive barometer of feeling. The sentences, like the relationships, are full of nuances. It is the inner life rather than the outer that is important, and the inner life is revealed through long conversations and sentences that abound in qualifying negatives." See also Richard Locke, review of *Rabbit Redux*, New York *Times Book Review*, 14 November 1971, p. 20; Locke calls *Of the Farm* "one of the finer American psychological novels."

6. Charles Thomas Samuels agrees: "Only a confused and decadent criticism can accuse Updike of lacking matter. His matter is the sum total of every precisely recorded gesture, thought, and word. . . . I recoil when critics fabricate gratuitous comparisons between new and established writers in an attempt to create excellence by association. But I cannot read Updike without recalling a much larger writer whose genius has eluded some in a manner recalling Updike's present reputation. Henry James also cultivated style to the point of preciosity, presented characters largely through their sensibilities, so narrowed his range that he seemed to be 'chewing more than he bit off,' and so blended statement and imitation that he was frequently thought to have abandoned statement altogether." See "The Question of Updike," *Kenyon Review*, 28 (March 1966), pp. 273-274.

7. Richard Burgin, "A Conversation with John Updike," *The John Updike Newsletter*, 10 and 11 (Spring and Summer, 1979), p. 10.

8. For what it is worth, I count myself among those who name *Of the Farm* as their favorite Updike novel, perhaps because I am also an admirer of Henry James's fiction.

9. Lewis Nichols, "Talk with John Updike," New York *Times Book Review* 7 April 1968, p. 34.

10. Eric Rhode, "Grabbing Dilemmas: John Updike Talks about God, Love, and the American Identity," *Vogue*, 1 February 1971, p. 184.

11. Frank Gado, "Interview with John Updike," *First Person: Conversations on Writers and Writing* (Schenectady, New York: Union College Press, 1973), p. 104.

12. See Roger Sale, "High Mass and Low Requiem," *Hudson Review*, 19 (Spring 1966), especially pp. 129-131; Bryant N. Wyatt, "John Updike: The Psychological Novel in Search of Structure," *Twentieth Century Literature*, 13 (July 1967), pp. 89-96; and Marcus Klein, "A Mouse in the Barn," *Reporter*, 16 December 1965, pp. 54-56.

13. See D. J. Enright, "Updike's Ups and Downs," *Holiday*, (November 1965), pp. 162-166; and Anthony Burgess, "Language, Myth and Mr. Updike," *Commonweal*, 11 February 1966, pp. 557-559. Burgess goes on to lament the "clumsy

muscularity" of contemporary American fictional style and to praise Updike as the exception.

14. Walter Sullivan, "Updike, Spark and Others," *Sewanee Review,* 74 (Summer 1966), especially pp. 711-713; and Joseph Epstein, "Mother's Day on the Updike Farm," *New Republic,* 11 December 1965, pp. 23-26. With fine humor, Epstein thanks Updike for the character of Mrs. Robinson: "If it accomplishes nothing else, Updike's creation of the mother in *Of the Farm* provides a tremendous service for Jewish mothers everywhere. In effect, it lets them off the hook. . . . Next to Updike's creation, the mother in Bruce Jay Friedman's novel, *A Mother's Kisses,* for example, seems like a favorite aunt."

15. Peter Buitenhuis, "The Mowing of a Meadow," New York *Times Book Review,* 14 November 1965, pp. 4, 34; Charles Thomas Samuels, "The Question of Updike."

16. The generally lukewarm response in the British press is illustrated by Robert Taubman's complaint: "Switching from mythology, Updike has contrived a neo-classical tragedy. As before, the point is very largely in the contrivance, and it satisfies so long as nothing else is asked of it. The dazzling exchanges between Joey, his mother and the new wife are best enjoyed for themselves alone. To look for more can hardly fail to raise doubts." See "Updike," *New Statesman,* 12 August 1966, p. 233.

17. On the Dick Cavett Show for 15 December 1978, Updike revealed that he often wrote the material for the dust jackets of his books.

18. See Updike's poem "Leaving Church Early," *Tossing and Turning* (New York: Knopf, 1977).

19. See Updike's short story "The Bulgarian Poetess" in which he expresses a similar idea: "We fall in love, I tried to say in the book, with women who remind us of our first landscape." "The Bulgarian Poetess," *The Music School* (New York: Knopf, 1966), p. 229.

20. Compare Updike's short story "Should Wizard Hit Mommy?," *Pigeon Feathers* (New York: Knopf, 1962).

21. For a similar view, see the following comment by Wesley Kort: "The presence of those remembered lives forms the answer to death which the minister in this book refers to as 'the concrete reality of Christ.' For the point at which religion and art join in Updike's work is where these portraits of recall move out to that all-important resurrected presence, and the art becomes a sacrament."; "A Confession of Debt," *The Christian Century,* 19 January 1966, p. 82.

22. But see Buitenhuis who argues that the tension is resolved affirmatively.

23. Samuels, *John Updike,* p. 154. See also Updike's introduction to what was to have been the Czech edition of *Of the Farm, Picked-Up Pieces* (New York: Knopf, 1975), pp. 82-83: "The underlying thematic transaction, as I conceived it, was the mutual forgiveness of mother and son, the acceptance each of the other's guilt in taking what they had wanted, to the discomfort, respectively, of the dead father and the divorced wife."

# FALTERING TOWARD DIVORCE

*Couples* (1968)
*A Month of Sundays* (1975)
*Marry Me: A Romance* (1976)

# Couples

*"Every marriage tends to con-
sist of an aristocrat and a peasant."*

—*Couples*

In 1963, five years before the publication of his biggest selling novel, Updike wrote a short story titled "Couples." Rejected by the *New Yorker,* the story was not made public until 1976 when Updike published "Couples" in an edition limited to 250 signed copies.[1] In the meantime, of course, the novel *Couples* (1968) had appeared with all the fanfare one expects of a best-seller that brings its author, whether he looks for fame or not, a lucrative sale of movie rights, a *Time* cover story, and resulting publicity. "Couples" is thus the forerunner of *Couples,* but as Updike explains in the introduction to the limited edition, the plot is too crowded to be developed successfully in a short tale.

Yet the story is important because it is among Updike's earliest attempts to write about adultery in the suburbs of the upper middle class. As he notes in the 1976 introduction, suburban adultery is a subject that, if "I have not exhausted it, has exhausted me. But I have persisted, as I earlier persisted in describing the drab normalities of a Pennsylvania boyhood, with the conviction that there was something good to say for it, some sad magic that, but for me, might go unobserved." The magic is sad because time tarnishes the glow of the once innocent party pleasures that used to keep the revelers happy. Both the tale and the novel chronicle another of America's perpetual falls from innocence, from the moment in the 1950s "when everyone was pregnant" to the moment in the 1960s when everyone was guilty. Updike writes in the introduction to the story, "The lofty and possibly unkind sociological tone of that novel [*Couples*], and the note of personal emotion struck in a number of short stories less clumsy than this one, are here still fused." Marital illusions give way with the changing decade.[2] The safeguard to being surrounded by other couples breaks down. Friendship turns to betrayal.[3]

The decision to expand the short story resulted in one of Updike's longest novels. *Rabbit Is Rich* (1981) has nine more pages than *Couples*, but the latter takes much more time to read. Divided into long chapters with descriptive titles reminiscent of the traditional well-made novels of social observation and the human comedy, *Couples* is Updike's bow to Victorian methods of story telling. He explains, "*Couples* was in some ways an old-fashioned novel; I found the last thirty pages—the rounding up, the administering of fortunes—curiously satisfying, pleasant. Going from character to character, I had myself the sensation of flying, of conquering space."[4] Yet he does not like to think of his novel as Victorian, and he takes issue with an implication in the *Time* cover story (26 April 1968) that his fiction resembles not the art of his contemporaries but the creations of an earlier century: "Gee, I hope it's not true, although the book they were referring to is, I suppose, an old-fashioned book—a big roomy book with a lot of little chambers and many characters—and in that respect it could be called Victorian. And, yes, it is kind of a cozy, close book. But I don't feel 'Victorian' and I don't much enjoy reading Victorian novels."[5]

But he clearly enjoyed writing *Couples*. Long, leisurely, and full of luxuriously observed detail, *Couples* is a serious account of an effort by upper middle-class Americans to establish an erotic utopia. The characters' swerve toward romance, however, is often halted by the omniscient narrator's puncturing edge of irony. Freedom within the staked-out boundaries of marriage is at issue, as it is for Joey Robinson and Harry Angstrom. When Gallagher, Piet Hanema's business partner, tells him, for example, that the Roman Catholic Church defines marriage as a sacrament celebrated by the couple themselves, Piet answers, "Maybe some of the sacrament should be giving the other some freedom."[6] The point is that certain religious beliefs inhibit what Gallagher calls "room for maneuver." Since he believes that fidelity can never be questioned, freedom must be sought in places other than the bedroom. But Piet is not convinced. His need for freedom is the heart of this novel about declining beauty, diminishing potency. Despite the surface connections with Victorian fiction, then, *Couples* differs radically in theme, for it begins where novels of manners used to end—with marriage—and it develops toward dissolution of the social bond. As Updike writes in a short story published just two years before *Couples*, "We are all pilgrims, faltering toward divorce."[7]

Piet's faltering takes him in and out of bedrooms, in and out of mistresses, and in and out of trouble. His stumbling away from hearth and home is both comic and moving. It is also puzzling to him because he is one of the few religious believers in his circle of couples. Beyond the paradise of the female body lies his fear of damnation. Thus the larger issue in *Couples* may be not sexual freedom but freedom from the terror of death. Piet's longing for a pre-lapsarian Eden, for the pastoral enclosure of his dead parents' greenhouse, restricts his acceptance of a post-lapsarian world. Abandonment of angelic wife Angela for sensual mistress Foxy may be his fall from grace, but it is also his entry into the mundane where death is an unglamorous natural fact along with Foxy's scratchy armpits and used underwear. The streets of Tarbox named Charity and Divinity are in view of the old Congregational Church with its "flashing cock" on the steeple, and the children of the town identify the weathervane with God. Although one may wonder if sex replaces religion as Piet's armor against death, the point is that the Tarbox commune fails. No one is hurt when God's "own lightning" strikes the church, but Piet and Foxy are expelled from the community and turned to the world.

What are the wages of sin if adultery is the cornerstone of what another of Piet's mistresses calls the "post-pill paradise"? Expulsion is one thing, but damnation is quite another, and it seems unlikely that Foxy will be made to wear an *A* either literally or figuratively.[8] The religious sacraments that restrain Gallagher's need for freedom are shaky when applied to Piet. In this sense it is instructive to consider *Couples* in light of Tony Tanner's *Adultery in the Novel*. Paraphrasing Vico, Tanner points out that all human relationships begin with and then depend on restraint. The social restriction of marriage, as opposed to the freedom of adultery, has a historical connection with the origins of man's ability to define boundaries, for definition helped to differentiate man from the chaos of promiscuity where all things are in common, that is, unbounded, unrestrained. Marriage is thus a contract, an exchange, a possibility for both individual and social stability.

But what if marriage fails, as it does in Updike's Tarbox? What is the relationship between marriage and the novel? Norman Cousins paraphrases one of Updike's answers: " . . . he quoted the French as saying that the novel cannot exist without adultery. Readers, he said, tend to be quickly sated with tales involving fame or wealth, but they sit upright when the novelist burrows into the inner lives and desires of people."[9] He may be correct. The history of the novel shows that since the eighteenth century fiction has laid bare what Tanner calls the "radical instability" of the institution: "If marriage is at the center, and the center cannot hold, what then? . . . For nineteenth-century bourgeois society one might almost say that marriage sanctioned religion, and if it is in any way called into question or it disintegrates, then for those implicated and involved in its unstabilizing, the problem does indeed arise—is there another form by which they may exist in the world at all? That is the social problem that the novel concerned with adultery finally must confront."[10] Since the sanction behind marriage is religion, a corresponding problem is what happens to marriage, and by implication social stability, if religion fails? How, in other words, do people live as humans if the forms that grant definition and restraint are abandoned? Tanner again paraphrases Vico: "Chaos is a state in which there are no marriages, and hence no identification of offspring, and hence an inability to establish names."[11]

The primary couples in Updike's novel dodge the church and change the names. Piet and Angela Hanema and Ken and Foxy Whitman become Piet and Foxy Hanema. Angela and Ken, the left-over spouses, are all but canceled. Thus chaos is partly skirted, but the ancient church in Tarbox burns anyway. Piet longs to hold back the night, but he fears that his freedom is at stake. According to Tanner, the eternal question is "just what, in terms of law, can bind the variant volatility of a committed pair?"[12] There are no easy answers, but Tanner quotes Denis de Rougemont's *Love in the Western World*, a work Updike is familiar with, to the effect that in desiring literature based on adultery, readers are "constantly *betraying* how widespread and disturbing is our obsession by the love that breaks the law. Is this not the sign that we wish to escape from a horrible reality?"[13] In other words, and this is a key point in *Couples*, lovers are drawn as much to what destroys marriage as to what supports it. As Freud noted, and as literature has long confirmed, obstacles are necessary for the intensity of passion. If society weakens to the extent that the social institutions limiting love waver, institutions such as church, home, and marriage itself, then the traditional novel of adultery disappears.

Tanner argues that *Couples* illustrates this loss: "When a society ceases to care much about marriage, and all that is implied in that transaction, by the same token it will lose contact with the sense of intense passion. This would mean that the novel of adultery, as I have been describing it, would vanish—as indeed it has. A novel like John Updike's *Couples* is as little about passion as it is about marriage; the adulteries are merely formal and technical. Adultery, we may say, no longer signifies."[14] Updike might disagree and reply that *Couples* only illustrates an adjustment in fiction, that the traditional question, who loves whom, is still at the heart of his novel:

The bourgeois novel is inherently erotic, just as the basic unit of bourgeois order—the family unit built upon the marriage contract—is erotic. Who loves whom? Once this question seems less than urgent, new kinds of novels must be written, or none at all. If domestic stability and personal salvation are at issue, acts of sexual conquest and surrender are important. If the issue is an economic reordering, and social control of the means of production, then sexual attachments are as they are in Mao's China—irrelevant, and the fewer the better.[15]

Unlike Tanner, Updike celebrates both domestic stability and personal salvation. In his fiction, the needs of the individual are every bit as important as the demands of society, and this is why Piet Hanema is all but handcuffed by the competing requirements of sexual desire and religious restraint. No wonder he veers toward doubt.

As Joyce Carol Oates points out, Updike's sympathies are usually with his doubters despite the overview of orthodox religious faith in his novels.[16] His believers long for but question the certainties of salvation, and thus they accept in exchange the possibility that their own lives may be a work of art. Colonel Ellelloû and Peter Caldwell write their stories; Joey Robinson tells his as a kind of ironic Virgil of the farm; and Rabbit Angstrom acts his life convinced that it has value. Tragedy seems impossible for these people because the creations of their imaginations bring them closer to salvation than their doubting beliefs. Piet joins the list of Updike's religious men who rely finally on the validity of the imagination rather than the sacraments of faith. If, as Piet apparently believes, God has already judged, then the challenge of his life is not to obey conventional moral strictures but to find happiness in freedom.

Piet in turn encourages imagination in his many women so that the adulteries seem more to him than uncontrolled lust; they are creative, full of promise, and eventually rejected when a mistress like Georgene Thorne makes the affair too easy. Adultery for Piet requires not ease but skill. Too much facility resembles marriage. Unlike Ellelloû and Rabbit, Piet does not yearn to be the hero of his own life. But he does want happiness and he does need sex. If, as Oates shows, he is an artist, "it is at compromises he is best. . . ."[17] Architecture gives way to contracting which yields to inspecting military barracks; failure with one wife leads him to take another; embarrassment in Tarbox means only that he moves to the next suburb. When he accepts the human in Foxy in place of his ideal of her, marries her, and relocates in a neighboring town where they become just another couple, he acknowledges mortality, doubt, and limitation to freedom. No one is at fault, but neither he nor Foxy can live up to the artistic demands of his imagination that they linger forever in their little kingdom by the sea. Oates's comment is instructive: People "forever elude the word-nets we devise."[18] True, but one may add that the "word-nets," the tales themselves, are the surest guarantees of immortality, acts of faith beyond the uncertainty of God's plan. Piet may compromise, but he holds on to the hope of creation as he steps toward tomorrow with a new wife.

Sex is his art form even though it leads to a fortunate fall. Updike is candid about the prominence of sex in *Couples*: "It's wonderful the way people in bed talk, the sense of voices and the sense of warmth, so that as a writer you become kind of warm also. The book is, of course, not about sex really: It's about sex as the emergent religion, as the only thing left. I don't present the people in the book as a set of villains: I see them as people caught in a historical moment. . . . The people in the book exist within a society, but have no wish to restructure it; rather, within its interstices they are seeking through each other's bodies, and really through each other's voices too . . . to console themselves."[19] Consolation from what, the reader asks himself; from the breakdown of religious restraint, answers the author. Recall Tanner's argument that for the traditional nineteenth-century novelist marriage and religion were so intertwined that marriage almost sanctioned religion rather than vice-versa, and then note Updike's comment: " . . . in this novel I was asking the question, after Christianity, what? Sex, in its many permutations, is surely the glue, ambience, and motive force of the new humanism."[20]

Updike's sense of the tension between social stabilities as sanctioned by religion and individual desire as illustrated by sex results in his convincing portraits of women. American fiction is, as he says, "notoriously thin on women." Thus he has consciously tried to create female characters who, in Couples at least, "are less sensitive perhaps to the oppressive quality of cosmic blackness, and it is the women who do almost all of the acting . . . the vitality of women now, the way many of us lean on them, is not an eternal phenomenon but a historical one, and fairly recent."[21] The phenomenon is recent because in being less paralyzed than their husbands when faced with what Piet sees as the contemporary stalemate between social institutions and personal freedom, women shed their traditionally passive roles. Foxy attends religious services, for example, but she also seduces Piet. She, not he, knows exactly what she wants. It may not be a joke that Updike claims he plotted Couples in church.[22]

The sense of God that he envisions for Couples is a fierce God, a judging God. Aware that the adults in the novel want God to be a kind of nice daddy who will take care of Nancy's dead hamster, Updike differentiates Piet by giving him faith in a God of absolute power. This is the God that throws the lightning bolt at the Congregational Church and persuades Piet of the reality of Sodom and Gomorrah. Updike comments, "What is new, and what I can't quite explain, is that the withdrawal and wrath of God are felt by the hero, Piet Hanema—he and Foxy are the only orthodox Protestants in the book—as a relief. When the rooster is brought down, and exposed to the children, Piet somehow dies—dwindles, moves to Lexington, lives happily ever after."[23] More will be said later about Updike's claim for Piet's eventual happiness; for the moment it is significant that Couples illustrates another of what he calls his "yes, but" attitudes: "No, in Couples, to a religious community founded on physical and psychical interpenetration, but—what else shall we do, as God destroys our churches?"[24]

Answers to such questions are not easy, but reactions to Updike's asking them were loud and long. With its mixture of religious concerns, sexual frankness, and social observations, *Couples* attracted more attention at publication than any other of his many books. Despite the autobiographical overtures, Updike disavows connections between how he lives and what he writes, especially when he is not writing about Olinger. The town of Ipswich, Massachusetts, for example, the town where he lived when he wrote the novel and which served as a rough model for Tarbox, was, he reports, "a little startled at first by the book," but "was reassured, I think, by reading it."[25] For many reviewers, however, reassurance was not forthcoming.

Part of the problem may have been the immediate notoriety. Splashed across America with a banner proclaiming "The Adulterous Society," Updike's portrait graced the cover of *Time* magazine from newsstands and bus stops to local libraries. The tone of the cover story is pure show biz: "The biblical woman accused of adultery would be safe in Tarbox; here no stones are thrown, only envious glares."[26] A serious reader might have pointed out that not a woman but Piet Hanema is the primary transgressor, but it was too late. The howls of outrage had already begun, and they began with Diana Trilling's review that even Updike defined as a "banshee cry of indignation."[27] Calling the novel "morally ambiguous," Trilling laced into Updike's inability to suggest any meaning "except such as the reader may himself supply. . . . With nice economy the book is called *Couples*. It would have been more precise to have called it *Couppling*."[28] One need not add that Ms. Trilling misses the point. After that banshee cry, the negative comments rolled in with *Commentary*, of course, in the lead. Jack Thompson criticizes the style, calling *Couples* a "well-raisined fruitcake." The *Virginia Quarterly Review* criticizes the sex scenes, urging Updike to "realize his substantial promise, or else dwindle into the evanescence simple lubricity will provide." Elizabeth Dalton criticizes the details, dismissing the "compulsive sociological detail that makes the novel seem almost a parody of the realistic convention." Jose Yglesias criticizes the point of view, asking Updike to commit himself to a definite perspective so long as he continues to write about middle-class society. Anatole Broyard criticizes the main character, arguing that one cannot respond to sex scenes that involve "a fornicator, not a lover." And finally, Richard Locke criticizes *Couples* as a "thesis novel," calling it "a noble failure."[29]

Listening to such protests about a long book by a major novelist, one marvels that *Couples* was read at all. Yet it was read, and many notable critics responded with reviews of high praise. William Pritchard, for example, calls parts of the novel "beautiful and rare," and he suggests that the tone of nostalgia is not the characters' but Updike's: "As I see it there are no consequences to be drawn, lessons to be reaped from these adventures, except that life is very strange and people don't seem satisfied with what they have. With the exception of Saul Bellow, no American novelist says this as strongly as Updike. . . . " Wilfred Sheed also praises the theme, especially Updike's handling of "an authentically decadent community" that falls apart when the priest and scapegoat stop their infighting. Finally, Granville Hicks wittily calls attention to the style: "Although quantitatively, so to speak, *Couples* reminds me of the works of Updike's fellow-Pennsylvanian John O'Hara, there is no comparison in quality. Updike's style can carry the burden of details with which the book is filled. He uses even the four-letter words with distinction."[30]

It is interesting that the reviewers who blanched at the sexual frankness ignored the equal emphasis on death. *Couples* is laced with death, as one of the epigraphs shows:

> We love the flesh: its tastes, its tones,
> Its charnel odor, breathed through Death's jaws . . .
> Are we to blame if your fragile bones
> Should crack beneath our heavy, gentle paws?

The lines are from Alexander Blok's "The Scythians," and they suggest the equation of sex and death, hedonism and decadence. Updike's second epigraph, from Paul Tillich's *The Future of Religions*, comments on the tendency of average but intelligent people to consider the decisions that affect the life of their society to be a matter of fate over which they have no control. This situation, says Tillich, may encourage religious belief, but it is harmful to democratic processes. The couples of Tarbox cannot permit even the assassination of a president to shake them from their lethargy in the face of fate. Their parties are too much fun. As Angela Hanema observes about despicable but comic Freddy Thorne: "He thinks we're a circle. A magic circle of heads to keep the night out. He told me he gets frightened if he doesn't see us over a weekend. He thinks we've made a church of each other" (7). *Couples* depicts the little disasters that result from this combination of sex, death, and religion.

The elaborate dust jacket is a case in point. A reproduction of William Blake's water-color drawing "Adam and Eve Sleeping," the jacket reveals the original couple resting in pre-lapsarian innocence under the watchful eyes of God's angels. All seems peaceful and lovely and quiet until one notices the small, ugly toad staring at the sleeping Eve. Not quite a snake, perhaps, but something other than the beautiful has crept into Eden. The jacket blurb echoes both the effect of Blake's drawing and Angela's comment about Freddy Thorne: "The circle of acquaintances is felt as a magic circle, with ritual games, religious substitutions, a priest (Freddy

Thorne), and a scapegoat (Piet Hanema)." Tarbox is a long way from the garden.

The year is 1963, President Kennedy is in the White House, and Vietnam and civil rights still hide behind the toad. Most of the couples do not yet agree with Roger Guerin's description of their town: "There's nothing romantic or eccentric about Tarbox. The Puritans tried to make it a port but they got silted in. Like everything in New England, it's passé, only more so" (31). Updike is superb as he describes the dinner party at which this crack is made. The detail is so closely observed that one wonders if the author were the unobserved guest. The awkward pause before the hostess lifts her spoon, the silly jokes, the empty banter, the allusions to sex— Updike knows what it means to sit down to dinner in upper middle-class suburbia. The repartee envelopes the couples until all the revelers seem alike, caught in small talk and retort. As newcomers Ken and Foxy Whitman see immediately, guilt somehow unites these adults. They want too much to be loved. Like children on the other side of Eden, they do not know how to act once the party is over. One of the most effective passages in the novel is Foxy's thought as a languid Sunday afternoon of play winds down:

She was to experience this sadness many times, this chronic sadness of late Sunday afternoon, when the couples had exhausted their game, basketball or beachgoing or tennis or touch football, and saw an evening weighing upon them, an evening without a game, an evening spent among flickering lamps and cranky children and leftover food and the nagging half-read newspaper with its weary portents and atrocities, an evening when marriages closed in upon themselves like flowers from which the sun is withdrawn, an evening giving like a smeared window on Monday and the long week when they must perform again their impersonations of working men, of stockbrokers and dentists and engineers, of mothers and housekeepers, of adults who are not the world's guests but its hosts. (73-74)

Couples are children who do not want to grow up.

Raised in the relative prosperity of the 1950s, they think of their nation as protecting a culture where "adolescent passions" are not quite triumphant, where the climate is still *"furtively* hedonist." As the narrator suggests, their Eden is now found in pastoral towns like Tarbox, a place where games are improvised and where duty and work yield "as ideals to truth and fun" (106). Mostly fun. The narrator occasionally breaks in to keep the reader in touch with the times, with the first invitation to horror in Vietnam, with the uneasiness of the stock market, but the couples do not care about the news. They are too self-centered, too encapsulated to care. News happens to other people. Given this situation, Freddy reacts predictably to the reports of President Kennedy's assassination: "But I've bought all the *booze*" (294). How can he cancel the party? How can the guests not attend? Foxy feels empty, and Piet gropes for a religious balm; but later that evening, dressed in low-cut gowns and black ties, they ring Freddy's doorbell. The dinner-dance goes on because they have nothing else to do. The chemistry of the group determines the reactions of the couples. Wondering if they are "gliding on the polished top of Kennedy's casket," Piet looks around the room and sees his own death on one side and salvation by Foxy on the other. As the narrator reveals later, the most flattering invitation in Tarbox is to share someone else's intimacy, quarrel, or grief.

A nagging problem in *Couples*, however, is that the reader is asked to share too much. There are too many chatty letters from Foxy to Piet, too many accounts of small talk at parties long after the use of conversation to indicate individual personalities and attitudes has been established, and too many details of games. It is not that these matters are irrelevant but that they are overdone. The most important of them is the description of the various entertainments. Alan McKenzie calls them parlor games, and Howard Eiland describes them as play, but in either case the amusements illustrate the couples' efforts to achieve spontaneity in a largely artificial situation.[31] Their word games and sports expose their personal characteristics as players in the Tarbox Eden. Freddy Thorne, for example, talks a good game of basketball and sex, but he fails in the clutch. With their avoidance of church services, the backyard basketball court becomes a place of ritual as nearly important as the bedroom. Henry James would have had them playing bridge in the drawing room, but the effect is the same. Just as the rules of the games provide boundaries for the players, so adultery may be committed so long as transgressors and witnesses remember how to act. Eiland points out that the various guises of play in *Couples* permit self-dramatization of the participants and encourage them to perform in their social circle. All they have to do is stay on the court. Those who wander off, like Piet and Foxy, are expelled from Updike's ironic Eden. The toad hops closer to Eve.

Piet speaks the opening line which is the question of the novel. His query rings with irony because while the individuals are always the same, the couples are always new: "What did you make of the new couple?" Although Piet asks Angela about the Whitmans, the question directs the reader to the Hanemas; they are the new couple when the reader opens the book. Piet is a fearful man who nevertheless embraces life, a man whose name echoes the sounds of piety, anima, amen, and even Freddy Thorne's disparaging epithet, enema. Updike immediately sketches Piet's differences from his wife to hint at the discord between his intimacy and her inhibition. Angela seems tall, graceful, and aristocratic; Piet is short, bouncy, and thinks of himself as coarse. As Updike himself notes, they are "ordained for divorce."[32] Angela is all but unobtainable, like Iseult, and when they admit their dissolution as a couple, they accept reality.

The irony is that their divorce goes against Piet's grain, for he is a builder, a contractor who believes in the arts of carpentry and restoration instead of the pre-fabricated junk of the newer houses in Tarbox: "All houses, all things that enclosed, pleased Piet" (5). Presumably these enclosures include the vaginal canal, for he is more successful at adultery than at contracting. Yet he is also the only believer in religious sureties, the only one of the players who goes to church regularly despite Freddy's quip that their circle of couples is the new church of security and ritual. When clearing land for a housing development, for example, only Piet worries about desecrating sacred burial plots. But as a man longing for the old Eden of his childhood while stuck in the new paradise of Tarbox, he equates religious faith and sexual ecstasy, prayer and masturbation. The weather-cock on top of the Congregational Church which Piet attends is the symbol of the equation, and the children of the town believe that the bird is God.

Occasionally Piet does too. He enjoys the feeling of continuity in church, the sensation of joining the long dead carpenters who built the sanctuary and whose skill will never be replaced. He even tries to pray on command. Yet Piet goes to church primarily because of the memory of his dead parents, owners of a greenhouse, an early Eden enclosed with glass and flowers. Their deaths in a car wreck have given him a sense of the world as a "slippery surface" as if he were stranded on ice waiting for the first warning crack. No wonder he gravitates toward religion and sex. Praying for his dead parents, he is conscious of his own death. He lacks, he persuades himself, the courage to break with faith, for religious belief and sex offer a sense of immortality in a world where capricious accidents lurk around the next bend. Resisting the break is important to him because he needs the ritual, the discipline, the feeling that religion keeps each in its ordered place.[33] Only Foxy's husband Ken understands Piet's notion of the relationship between life's complexity and belief in God, but his idea of God is too scientifically narrow to be of use in the post-pill paradise. If, as Vico and Tanner have argued, religious sanctions under-gird such social institutions as marriage which are necessary to the stability of a culture, how is the believer to respond to Marcia's account of a newspaper article that predicts a television in every room? " 'The article said' —she faltered, then swiftly proceeded— 'nobody could commit adultery.' An angel passed overhead" (30). Frank's retort that "they'll undermine the institution of marriage" may be truer than he knows. Cultural changes are inevitable when adultery replaces angels as a sign of the new religion.[34]

Dr. Freddy Thorne, dentist, speaks for this new community. The *Time* cover story calls him a "faithless St. Augustine," but he is more likely the local lord of misrule, a specialist in decay and death, a prober of rot. Although he reads Sade and writes pornographic plays about the couples, his wife Georgene says that he is lousy in bed. Angela dismisses him as "a jerk," but she admits that he talks about matters that interest women such as food and children's teeth. Piet fears his appetite for dirty gossip, Foxy realizes that he savors rejection and that the others find a kind of unity in despising him, and the narrator calls him repulsive, a "king of chaos." Even Freddy describes himself as "an indestructible kind of prick." He and Piet are symbolic antagonists in the new Eden, the priest and the scapegoat, the voyeur and the lover. Yet Freddy is the only one who admits that love often poses a threat, that people in love fear being hurt: "People hate love. It threatens them. It's like tooth decay, it smells and it hurts" (145). In his new theology, sex has replaced God, and everything from stars to germs is tragic. When he claims that only Christianity and naked women are comic, we know that he is Blake's squatting toad staring at the sleeping Eve. He later plays his part perfectly when all he can do is look at naked Angela beside him in bed. His impotence in front of disrobed Angela is an ironic comment on the adulterous society, for he is its spokesman: "We're a subversive cell . . . like in the catacombs. Only they were trying to break out of hedonism. We're trying to break back into it. It's not easy" (148). Guilt causes the difficulty, and guilt stems from their Calvinist heritage. As Angela realizes, they are all involved. Freddy is not truly evil, she says; he just "loves a mess."

Yet his relationship to the social messes in Tarbox is primarily that of observer, the watcher who can give a party the night of an assassination or provide a contact for those in need of abortion. Freddy witnesses the messes, but Piet makes them. Needing the couples as much as God, Piet is stuck between requiring the order of home and insisting on the freedom of pursuit. Angelic Angela seems above him, unwilling to fulfill his sexual desires. He views his wife as a woman raised to live in a world that no longer exists, as a woman who believes in families whereas he longs to believe in couples.[35] Piet is the dreamer, not Angela. He is ready for sex after a party; she resists. He thinks of Egyptian handmaids and sheer blouses; she falls asleep. The narrator suggests that their dilemma is not unusual. "They were growing old and awful in each other's homes. . . . The men had stopped having careers and the women had stopped having babies. Liquor and love were left" (11, 12).

But standing on the other side of the bedroom wall, always there and always waiting, are the children. Angela tells Piet that the children just get yanked along without the fun, but the adults shut their eyes, dance the

Twist in the children's playroom, and play the parlor game of guessing who is enjoying adultery with whom. Their nostalgia is for an old order, for a time long gone when, like children, they were the world's guests. That day is on the far side of Eden, so they look to Piet as their old-fashioned man, the artist who builds and restores. Attracted to his neatness and order, they are puzzled by his adultery and faith. Piet is puzzled too, for he knows that "all love is a betrayal, in that it flatters life" (48). He understands that the ecstasy of love blunts the threat of death, blinds the lovers to the presence of a jealous God, betrays them with the illusion that the moment is forever. So far as the couples are concerned, the moment may last forever if spouses return to one another after visiting neighboring bedrooms. Adultery is thus only a game. But Piet and Foxy eventually violate the unwritten rule in Tarbox that adultery with lovers does not negate faithfulness to spouses, and for their transgression, their mess, they are expelled from the circle.[36]

Guilt and the fear of death keep Piet in the fold for a while. Sex with unrestrained Georgene Thorne is thrilling because it is so different from sex with beautiful Angela where everything is inhibited by tact, but Piet cannot join Georgene in saying that "God's a woman. Nothing embarrasses Her" (54). Jealous gods throw lightning bolts, and Piet remains haunted by the deaths of his parents. More immediate is the death of his daughter's hamster. Mangled by the family cat, the dead hamster precipitates a crisis of confidence in the little girl, a slowly dawning realization that life ends. But the affair also bothers Piet and Angela because the death exacerbates the tension between their opposing approaches to life. His insistence that the hamster is in heaven serenely running on its squeaky wheel conflicts with her desire for instant replacement, for a new hamster that will in time become the old one, for a "religion of genteel pretense." Convinced that religious sureties complicate a child's reaction to death, Angela resists when Piet tries to "sell" heaven to unbelievers and innocents.

He is, says Janet Appleby, "too thick in the conscience," and thus he relies on the order of faith to assuage the nagging of guilt. When Angela surprisingly but honestly admits that their marriage is failing sexually, Piet's thick conscience accepts the confession, mixes it with religious beliefs, and wonders if he was wrong to take his "angel" from her "omnipotent" father. He longs for the paradox of a marriage sanctioned by God and sexual freedom sanctioned by Tarbox. That way he can remain faithful and wander at the same time, pray and enjoy adultery simultaneously: " . . . he gave thanks that, a month earlier, he had ceased to be faithful to Angela and had slept with Georgene. It had been a going from indoors to outdoors" (224). Piet offers this prayer while playing golf, another game, but Updike understands that their games border on aimlessness and their aimlessness makes them childish. They are like nineteen-year-olds at a fraternity party, and they do not know how to act when the band goes home and the music stops. Piet is one of the revelers, but he is also different because he truly believes in the possibility of happiness. Misery constantly creeps toward the garden. Happiness can occasionally keep it at bay. Only he realizes that the toad is already there, that the couples accept the world as unhappy, that the endless round of parties is their antidote. Only he still hopes that life is wonderful. Freddy, a dentist, makes his living from decay; Piet, a contractor, longs for growth. No wonder he loves pregnant women.

Foxy is pregnant. Just as significant, she believes in God. Piet first views her upper thighs as she descends the stairs at a party; the next day after church her dress reminds him of bridal white. Sex and religion merge. Yet at the beginning she is clearly the new girl on the block. Her first reactions to Tarbox are of being enclosed by the couples. Unaware that adultery is the primary game among them, she speaks the key line in the first part of the novel, "Well, they say a man gets his first mistress when his wife becomes pregnant" (39). Her quip later becomes comic, for not Ken but she takes a lover. Ken's air of superiority challenges her stubborn will to defy, though neither of them considers divorce when they first move to Tarbox. Yet her own parents have divorced, and she is used to couples disappearing. As she says, "Every marriage is a hedged bet," a meeting of "an aristocrat and a peasant" (42, 60). Understandably she feels drawn to the reliable security of church. When asked at a party to name her most wonderful thought, she names the Eucharist.

But for all the emphasis on her faith, her pregnancy, and her bridal white, Updike stresses Foxy's whorishness, especially with the analogy to Christine Keeler, a British call girl whose involvement with government officials caused scandal and banishment. As her name suggests, Foxy is a predator. She is also a master of roles: Southern belle, sexy slave, spurned mistress, loving mom. From the moment that Piet looks up her dress and Foxy stares him down, she wants to own him. Piet is not dumb; he often wonders if she has gulled him. Yet his fall from grace is a condition he aspires to, and it occurs when he abandons his angelic wife for his predatory mistress. From the garden of his parents' greenhouse to the temptation of Foxy's bed by the sea is a long way.

Piet makes the journey willingly. Adultery is freedom, an untraditional invitation to worship another, a chance to give. Guilt is a natural consequence, and when Piet longs for Angela to guess so that secrecy is no longer an issue, one can understand his torment. But when he lies to Foxy about his having stopped seeing Georgene, one wonders if, despite Updike's obvious sympathy for him, he is capable of truth. A cynical point in *Couples* is that deception is a staple of marriage. Thus Piet's deceiving

Foxy is a more important step toward their marriage than the first time they slip into bed together: "Thus, in being deceived, Foxy closer approached the condition of a wife" (266).

The misery of secrecy clashes with the promise of the unknown, and the Hanema marriage slides downward to a painful conclusion. Piet does not want to hurt Angela, and Foxy does not want to hurt Piet by taking advantage of him. All this is seriously considered, a significant part of Updike's continuing examination of middle America. But how does one react to the scene where Piet walks into the bathroom while Foxy is still sitting on the toilet, sucks her milk-filled breasts, hears his wife knock on the door, and jumps out the window, all the while dressed in a tuxedo? The scene is ludicrous, but one suspects that Updike does not intend only comedy. Daniel Gordon defends the scene: "Much that seems ridiculous by realistic standards, especially the intimacies of Piet and Foxy, makes more sense if we can believe in 'the incomparable solemnity of their sin.' " Perhaps, but the *Time* cover story is closer to the point: "Scenes that other writers would play as burlesque, Updike plays straight, no matter how absurd they are." John Ditsky is more critical: "One cannot separate the intentionally ludicrous from the clumsily awful in this novel. . . ."[37] Worse, the ridiculousness of this passage inadvertently undercuts Piet's serious confession to Foxy that he must have her because deception and guilt are making his stay in Tarbox a circle of fear: "My whole life seems just a long falling" (312). The falling he shrinks from is a life and death matter to him, but one cannot take him seriously after laughing at his other fall—from the upstairs bathroom: "Button. Caught. Ah. There. He slid out on his chest and dangled his weight by his hands along Thorne's undulate shingles. Loose nails, might catch on a nostril, tear his face like a fish being reamed. Air dangled under his shoes. Ten feet. Eleven, twelve. Old houses, high ceilings. Something feathery brushed his fingers gripping the sill inside the bathroom. Foxy begging him not to dare it? Angela saying it was all right, she knew? Too late. Fall" (314). But this silly leap is not the fall he needs, and the reader begins to wonder how seriously he should consider Piet's desirable fall from the greenhouse of his parents to the hard rock of the world.

For the moment Piet yearns to believe that adultery takes place in "God's playroom," but afraid of tempting God by renewing the affair after the birth of Foxy's baby, he turns to Bea Guerin for his next mistress. He seeks sex along with grace. Orgasm holds off death. Finally, however, his bedding of Foxy results in another pregnancy, another slap at death perhaps, but hardly what he has in mind as a guarantee of his own immortality. Abortion goes hand-in-hand with this pregnancy. How can he approach salvation if he finds God only between Foxy's legs: "Piet struggled to see his predicament as relative, in any light but the absolute one that showed it to be a disaster identical with death. Pregnancy was life. Nature dangles sex to keep us walking toward the cliff" (345). But all he glimpses are the specters of disgrace, extinction, and "eternal namelessness." Recall Tony Tanner's paraphrase of Vico that chaos is a situation in which there are no marriages and hence no identification of offspring and no names.

Abortion with the aid of court jester Freddy Thorne is a solution, and when Piet makes arrangements with the specialist in decay, he notices the Congregational Church through the window. Freddy demands Angela as payment, and guilt creeps through suburbia. Suffocating in what he defines as sin, Piet prays not for Foxy but for the rebirth of his innocence when Foxy drives to Boston for the abortion. Like many of Updike's lovers, all he wants is freedom. He gets it. Divorce comes to Tarbox and the couples realign. His first reaction at losing Angela is that he has lost the guardian of his soul. His solution, which is childish given the circumstances, is to ask forgiveness of the women he may have hurt. As his partner Gallagher tells him, all he ever does is let things happen and then pray.

It is not easy to sympathize with Piet in the final third of *Couples*. He is a man who plows through many women with little thought of the consequences beyond concern for his spirit. Like a boy with one hand in the cookie jar, he apologizes and then goes right on eating. When Angela asks him, for example, if he feels guilty for causing the Whitmans' divorce, he replies that he has been a blessing for bringing their marital tension to a head. His Calvinist God has already judged; thus men are free to love whom they please. Leaving Angela, he fears that he may be "damned eternally," that the aura of her golden light will give way to nameless children and weeds in the lawn, but he blames no one except himself. Forced from his parents' garden and his wife's glow, he accepts the reality of death and steps toward the world. His visit to a dying friend confirms how easily death shows its face, how it can be as unspectacular as divorce or a mangled hamster. The universe, he realizes, does not care so much about lovers as he once thought.

But God might still care. *Couples* ends with the sensation of apocalypse, a sudden thunderstorm that nourishes "God's own lightning" to strike the church. The weathercock whirls in the wind: "Through the great crowd breathed disbelief that the rain and the fire could persist together, that nature could so war with herself: as if a conflict in God's heart had been bared for them to witness" (443). The spectacular destruction of the church shows Piet that something beyond him does indeed exist, that separation from wife does not mean abandonment by God. The weathercock survives above the fire, rescued by a daring young man on a huge demolition ball, but it is removed to make way not for restoration of the old church but for construction of a modern concrete edifice that will have no need of an ambiguous sign of God.

True to the requirements of the traditional well-made novel, Updike rounds out the lives of the major characters, ties up the strands of the story, and brings *Couples* to a gentle close. And Piet and Foxy? They marry, move to a different suburb, and become just another couple. The resolution is clear, but its meaning is debatable. Two pertinent comments by Updike indicate his intention that the novel end happily:

It has a happy ending. It's about a guy meeting a girl and the guy getting the girl. But I know that they don't see it that way. You know, they were talking about it as satire! Satire—this wonderful story. It's a loving portrait of life in America.[38]

So that the book does have a happy ending. There's also a way, though, I should say (speaking of "yes, but") in which, with the destruction of the church, with the removal of his guilt, he becomes insignificant. He becomes merely a name in the last paragraph: he becomes a satisfied person and in a sense dies. In other words, a person who has what he wants, a satisfied person, a content person, ceases to be a person. Unfallen Adam is an ape.[39]

The words of the author always carry a certain though limited weight so long as the reader keeps in mind D. H. Lawrence's dictum to trust the art and not the artist. Still, one detects irony in the first statement and earnestness in the second. Boy does indeed get girl, but *Couples* is hardly a fairy tale in which boy and girl are guaranteed to live happily ever after. *Eros* defeats *Agape*, people die, churches burn, couples divorce, and Piet and Foxy drive away from Tarbox. If Piet's fall from the memory of the paradisaic greenhouse is necessary, it also forces him into the role of one half of a new couple. Given the longing for newness, the intimacy, and the ensuing deceit that Updike finds in affluent suburban couples, one can only wonder how long this new alignment will last. The end of *Couples* does not promise religious or cultural reconciliation. Politically active younger couples move into the void caused by the collapse of the post-pill Eden, and the tenor of Tarbox takes another turn.

## NOTES

1. John Updike, "Couples," (Cambridge, Massachusetts: Halty Ferguson, 1976). Quotations from the introduction are taken from this edition.
2. Updike explains in another context, eight years before the publication of the story "Couples": "*Couples* was first conceived as a short story, whose purpose was to show a group of couples as an organism, something like a volvox, making demands on and creating behavior in the individuals within it. The story was too cramped, and a novel, with enough space to work out a number of configurations, felt necessary. I didn't intend the book to be quite so long; but even so, there remain things—scenes, bits of gossip, further twists of

fate—that happen, as it were, on the other side of the margins." Lewis Nichols, "Talk with John Updike," New York *Times Book Review*, 7 April 1968, p. 34.

3. For a comment on the story "Couples," see my *The Other John Updike: Poems/ Short Stories/Prose/Play* (Athens, Ohio: Ohio University Press, 1981), 192-194.

4. Charles Thomas Samuels, "The Art of Fiction XLIII: John Updike," *Paris Review*, 12 (Winter 1968), p. 111.

5. Frank Gado, "Interview with John Updike," *First Person: Conversations on Writers and Writing* (Schenectady, New York: Union College Press, 1973), p. 100. Other commentators have noted the resemblence of *Couples* to Victorian fiction. See Josh Greenfeld, "A Romping Set in a Square New England Town," *Commonweal*, 26 April 1968, p. 185: "And he can bring to a description of anything . . . all of the energy and enthusiasm of a Victorian novelist confronting his first sunset."

6. John Updike, *Couples* (New York: Knopf, 1968), p. 220. Further references will be noted in the text.

7. John Updike, "The Music School," in *The Music School* (New York: Knopf, 1966), p. 190.

8. For intriguing suggestions about the relationships between Nathaniel Hawthorne and Updike, especially concerning such topics of mutual concern as sex and religion, longing and guilt, and romance and irony in *The Blithedale Romance* and *Couples*, see David Lodge, "Post-Pill Paradise Lost: *Couples*," in *John Updike: A Collection of Critical Essays*, eds. David Thorburn and Howard Eiland (Englewood Cliffs, New Jersey: Prentice-Hall, 1979), pp. 84-92. Lodge also suggests that we read *Couples* as an illustration of the contemporary effort to negate the effects of pornography by incorporating its characteristics into art.

9. Norman Cousins, "When American and Soviet Writers Meet," *Saturday Review*, 24 June 1978, p. 42.

10. Tony Tanner, *Adultery in the Novel* (Baltimore: Johns Hopkins University Press, 1979), p. 61.

11. Tanner, pp. 61-62.

12. Tanner, p. 74.

13. Tanner, p. 87. For Updike's thoughts on de Rougemont's theories, see his essay "More Love in the Western World," *Assorted Prose* (New York: Knopf, 1965), pp. 283-300.

14. Tanner, p. 89. See also p. 369: "The fact is that from the start, the novel had a conservative drive, serving to support what were felt to be the best morals and manners and values of the period, and giving new prominence to that phenomenon only visible so comparatively recently, the family. But in addition to that conservative drive, the novel has also always contained potential feelings for that which breaks up the family—departure, disruption, and other various modes of disintegration."

15. John Updike, "If at First You Do Succeed, Try, Try Again," *Picked-Up Pieces* (New York: Knopf, 1975), p. 402.

16. Joyce Carol Oates, "Updike's American Comedies," *Modern Fiction Studies*, 21 (Fall 1975), pp. 459-472; rpt. *John Updike: A Collection of Critical Essays*, eds. David

Thorburn and Howard Eiland (Englewood Cliffs, New Jersey: Prentice-Hall, 1979), pp. 53-68.

17. Oates, p. 62.

18. Oates, p. 66.

19. Eric Rhode, "Grabbing Dilemmas: John Updike Talks About God, Love, and the American Identity," *Vogue*, 1 February 1971, p. 185.

20. Nichols, "Talk with John Updike," p. 34.

21. Samuels, "The Art of Fiction XLIII: John Updike," p. 100; Rhode, "Grabbing Dilemmas," p. 184.

22. Samuels, "The Art of Fiction XLIII: John Updike," p. 97.

23. Nichols, "Talk with John Updike," p. 34.

24. Samuels, "The Art of Fiction XLIII: John Updike," p. 100. See also p. 105 where Updike mentions Piet as Lot and Don Juan, and Piet and Foxy as Tristan and Iseult.

25. Samuels, "The Art of Fiction XLIII: John Updike," p. 90.

26. "View from the Catacombs," *Time*, 26 April 1968, pp. 66-68, 73-75.

27. Samuels, "The Art of Fiction XLIII: John Updike," p. 90.

28. Diana Trilling, "Updike's Yankee Traders," *Atlantic*, 221 (April 1968), pp. 129-131.

29. See Jack Thompson, "Updike's Couples," *Commentary*, (May 1968), pp. 70-73; "Notes on Current Books," *Virginia Quarterly Review*, 44 (Summer 1968), p. XCVI; Elizabeth Dalton, "To Have and Have Not," *Partisan Review*, 36 (Winter 1969), pp. 134-136; Jose Yglesias, "Coupling and Uncoupling," *Nation*, 13 May 1968, pp. 637-638; Anatole Broyard, "Updike's Twosomes," *New Republic*, 4 May 1968, pp. 28-30; Richard Locke, review of *Rabbit Redux*, New York *Times Book Review*, 14 November 1971, p. 12.

30. See William Pritchard, "Fiction Chronicle," *Hudson Review*, 21 (Summer 1968), pp. 375-376; Wilfrid Sheed, "Play in Tarbox," New York *Times Book Review*, 7 April 1968, pp. 1, 30-33; Granville Hicks, "God Has Gone, Sex Is Left," *Saturday Review*, 6 April 1968, pp. 21-22. The British reaction to *Couples* is not so generous. R. G. G. Price, for example, thinks that the novel is excessively bulky and needs to be trimmed of fat; Frank Kermode compares *Couples* a bit unfavorably to Ford's *The Good Soldier*; and Francis Hope says that the novel is "very good" at its best but "intolerably clogged with fine writing." See R. G. G. Price, "New Novels," *Punch*, 13 November 1968, p. 710; Frank Kermode, "Shuttlecock," *Listener*, 7 November 1968, p. 619; Francis Hope, "Screwing in Turn," *New Statesman*, 8 November 1968, pp. 639-640.

31. See Alan T. McKenzie, " 'A Craftsman's Intimate Satisfactions': The Parlor Games in *Couples*," *Modern Fiction Studies*, 20(Spring 1974), pp. 53-58; and Howard Eiland, "Play in *Couples*," in *John Updike: A Collection of Critical Essays*, eds. David Thorburn and Howard Eiland (Englewood Cliffs, New Jersey: Prentice-Hall, 1979), pp. 69-83.

32. "View from the Catacombs," *Time*, p. 68.

33. For an interesting analysis of the religious theme in *Couples*, see James Gindin, "Megalatopia and the Wasp Backlash," *Centennial Review*, 15(Winter 1971), esp. pp. 43-52.

34. The religious allusions have been thoroughly explored, with opposite conclusions, by Robert Detweiler and Linda M. Plagman. See Robert Detweiler, "Updike's *Couples*: Eros Demythologized," *Twentieth Century Literature*, 17(October 1971), pp. 235-246; and Linda M. Plagman, "*Eros* and *Agape*: The Opposition in Updike's *Couples*," *Renascence*, 28(Winter 1976), pp. 83-93.

35. See Robert Detweiler's essay for a discussion of Piet as both Tristan and Don Juan in light of Updike's remarks about Denis de Rougemont.

36. See Roger Sharrock, "Singles and Couples: Hemingway's 'A Farewell to Arms' and Updike's 'Couples,' " *Ariel*, 4(October 1973), pp. 21-43: ". . . the crux of the problem for Piet, Angela and Foxy, as for all the other couples is not so much their desire to be unfaithful as their continued pleasure in remaining faithful at the same time; it has to be put like this because it is a matter of desire and pleasure, not of conventional conformity to the legal bonds of a sterile institution. . . ."

37. See Daniel J. Gordon, "Some Recent Novels: Styles of Martyrdom," *Yale Review*, 58(Autumn 1968), p. 119; "View from the Catacombs," *Time*, p. 73; John Ditsky, "Roth, Updike, and the High Expense of Spirit," *University of Windsor Review*, 5(Fall 1969), p. 113. Similarly, one cannot tell if the adultery of the "Applesmiths" is meant always to be comic. Janet is sexually desirable and vulgarly direct; Howard always follows his comments with a French phrase; Frank quotes Shakespeare on any occasion. How can one take them seriously?

38. Gado, "Interview with John Updike," p. 97.

39. Samuels, "The Art of Fiction XLIII: John Updike," p. 101. See also Detweiler, who argues that the ending is positive, and Plagman, who argues that it is negative.

# A Month of Sundays

*"Adultery is not a choice to be
avoided; it is a circumstance to
be embraced."*
—A Month of Sundays

Piet Hanema's fall from the garden of his memory to the ironic Eden of the post-pill paradise carries with it suggestions of God's continued motions in the world. Lightning strikes the church, and Piet exits Tarbox to begin life again in a new town with a new wife. God still lingers for those who care to believe in *A Month of Sundays* (1975), but unlike Piet's, Reverend Tom Marshfield's life faces disintegration when he is expelled from church and home to search for reconciliation in the desert.[1] Belief is not an issue for him. He knows that God may burn churches or scorch deserts, and that man may be puny in His sight. What does trouble Marshfield, however, is the difficulty of harmonizing the needs of the soul with the expectations of the body. In a word, he is an adulterer.

I find *A Month of Sundays* to be Updike's most difficult novel, but he names it a favorite: "When asked my favorites I tend to name books like *Buchanan Dying* or *A Month of Sundays* that nobody else much liked—the neglected child syndrome, I guess."[2] It is not that the novel was neglected at publication but that its reception was lukewarm. Unlike many of Updike's supporters who wish to find in his fiction either a religious aura that raises the canon to the level of high seriousness or a sexual underpinning that balances the seriousness at the level of comedy, George Steiner understands that "where eros and sadness meet, theology begins."[3] The point is that sex and religion are not to be separated in Updike's novels. To do so is to deny the enigma of sex and the natural frailty of all couples since the garden. Recognition of the stunning power of lust in a believer is one lesson that Updike has found in the writings of St. Augustine and Kierkegaard, and he has taken the tension between the religious stricture and the sexual imperative as a primary theme: "Also a book like *A Month of Sundays* is full of ideas in a way—that is, the man is, unlike my usual heroes, somewhat learned. My central idea there was that clergymen are exposed more than most men to sexual temptations and that, further-more, there is some deep alliance between the religious impulse and the sexual. Both are a way of perpetuating our lives, of denying our physical limits."[4]

Years ago in 1970, Updike discussed the relationship between natu-ralistic descriptions of sexual activity and the requirements of an author's style, and he pointed to D. H. Lawrence, James Joyce, and Vladimir Nabokov as three artists who led the way in showing the actualities beneath the elegance of language.[5] The balance between depictions of sex and nuances of style is a primary factor in *A Month of Sundays*, for Marshfield is the main character in a novel in which he plays the role of a first-person narrator writing a journal in which he is the main character. Extremely conscious of his dual positions as wayward adulterer and punning author, he struggles to reconcile the demand for style with his two roles. Thus when Updike argues that "to be a person is to be in a situation of tension, is to be in a dialectical situation," he suggests that perfect adjustment denies meaningful identity.[6] According to this defini-tion, Reverend Marshfield may know his identity better than he realizes. Few would call him perfectly adjusted. The tension between body and soul in his life mirrors the conflict between language and communication in his art. In both cases sex sits at the center.

Steiner goes so far as to say that "the erotic has provided Updike with an essential coherence." He may be correct. For Updike, investigation of the erotic involves pursuit of the aesthetic:

Through detailed accounts of sex, ranging from the physiological to the alle-gorical, Updike has found a center, a discipline for the prodigality of his art. At its best, the result is poignant and ironic: what is in lesser writers a dispensation is in Updike a severity. The more urgent, the more acrobatic the sexual moment, the tauter, the more contemptuous of facility is the writing. Eroticism is, in a serious artist, an ascetic pursuit. . . . The eroticism of his fiction has been a long prelude to a radically theological view of American existence.[7]

Little wonder, then, that *A Month of Sundays* bows to *The Scarlet Letter*, the first great American tale of the erotic within religious sensibilities. But where Hawthorne saw the lure of sexual pleasure as a sign of man's weakness, Tom Marshfield argues that not Calvinist prohibition but de-lightful emancipation is the message of the commandment "be fruitful and multiply." Thus, Marshfield concludes, marriage is merely a non-binding sacrament. Man longs for freedom, as God the Father recognizes; without the restraint of marriage there would be no adultery.

Six years after *A Month of Sundays,* Updike formalized his ideas about Nathaniel Hawthorne in an essay titled "Hawthorne's Creed." He had originally called his comments "Hawthorne's Religious Language" and had delivered them as the Evangeline Wilbur Blashford Foundation Address at the annual ceremony of the American Academy and Institute of Arts and Letters on 24 May 1979. The address was first published in the *Proceedings* of the Academy and Institute (Second Series, Number 30), then published as "On Hawthorne's Mind" in the *New York Review of Books* (19 March 1981), before being issued as "Hawthorne's Creed" in a limited, signed edition of 250 copies.[8] Unlike Tom Marshfield, Updike's Hawthorne seeks to dodge the outward forms of religion. Where Marshfield commits himself to following his father into the ministry, Updike reports that Hawthorne wrote to his mother that the life of the cloth was "dull," that Unitarianism deserved his satire, and that the services of the Church of England were "mummery." Yet while Marshfield strays and Hawthorne complains, both are confident that, in Hawthorne's words, "never can my soul have lost the instinct of my faith." Musing on the problem of defining Hawthorne's belief, Updike writes, "a very vivid ghost of Christianity stares out at us from his prose, alarming and odd in not being evenly dead, but alive in some limbs and amputate in others, blurred in some aspects and basilisk-keen in others, even in part upside down" (*HC,* 8).

Marshfield's faith suffers a similar topsy-turvy fate, and like Hawthorne's heroes he turns to women for relief. Updike explains, "In Hawthorne, matter verges upon being evil; virtue upon being insubstantial. His insistence on delicate, ethereal heroines goes not only against our modern grain but his own. . . . Where the two incompatible realms of Hawthorne's universe impinge, something leaks through; there is a *stain*" (*HC,* 9-10). Marshfield would not agree that matter is evil. Indeed, his return from the motel in the desert to an altar in the suburbs depends partly on his ability to find salvation in the body. Nor does he seek ethereal heroines. His women for the most part are solid, sexy, and ready; whether or not they believe is often irrelevant. Updike creates Reverend Marshfield as the modern opposite of Dimmesdale's weakness and Hawthorne's doubt. Both Marshfield and Hawthorne may sense a stain when matter and spirit collide, but where Hawthorne's symbol for the stain may be poison or dreams or mirrors, Marshfield's is ironically the stain of sexual juices. No wonder, then, that guilt does not dog him the way it torments Hawthorne: "Guilt, of which Hawthorne was such a connoisseur, pervades his work without any corroborating conviction of sin. . . . He believed, with his Puritan ancestors, that man's spirit matters; that the soul can be distorted, stained, and lost; that the impalpable exerts force against the material. . . . The territory that Hawthorne defined as that of his art, 'where the actual and the imaginary might meet,' is the borderland where we still live" (*HC*, 11, 13). Worried about the friction between the impalpable and the material, Hawthorne tried to unite them with metaphors of the imaginary and the actual. Marshfield is similarly aware of this border. As he strides toward it, however, he finds that the borderland offers not clarity of matter and spirit but ambiguity. His solution, which he does not work out until the end of his journal, is that the body—matter—does count, that body and soul are somehow, ambiguously, one.

Hawthorne might not agree with Marshfield's conclusion, but his spirit lingers behind the minister's confession and Updike's novel. The way to control duality is through art. Yet where Hawthorne winces, Updike winks. Marshfield's combination of colloquial language and theological rhetoric is Updike at his comic best, but the musings about the tension between the erotic and the religious are serious and perceptive. What good is grace, Marshfield (and Updike?) wonders, if it is not to be part of this world? Since God made man sexual, may grace not be found in sensual pleasure? Only there do spirit and flesh, Updike's answer to Hawthorne's impalpable and material, truly meet. In Steiner's words, "He is making an insistent point about the ephemeral substance of reality, about the possibility, profoundly heretical and grievous, that there is beyond the skin of things no firmer realm, no compensating deep."[9]

As in sermons, language is the key to Marshfield's confession and Updike's novel. Puns, linguistic jokes, and Freudian slips run riot as the Reverend types away, fully aware of each leering typo, each erotic pun: "pric, pic, truthpic." Steiner is not convinced by such stylistic acrobatics: "Whether 'A Month of Sundays' is substantial, controlled enough to make this vision emotionally plausible is less certain. It is an impatient text enforced by rather than enforcing its pyrotechnics."[10] Such judgments are matters of personal preference. Another literate reader might call these passages witty. The problem, it seems to me, is not the self-conscious language but the difficulty of determining the extent of Updike's sympathy with his narrator. He may join Marshfield and revel in the linguistic escapades, but does he agree with Marshfield's opinions?

Bernard Schopen believes that he does: "There is little question that Tom Marshfield's views on faith and morality are shared by his creator. Indeed, they pervade Updike's fiction. Unfortunately, they are rarely considered in the criticism of it."[11] In view of Updike's own thoughts about the temptations facing the believer in a morally ambiguous world, Schopen may have a point. Yet one hesitates to identify an author with his character, as Updike himself notes: "I disavow any essential connection between my life and whatever I write. I think it's a morbid and inappropriate area of concern, though natural enough—a lot of morbid concerns are natural. But the work, the words on the paper, must stand apart from our living presences; we sit down at the desk and become nothing but the excuse for these husks we cast off."[12] These comments suggest Updike's determination to keep his private life free from the public lives of his characters, but that does not mean that he sets the characters loose only to undercut them with irony. The author still sends signals that the careful reader must decipher. The problem is figuring out the code. Thus Updike wonders if today's readers and authors are mistaken when they dismiss authorial intrusions that signal above the heads of the characters to the reader: "Yet I feel that something has been lost with this authority, with this sense of an author as God, as a speaking God, as a chatty God, filling the universe of the book."[13] Marshfield talks to God in *A Month of Sundays*, but one is not sure when Updike nudges the audience.

First person narrative often poses this dilemma. The reader cannot always decide whether the author treats the teller ironically or even whether the teller is aware of the irony of his statements. This is especially true when Marshfield exults over the fun of jotting down his confessions. Because of the multiple word games and linguistic curlicues, one may assume that Updike enjoyed writing this novel. The parlor games of *Couples* seem just around the next corner. But as Marshfield self-consciously organizes his journal, one is not sure whether he is commenting ironically on his therapy or whether he truly likes each trick of the pen. The latter seems to be the case, for the minister loves himself too much to care about the characters in his tale as little more than puppets to be linguistically manipulated: "This is fun! First you whittle the puppets, then you move them around" (12). Confronted with such delightful ambiguities, some readers may not be convinced that Updike has unified his interests in sex and religion to suggest anything more serious than a man of God writing a novel to explain why he has gone astray.

Yet as Robert Detweiler has shown, Updike's fascination with the nature of language makes *A Month of Sundays* more than just a comic exposé of a minister caught in adultery. Offering a structuralist interpretation, Detweiler bases his remarks largely on Jacques Lacon's structuralist psychoanalysis and notes, correctly, that with *A Month of Sundays* Updike joins other contemporary novelists in expressing dissatisfaction with traditional forms of fiction. The combination of confession and sermon supports his interest in language to shape a novel that is about the nature of narrative itself. "The implication," writes Detweiler, "is that sex and religion as forms of communication are fundamentally flawed, consisting of paradoxical structures that render one's involvement in them ambiguous, uncontrolled, full of distortions, and somehow always partial and broken." Detweiler goes on to argue that Marshfield's dilemma is Updike's: "This depressing assessment seems also to be Updike's own and is illustrated by the depiction of the inability of language itself to communicate adequately. . . . In *A Month of Sundays* that effort has evolved to the point where language has become so self-conscious that it is self-critical. . . . All of these suggest a language sliding out of control, struggling to speak itself out of the unconscious and to say something other than what the speaker actually utters."[14]

The irony, of course, is that Updike himself is very much in control as he uses language to show how language slips out of control. Even Tom Marshfield, the ostensible novelist, the artist figure against whom letters and words seem to rebel, is convinced that language occasionally conveys what the speaker or writer means: "God. Since before language dawned I knew what the word meant: All haggling as to this is linguistic sophistry" (25). The question of language as an inadequate form of communication interested Updike in the 1970s. In March 1974, for example, one year before the publication of *A Month of Sundays*, he gave an address in Adelaide, South Australia, entitled "Why Write?" Toward the end of the speech he denies the role traditionally assigned to the serious author as a keeper of grammar, a guardian of correct usage, an exemplar of precision. Pointing out that language evolves and changes in the street and in the spoken media, he insists that it does not look to well-written books for direction: "I see myself described in reviews as a doter upon words. It is true, I am grateful to have been born into English. . . . But what I am conscious of doting on is not English *per se,* its pliable grammar and abundant synonyms, but its potential, for the space of some phrases or paragraphs, of becoming reality, of engendering out of imitation another reality, infinitely lesser but thoroughly possessed, thoroughly human."[15] The dilemma in *A Month of Sundays* is that Marshfield's phrases and paragraphs may not engender a satisfactory reality. He is not defrocked, but he is confused.

Updike's jacket blurb suggests the comic tone of what is described as "a testament for our times." The less-than-solid Reverend Marshfield is banished to the desert for one month to solidify his shaky status as a minister, and he finds an omega-shaped motel managed by an "impregnable" Ms. Prynne. No little Pearl for her. "In his wonderfully overwrought style," Updike writes for the blurb, "the errant cleric spills day by day his confession" of everything from seduction of his "organist" to his unreliable golf game. It is as if Rabbit Angstrom merged with Reverend Eccles and Piet Hanema and then headed west to find Nathaniel Hawthorne.

One of the two epigraphs extends the comic associations of religion, sex, and art: "My tongue is the pen of a ready writer" (Psalm 45). Such a writer, the Psalm continues, should sing his song to God, but Marshfield's hymn is also to himself. No one will sing his praises unless he does so.

The second epigraph, a comment by Paul Tillich, defines the ambiguity confronting the man who would understand his own soul: "This principle of soul, universally and individually, is the principle of ambiguity." George Hunt illuminates Tillich's comment:

Unlike most modern novelists, Updike sees man in such a radically "boundary" situation. Hence man's life is inevitably ambiguous—and not merely ironic or absurd as atheists would have it—precisely because man is created simultaneously to affirm two meanings, the meaning of heaven, or transcendence, and the meaning of earth, or the goodness of creation. As Tillich's quotation implies, never is man's dual affirmation a wholly unambiguous response.[16]

Tom Marshfield finds himself on the kind of boundary that plagues George Caldwell in *The Centaur:* Faith in the Christian religion places man on a border where his acts often take on opposing meanings. Sex, for example, lures Marshfield to the uncertainties of adultery, but as a minister he knows that sex is often a Biblical metaphor for the love between Israel and God. What is he to do; how is he to understand Tillich's "principle of soul"?

Marshfield finally realizes that to deny the body is to reject Paul's message, preached in the final sermon in his journal, that Christ rose bodily from the grave. In other words, the soul is also the body: "For we do not want to live as angels in ether; our bodies are us, us; and our craving for immortality is . . . a craving not for transformation into a life beyond imagining but for our *ordinary life,* the mundane life we so driftingly and numbly live, to go on forever and forever. The only Paradise we can imagine is this Earth. The only life we desire is this one. Paul is right . . . " (209). Affirmation of this ambiguity, of the principle of soul that nudges man to recognize both transcendence and the mundane, is why Ms. Prynne comes to his bed at the end. Marshfield learns that man remains in the ambiguous state of perpetually sinning while always having grace. His problem is his relationship not with man but with God.

Compared with the ambiguity of morality, which is man-made, the question of faith is relatively simple. One either believes or does not believe. Updike's fictional worlds are always morally ambiguous, and thus acceptance of the dilemma becomes both the issue and the solution. Marshfield must accept on faith that his morality or immorality is finally not an issue. Only belief matters. Updike's perspective on this question is clear: "I believe that all problems are basically insoluable and that faith is a leap out of total despair."[17] Behind Updike's comment stands the theologian Karl Barth. Bernard Schopen's observation is instructive: "Barth is not suggesting that moral standards and precepts are in themselves harmful or unnecessary. He is, rather, attacking moralism, or the self-righteousness of humanistic morality, as well as the assumption that a rigorous adherence to moral principles will solve human problems."[18] The point is that any ethical system, no matter how fine, gives way before the ambiguities of human life. Marshfield significantly calls on Barth when he contrasts himself with his wife: "She was moderate, I extreme. She was liberal and ethical and soft, I Barthian and rather hard" (48-49). He does not mean that ethics are bad; he means that they are not good enough. His wife is soft because she is good; he is hard because he believes. Hunt notes that in one sense Barth's theology rests on his interpretation of the first article of the Apostles' Creed, the assertion that one believes in God's existence: "However, Barth will emphasize boldly that the first article of the Creed . . . can be understood *only* in the light of Jesus Christ as He is revealed to us in Scripture. The meaning and import of that first article is revealed; any other approaches in attempting to understand it, according to Barth, are at best empty efforts at speculation."[19] Marshfield need only stop worrying about the revelation.

Updike's critics find the task more difficult. Apparently ill at ease with the comic yet sophisticated merger of Barthian theology, sexual escapades, Hawthornian allusions, and linguistic highjinks, most reviewers greeted *A Month of Sundays* with what may only be called a lukewarm response.[20] No more than a few dismissed the novel outright, but those who did were clearly disappointed. The unsigned complaint in *The Critic* is typical: "What the point of the whole thing is supposed to be is known only to God and Mr. Updike who proves conclusively that not even a layman can produce an interesting sermon." Carlos Baker is just as witty and just as disappointed, describing a reading of *A Month of Sundays* as like dropping in on a lecture by Bertrand Russell after just viewing *Deep Throat*.[21] Gilbert Sorrentino and Blanche Gelfant are more upset. Criticizing the "purple blush that suffuses the work," Sorrentino argues that "we are given wit and talent and we are given invention. But we are not given literature." For some reason, Gelfant is outraged: "I think the reader of *A Month of Sundays* should resist that charm. I think the reader should be stern, take Updike seriously so that he might take himself more seriously and forego the tricks of his trade—titillation, verbal pyrotechnics, philosophical chicanery, and factitious mushy theologizing. I think we must say No No to the obsessively repetitive sexual encounters, and No No to the obsessive naming of anatomical parts."[22]

Reading Gelfant's tirade, I can only wonder if my efforts in this chapter are in vain. She makes no mention of Karl Barth, communication theory, Nathaniel Hawthorne, or the Bible; the explicit descriptions of coupling from the male point of view seem to disturb her sense of sexual politics. The lukewarm commentators are more balanced in their assessments. In a calmly written essay, for example, Janet Karsten Larson questions what she considers to be the fuzzy ironic perspective: "The jester is so insistent

. . . that one scarcely knows when to take him seriously." Similarly, Joan Joffe Hall thinks that the novel is witty but plagued with jokes; the linguistic fun has little to do with serious investigation of how we communicate: "One may be saved by faith and works but not by speech, by the Word, but not by words." Paul Gray does not like the "bag of Nabokovian wordplays"; Ronald De Feo does not like the way Updike apparently subordinates character to style; and Benjamin De Mott does not like the absence of a clearly defined moral authority.[23]

With so many guarded responses from so many responsible critics and journals, it is inevitable that those who believe *A Month of Sundays* to be among Updike's best should be in the minority. Peter Prescott calls it Updike's "most playful, most cerebral, most self-regarding novel. . . . A special novel, then, for the happy few"; and George Hunt praises it as Updike's "finest work in the past 10 years."[24] Studying the reception of *A Month of Sundays*, one is struck by how often the language is emphasized, by how often the meaning is ignored. Unlike the astounding differences of opinion that normally greet an Updike book, the response to *A Month of Sundays* seems more puzzled than outraged, more wary than pleased. Leading the list of characteristics of the novel receiving comment is not the difficult theology or the Hawthornian echoes but the minister's style. How Marshfield says what he says is a key to his tale.

Told in the first person, the Reverend's story is a kind of journal, a written confession that is the core of what he calls his "soul therapy" at Ms. Prynne's desert retreat. Not his character but his voice is the focal point, and thus the novel is fun to read but difficult to understand. One is never sure of Marshfield's appreciation of the irony. Augustine's confessions hover around the edges, but Marshfield's amused tone contrasts with the agonized seriousness of that ancient document. One cannot imagine the repentant saint joining the wayward minister in urging his reader to bless the bishop's miter.

Officially ordered by his bishop to seek help for his "distraction," Marshfield accepts the temporary banishment, disagrees with his superior's diagnosis, and defines his malady as suffering "from nothing less virulent than the human condition" (4). Determination to preach that condition results in his novel, but he signals his refusal to take the soul therapy too seriously when he explains the typo "throughts" with a footnote: "meant to type 'throats,' was thinking 'thoughts,' a happy Freudian, let it stand" (5). Similar footnotes dot his confession. This is a novel in which the process of writing the novel is as important to the ostensible author as what he has to say. He finds that language misbehaves, jerks out of control, and makes the writer feel foolish. How can he command his thoughts if he cannot control his typewriter? How can he communicate about his life when words lead lives of their own? Marshfield's plight is Updike's sharpest picture of the frustrations facing the contemporary author, and he joins his sense of man's inability to say what he means to man's incapacity to direct either his sex life or his religious life. Man himself, not art, sex, or religion, is the pawn. The antics of *The Carpentered Hen* (1958) dance through Marshfield's balky vocabulary, but his predicament is indeed that of modern suburbanites.

Pale, displaced, and dazed, Marshfield and his fellow penitents sit at their typewriters in the omega-shaped desert retreat and feel freed of useless liturgical debates about "the shared chalice versus the disposable paper cuplet" (5). These burdens lifted, what, he asks, can he tell us? As it turns out, a good deal. Two questions direct his muse: "Who are you, gentle reader?" and "Who am I?" To answer them, he cranks up what the jacket blurb calls his overwrought style as if he were on the side of the poet in Wallace Stevens' "A High-Toned Old Christian Woman," declaring that not religion but poetry is the supreme fiction, that not widows but fictive things "wink as they will." Marshfield's style winks beautifully. Bowing to the fancy prose of Vladimir Nabokov's Humbert Humbert and Saul Bellow's Moses Herzog, he is urged by his runaway style to pen such ironic praises to the less-than-laudable as these words to his bathroom: "O, that immaculate, invisibly renewed *sanitas* of rented bathrooms" (7). Banished for his derelictions, both sexual and spiritual, he looks toward his immaculate bathroom mirror and sees not the mask of a sinner but a "face still uneasily inhabited, by a tenant waiting for his credit rating to be checked" (8).

Marshfield is always conscious that he is writing a novel, that he is creating, as it were, his own account of what the bishop calls his indiscretions, that he is waiting for his ideal reader. One almost wonders when he will join Humbert Humbert and ask for a literary agent. The problem of the ideal reader especially bothers him because he does not like the notion of writing for the void. Updike himself has raised this issue: "Not only is it difficult for me to picture my ideal reader, but there's also some confusion in my mind as to how he relates to what I write. Slowly, after years and years of writing . . . I've begun to realize that there is a collaboration between you and this reader, that the reader more or less supplies out of his own friends a basis for your characters. This is a link between you and his reality. . . . There is a contract between writer and reader about where the reality of the book exists."[25] Marshfield feels a similar confusion because while he senses the invisible presence of Ms. Prynne as his ideal reader, he cannot define her relationship to his tale. Without this definition, the question of the reality of his predicament is acute.

Not knowing why he writes or to whom, neither Marshfield nor the reader takes the first scribblings of his soul therapy too seriously: "On Saturdays he would type—ejaculations of clatter after long foreplay of silent agony" (18). Sex and writing blend as physical acts of faith that conclude in creation, but such high notions of the maker's art tumble under the weight of puns and play. The literal demands of authorship stand between him and his vision, so he jokes as much about his process as his plight. Recalling, for example, a furtive walk to his mistress' house while he is dressed only in pajama tops, he consciously breaks the erotic spell of his prose to comment on the narrative at hand. Thus when he resumes the titillating descriptions of the half-clad man of God sneaking across back yards to peer at his mistress in bed with his assistant minister, both he and the reader smile rather than gasp. Visions of a layout for *Oui* or *Rawhide* give way to comic accounts of how to tell the tale: ". . . and in one smooth parabolic step our ex-athletic cleric and voyeur swung his ungirded loins an airy inch or so above the pointed painted pickets and with cold toes trespassed upon the ill-tended turf . . ." (13). The alliterative cancels the erotic. Describing himself as the "ideal bare-bummed burglar" and as "cretinous and cunning as an armadillo," he exclaims in triumph, "More power to the peephole!" (14, 15). Both the minister as sinner and the author as word-master are being mocked. Fictive things may wink as they will, but that does not make communication any easier. Marshfield's trouble with his narrative is a metaphor for his difficulty in determining his relationship with God. He ends the scene as self-consciously as he begins it, telling the reader that before he abandons the typewriter for a Daiquiri, he must "move our bare-legged puppet up the stairs and put him to bed" (16). So much for the agony of confession. So much for the free will of man.

Like the novice author he is, he understands that his sentences come in no special order and that each might have been different while achieving the same effect. More important, he occasionally revises what he has written and what we have read, altering comments about himself and thus changing our reactions. At the end, he queries his own story because he knows the omission of details challenges the credulity of the reader: "My defiantly tricksome style of earlier has fallen from me; I limp, lame and fuzzy-brained, from one dim thought to the next. Spent an hour now rereading, between winces of embarrassment, the pages we (you and I, reader; without you there would be the non-noise of a tree crashing in the inhuman forest) have accumulated. Not, you say, a very edifying or conclusive narrative. . . . How much, I see backwards, has been left out, even in the zealous matter of sexual detail" (202). He suffers from, he claims, the human condition, but in truth his maladies are artistic control and sexual distraction. Using wit and linguistic absurdities, he blunts the reader's tendency to condemn his recklessness with other people.

It all began, he recalls, in childhood. Growing up with his minister father bred him into a belief in God. The result, for Marshfield at least, is not peace but a life of "inconvenience and unreason." Living an exemplary life but neither wise nor kind, the father was at his best, says Marshfield, when working with his hands. Only the furniture in the parsonage, the one constant in a childhood of changing houses and moving vans, convinces the boy Marshfield that God exists. It is curious, he now understands, for a believer to find proof of God not in the airiness of skies and sunsets but in the solidity of mantel clocks and sofas. Yet he plays even this potentially weighty subject for laughs: "I had no choice but to follow my father into the ministry; the furniture forced me to do it. I became a Barthian, in reaction against his liberalism . . ." (24).

Updike explains his attraction to the conservative theology of Karl Barth in his essay "Faith in Search of Understanding." Agreeing with the theologian that there is no way from man to God, Updike writes:

His theology has two faces—the No and the Yes. The No . . . is addressed to all that is naturalistic, humanistic, demythologized, and merely ethical in the Christianity that German Protestantism had inherited from the nineteenth century. . . . The real God, the God men do not invent, is *totaliter aliter*—wholly other. We cannot reach Him; only He can reach us. This He has done as the Christ of Biblical revelation, and the Yes of Barth's theology is the reaffirmation, sometimes in radically original terms . . . of the traditional Christian message.[26]

Just as his father had become a liberal minister in reaction against *his* father's anti-Darwinian fundamentalism, so Marshfield embraces Barthian conservatism in rebellion against his own paternity. Steeped in Barth's belief that man must wait for God to reach him, Marshfield dismisses the "merely ethical" in human affairs to the consternation of his good wife Jane and his liberal assistant Ned Bork. Good works and flower children are finally not enough. They are part of Barth's No, a dismissal that Bork does not understand.

If Updike ever comes close to standing with his narrator in *A Month of Sundays*, it is here in his sympathy with Marshfield's theological position. Bork is their foil, a sounding board against which they may explain their beliefs. A friend of drop-outs in the drug culture, the assistant curate resembles Conner in *The Poorhouse Fair*, the conventionally good person committed not to God but to man. Bork's debate with Marshfield exposes his inability to see the world with Barthian eyes: "It's atheism. Barth beheads all the liberal, synthesizing theologians with it, and then at the last minute whips away the 'a' and says, 'Presto! Theism!' . . . It sets up a diastasis with nothing over against man except this exultant emptiness. This terrible absolute unknowable other. It panders to despair." Marshfield merely shrugs in the face of such familiar liberalism and declines to remind Bork that the Bible itself is the something that Barth places in the face of nothing (89-90). The delinquent minister will not literally experience Barth's something until the end, when he sees life in the desert, but his rejection of Bork's good deeds shows that he, not his assistant, grasps the radical affirmation of Barth's theology, the fundamental power of his Yes.

Marshfield knows that the transparencies of his age, the very freedom Bork celebrates, are liberating but also terrifying. As he looks away from the solid furniture of his past through the erotic vistas of his mistress Alicia's bedroom, he wonders if transparence reveals the void, the absence of God. This is why he is later impotent with eminently desirable Frankie; her faith is so transparent that it inhibits him. What he longs for is the substance of solidity which he gets at the end when the formidable Ms. Prynne climbs silently into his bed.

*A Month of Sundays* is not, however, a dissertation on Karl Barth. Marshfield is confident of his theology but unsure of his journal. True to his struggle with his tale, he rereads his explanations of why he becomes a Barthian and then rewrites: "No. Two points arose as I rummaged in the bathroom for the Coppertone. One, I did not become a Barthian in blank recoil, but in positive love of Barth's voice, his wholly masculine, wholly informed, wholly unfrightened prose" (24-25). Whom do we trust—the young man who turns to Barth in reaction against his father's liberal theology, or the displaced minister who turns to Barth in love with the theologian's voice? In the long run it makes little difference, but Marshfield's difficulty in writing what he knows parallels his father's difficulty in saying what he means. The one is adulterous and the other is senile, but both men have trouble controlling words. Updike suggests that just as there is no way from man to God, so there is no way from vocabulary to meaning. A case in point is Marshfield's affair with Alicia Crick, his organist.

Thirty years old and divorced with two children, Alicia wears chartreuse bell-bottoms under her choir robe and next to nothing in her bedroom. Until Marshfield accepts the charms of his organist, he has not been unfaithful to his wife, but now as he sits before the typewriter, he is not sure whether he is recalling the truth or inventing the tale: "What do I mean, writing that? Am I imposing backwards upon the moment the later moment when truly she was behind glass, her foot and her hair, with Ned? Or did my knowledge that a process of seduction was at work, that this face could, if not now, later, be touched, secrete in panic a transparent barrier?" (30). Like loops of overlapping film, reconstruction of the past involves the imposition of various narrative strands. Thus the Alicia we meet in the confession may not be the organist he seduces in the church. Yet she is the one who reveals Marshfield's posing, who tells him that he teases the congregation with his mask of the believing unbeliever. Better, she informs him that his marriage with Jane is lousy. Sex in the pews is just around the corner, and he and Alicia rehearse it during Lent.

Marshfield's gentle reader can never be sure of anything he says. Like Colonel Elleloû of *The Coup,* he is a first-person narrator commenting on his own presence in the tale: "Or perhaps these words were never spoken, I made them up, to relieve and rebuke the silence of this officiously chaste room" (33). Inspired man of God or sneaking scribbler? That is the fun of this novel. Marshfield would have us believe that in the organist he finally meets his "own sexual demon." Quick to orgasm and utterly uninhibited, Alicia loves most of all her own sexuality. With her, Marshfield can laugh. Yet she also reaffirms his sense of God, for while glorying in the investigation of her wrinkles and calluses and pores, he realizes that his devotion to her flawed beauty equals that of the saints who so loved God that they forgave the pain of children and the ravishing of disease. But just as we accept his pious equation, he deliberately undercuts the mood with a direct comment not on the meaning of the narrative but on the story as physical object: "You've read it before (I *do* feel someone is reading these pages, though they have the same position on the desk when I return from golf, and my cunning telltales arranged with hairs and paper clips have remained untripped), I know" (38). The John Barth of *Lost in the Funhouse* is as much a presence in these pages as the Karl Barth of *Anselm: Fides Quaerens Intellectum.* Caught in the plight of the anonymous author in John Barth's "Anonymiad" (*Lost in the Funhouse*), Tom Marshfield is compelled to write his narrative for an audience that may not exist. His predicament is, suggests Updike, that of the contemporary author: Unsure of the identity of the ideal reader, he can only narrate his tale while describing the narration of his tale. Thus he hopes to justify not only his transgressions but also his book.

Little wonder, then, that when he writes his first sermon for the journal, he selects as his text Jesus' forgiveness of the woman taken in adultery: "Neither do I condemn thee" (John 8:11). Marshfield unrepentantly and comically exploits religious language to excuse his sins. To him the traps and trails of language are darker and deeper than Hawthorne's forest. Peter Prescott calls this sermon on adultery the best set-piece Updike has ever written, and he may be correct.[27] But John Gardner worries about the irony because he cannot be sure of it:

. . . the disparity between the surface and the sub-surface of his novels is treacherous. To the naive reader, a novel like *A Month of Sundays* seems a merry, bourgeois-pornographic book about a minister who likes copulation, while to the subtler reader of the novel it may seem to be wearily if not ambivalently satirical, a sophisticated attack on false religion. Since the irony—the presumably satiric purpose—is nowhere available on the surface, since the novel can easily be read as a piece of neo-orthodox Presbyterian heresy, one cannot help feeling misgivings about Updike's intent. His novels, properly understood, may be too much like sermons.[28]

Being too much like a sermon is precisely the point of Marshfield's story. Only the most uninitiated reader can fail to catch some of the irony. If each home is a temple as the New Testament suggests, then, reasons Marshfield, Christ's pronouncements on the threats to the household, particularly adultery and divorce, are central to Western life. And just as God forever forgives Israel which is forever faithless, so Jesus forgives the adulterer. Adultery, Marshfield concludes, is "our inherent condition. . . . Adultery is not a choice to be avoided; it is a circumstance to be embraced" (44-45). With inspired sophistry based on his rationalization that marriage isolates men and women from the bright sun of freedom, he argues that the sacrament of marriage is so impossible to observe that it must be a "precondition for the sacrament of adultery." What else, he asks, can Christ's easy forgiveness of the adulterous woman mean other than to lend a "covert blessing" to those who defy the hell of eternal marriages for the paradise of transient fornication? Time is man's element. Adultery quickens his awareness of the mutable.

Although there are bits of truth amid this specious reasoning, one wonders how aware Marshfield is of Updike's irony. Even if the minister is unaware, Updike laughs at his own touches of self-mockery. With such sentences as the following, it is as if he were gleefully slinging his prose back in the faces of all those negative critics who claim that his style is too ornate: "Hark! A far car drew nearer in the ghostly grid of snowglazed ways" (77). Updike may, of course, blame his narrator for such nonsense, but one knows that at bottom most of the fun is his. As he has Marshfield say, a "Higher Wisdom" directs his style. But not, perhaps, his love life. Alicia takes up with anti-Barthian Bork, and Marshfield decides that her tirade about the injustice visited on the female in an adulterous affair deserves his full ministerial concern: Sex. Yet her betrayal does little to increase his guilt. With comic gusto he implies that women fight for the privilege of shouldering his reservations: "Babies and guilt, women are built for lugging" (170).

Marshfield is surrounded by them. Alicia is all body, Frankie all faith, Jane all ethics. Marshfield is stuck in between and paralyzed. If Frankie's transparency results in impotence, Jane's goodness leads to stagnation. She is a good wife and ethical, but goodness is not enough: "Ethics is plumbing, necessary but dingy. Ethical passion the hobgoblin of trivial minds. What interests us is not the good but the godly. Not living well but living forever" (192-193). Marshfield is not ironic here; he is Barthian. Good works without belief are useless. What he needs is to balance the best qualities of his women, to convince his soul that he should accept the sacredness of the body so that harmony can be achieved: "Somewhere, amid these juxtapositions and their violent 'affect,' an American mystery was circumscribed, having to do with *knowing*, with acceptance of body by soul, with recovery of some baggage lost in the Atlantic crossing" (134-135). Ms. Prynne will personify that harmony, but for the moment there is his wife Jane to worry about.

Born to a father with the imposing name of Wesley Augustus Chillingworth, Professor of Ethics, Jane Chillingworth is Marshfield's "dear sainted sloven." One cannot help thinking of Roger Chillingworth's wife, but in Updike's update of Hawthorne's puritan world, not adultery but divorce is the ultimate social shame. Marshfield's parishioners view his sexual vagaries not as a sin but as an embarrassment. Suzanne Uphaus has a point: "In referring to *The Scarlet Letter* Updike makes us aware of his purpose—to reject that separation of body and soul, of faith from good works, which is our heritage, and which was most popularly and influentially portrayed in that novel. *The Scarlet Letter* embodies part of our religious, as well as our literary past; and in its redefinition, Updike has attempted to revise our religious and literary heritage."[29] Jane Chillingworth is no Hester Prynne, and her insistence on good works without belief is a problem in her marriage.

Updike's description of Marshfield's courtship of Jane is as different in tone from Hawthorne and as funny as anything in his fiction, for he parallels the progress of the groping hand with the development of Professor Chillingworth's course in ethics. Hating the way the professor turns the history of ethics into an empty academic exercise in which Augustine's *concupiscentia* gives way to Aquinas' *synderesis* and beyond, Marshfield remembers Spinoza because that part of the course coincides with the first kiss: "Our first kiss came during Spinoza, more *titillatio* than *hilaritas*. . . . As Kant attempted to soften rationalism with categorical imperatives and *Achtung*, Jane let me caress her breast through her sweater. By the time of Hegel's monstrous identification of morality with the demands of the state, my hand was hot in her bra, and my access had been universalized to include her thighs" (51-52). Never before has Updike so comically detailed the parallels between religion and sex. He does so here with such verve that Piet Hanema's serious ruminations on a similar topic in *Couples* seem as ponderous and dry as Professor Chillingworth's interminable lectures. That Jane and Marshfield toy with orgasm in a room directly above Chillingworth's study caps this set piece. Sly sex defeats dry ethics. When the Professor asks Marshfield what is so heartening about Barth, the aspiring minister might have answered, "Your daughter's thighs." Ethics, after all, mean little when one believes. With bluster and a fancy prose style he explains: "Impotent, I must say, I was (then) never: as ready to stand and ejaculate as to stand and spout the Apostles' Creed" (59-60). One can imagine Hawthorne's blush.

After years of marriage, however, his eternal uprightness, as he calls his unceasing readiness for sex, is in danger of falling limp before the complacencies of middle age. Marshfield shrinks from the crisis, but we laugh at what he describes as his "odious trick of clowning in the face of mystery" (62). Yet, Updike suggests, odiousness is not all that bad. Like Kurt Vonnegut's Bokonon thumbing his nose at "You-know-who," Marshfield can do little else except laugh. But is he always consciously ironic? How, for example, does one read these lines at the end of his description of his marriage: "Mock not my revelations. They are the poor efforts of a decent man to mitigate an indecent bind, an indecently airtight puzzle" (64)? It may be that, with Pascal, he finds his glory in knowing his misery. The sound of laughter keeps him sane; self mockery keeps him mellow. In the midst of angst he describes Alicia's clock as vanilla-colored with "needle-fine, scarcely visible hands, green-tipped for night-time luminescence, and a chic shy shape, that of a box being squeezed in an invisible press, so its smooth sides bulged" (74). What? asks the startled reader, and so, finally, does Marshfield himself when he immediately undercuts his own silly description.

Thus one admires the long-suffering Jane when Marshfield narrates Alicia's confrontation with her. Completely flustering the aggressive organist with a defense of diffidence and sympathy, Jane inadvertently goads Alicia from a declaration of love to an invective of vulgarity. Even Jane laughs with Tom at this unexpected proof of their "tough" marriage. Still, Marshfield imagines Alicia in "filmy dressing gowns carelessly buttoned," but he watches Jane grope for a nightie, "a dowdy tent of cotton she must have shopped for in a novel by one of the Alcott sisters" (97-98). The toughness of their marriage has a crack that Jane plugs with a renewed ardor born of fascination that her husband is desired by other women. But rather than rejoice, Marshfield panics. For in becoming athletic in bed, Jane completes her status as good wife and thus imprisons him even tighter. Perfection in an ethical wife, he implies, closes the loopholes to freedom, and loopholes, he believes, are necessary to a vital life. Rabbit Angstrom and Piet Hanema would agree. The question that he asks is how to get from love to free without resorting to word games.

As Marshfield says in one of his sermons, Christ's ways are not man's ways. Faithless and perverse describe his generation; he does not lament but accepts. Updike creates his fictional ministers to be scapegoats. The joke in *A Month of Sundays* is that Marshfield understands Updike's positions about faith versus ethics, body versus soul, and Barth versus liberalism, and he refuses to be beaten down. Instead of tearing his hair and jumping into sackcloth, he preaches a sermon on God's deserts. Concluding that life is a desert that is itself the palm of God's hand, he exhorts the faithful, his readers, to remember God's blessing and rejoice: "Do I detect an extra whiteness, as of erasure, in the blank space beneath the conclusion of yesterday's sermon? Holding the suspicious spot up to the light, do I not espy the faint linear impress of a pencilled word? There seems to be a capital 'N,' in a pedestrian school hand—can the word be 'Nice'? Ideal Reader, can it be you?" (167).

It can be you, though he would prefer it to be Frances "Frankie" Harlow, the third of his four special women. Wearing nicely-filled knit dresses and knee-length mink coats, Frankie is unhappily married and desirous of counseling. Marshfield is more than willing to help. The solution as always is seduction, and as more and more women come to him for advice, he begins to understand their collective female attitude toward husbands: The man's world no longer fits them. The problem, he argues, is not physical but theological, the failure of the soul to accept the body and thus sex as its natural extension. Listening to the varied complaints of Frankie and other frustrated women, he learns that adultery comes in several guises, that the "gaudy-winged disaster" of the freshly married differs considerably from the more stolid and domestic adultery of a couple in their thirties. Thus his impotence with the desirable and willing Frankie Harlow is comically ironic because it smacks of neither disaster nor domesticity. It is theological in origin. Dismayed at his inability to perform, he turns his failure into a testament of belief: "I would greet my impotence as the survivor within me of faith, a piece of purity amid all this relativistic concupiscence, this plastic modernity, this adulterate industry, this animated death" (139). In short, Frankie Harlow is too fine, too transparent, too much of faith and not enough of flesh. Eager to bed down with a man of God, she disarms the very body that could satisfy her. She is the other side of Alicia's emphasis on the physical. Marshfield needs a woman who combines the qualities of Alicia, Jane, and Frankie; he needs, finally, the mysterious Ms. Prynne.

He gets her. Large and "undeformed but unattractive," she is the opposite of Ken Kesey's Big Nurse. Ms. Prynne turns out to be Marshfield's Ideal Reader, a key to his cure because she combines solidity and mystery. As the unseen manager of the omega-shaped motel, she is god-like in her apparent absence and evident control. Marshfield longs for her to join him in bed, but she offers more than sex. She teaches him that what at first glance seems only a desert of nothingness is in fact the palm of God's hand, that life is everywhere, even in the endless sand: "And do we not see, around us (with the knowledgeable guidance of our dear Ms. Prynne), the Joshua tree lifting its arms awkwardly in prayer, and hear the organ-pipe cactus thundering its transcendent hymn?" (165). The nothingness of the desert is an illusion, for all of God's creations carry grace. With dinosaur fossils, she also teaches him about death, and she illustrates the combination of ethics and belief in her treatment of the drunken Indian: "The Indian understood; he looked up at the sky; he laughed, and his knees suddenly bent, and you reached forward to put a hand beneath his elbow. . . . Oh, I moved through you, understanding all this and more, and it came to me that love is not an e-motion, an assertive putting out, but a *trans*-motion, a compliant moving *through*" (217).

Only when Marshfield writes his sermon professing belief in the existence of God despite fear of the eternal silence does Ms. Prynne reveal herself as the Ideal Reader. She has prepared her revelation with a hint that she finds the sermon on the essence of life in the midst of death to be "nice": "To those who find no faith within themselves, I say no seed is so dry it does not hold the code of life within it . . ." (166). Ms. Prynne is finally won over when she reads Marshfield's confession that life is posited on an ambiguity, that only Jesus believes while man must be satisfied with professing belief. In short, Tom Marshfield reembraces Karl Barth.

Ms. Prynne is impressed. She has been his Ideal Reader all along, perusing his narrative while he plays golf, hovering like an unseen editor while he worries about runaway language. Her mission has been to return the minister to the world with its daily doses of ambiguity and illusion. Marshfield is willing. Yet before he turns again to pews and parishioners, he wants one thing: Ms. Prynne. With her sexual blessing, "the exterior sign of interior grace," he will be ready to meet the world as the chastened preacher but still prancing author: "I want my merit badge. You, Ms., pynne it on me" (223). Pin it she does. Silently answering his prayer, she undresses without comment and leads him to bed. Marshfield's reaction to her silence—"Wondrous strength and generosity of a woman's heart!"—ironically echoes Dimmesdale's praise of Hester Prynne at the scaffold. Dimmesdale and Hester remain forever separated by the minister's hypocrisy, but with Marshfield and Ms. Prynne human contact is once again restored.

Marshfield's final flourish is appropriately a prayer: "There was a moment, when I entered you, and was big, and you were already wet, when you could not have seen yourself, when your eyes were all for another, looking up into mine, with an expression without a name, of entry and alarm, and of salutation. I pray my own face, a stranger to me, saluted in turn" (228). Detweiler interprets this lovely conclusion as a recapitulation of Updike's suggestion that language lacks the ability to say what we mean, that language is inadequate to define the sexual and religious forces that come together silently at the end.[30] He has a point. The recalcitrance of language is a major consideration throughout *A Month of*

*Sundays.* But the conclusion also sparkles with affirmation. Baffled by contemporary man's tendency to separate body and soul, upset by contemporary man's inclination to disconnect ethics and belief, Marshfield feels adrift between anti-Barthian liberals and pro-adultery parishioners. His affirmation is possible because he comes to believe that the body itself is holy and that the profession of belief is a key to the kingdom. His closing prayer while making love with Ms. Prynne is, finally, for the communion of matter and spirit. Language, sex, and religion unify in the pages of his narrative, and ideal readers everywhere wish him well.

## NOTES

1. John Updike, *A Month of Sundays* (New York: Knopf, 1975). Further references will be noted in the text.
2. Richard Burgin, "A Conversation with John Updike," *The John Updike Newsletter,* 10 and 11 (Spring and Summer 1979), p. 10.
3. George Steiner, "Scarlet Letters," *New Yorker,* 10 March 1975, p. 116.
4. Burgin, "A Conversation with John Updike," p. 7.
5. Frank Gado, "Interview with John Updike," *First Person: Conversations on Writers and Writing* (Schenectady, New York: Union College Press, 1973), p. 99.
6. Charles Thomas Samuels, "The Art of Fiction XLIII: John Updike," *Paris Review,* 12 (Winter 1968), p. 101.
7. Steiner, "Scarlet Letters," p. 116.
8. John Updike, *Hawthorne's Creed* (New York: Targ Editions, 1981). Further references will be to this edition and will be noted by *HC* and page number.
9. Steiner, p. 118.
10. Steiner, p. 118.
11. Bernard A. Schopen, "Faith, Morality, and the Novels of John Updike," *Twentieth Century Literature,* 24 (Winter 1978), p. 534.
12. Samuels, "The Art of Fiction XLIII: John Updike," p. 93.
13. Samuels, "The Art of Fiction XLIII: John Updike," p. 111.
14. Robert Detweiler, "Updike's *A Month of Sundays* and the Language of the Unconscious," *Journal of the American Academy of Religion,* 47(December 1979), p. 611.
15. John Updike, "Why Write?," *Picked-Up Pieces* (New York: Knopf, 1975), p. 38.
16. George Hunt, "John Updike's 'Sunday Sort of Book,' " *America,* 21 June 1975, p. 479.
17. Jane Howard, "Can a Nice Novelist Finish First?," *Life,* 4 November 1966, p. 80.
18. Schopen, p. 525.
19. George W. Hunt, "Updike's Pilgrims in a World of Nothingness," *Thought,* 53(December 1978), p. 387. Hunt goes so far as to insist that some sense of Karl Barth's theology is necessary for any reader who hopes to understand Updike's fiction.
20. Hunt suggests that the reviewers hoped "not for a better book, but for a different book, one less ambivalent and less theological, and especially one

with more obvious evidence of hard work." See Hunt, "John Updike's 'Sunday Sort of Book,' " p. 478.

21. See review of *A Month of Sundays*, *The Critic*, (May-June 1975), p. 81; Carlos Baker, review of *A Month of Sundays*, *Theology Today*, 32 (October 1975), pp. 335-336.
22. Gilbert Sorrentino, "Never on Sunday," *Partisan Review*, 43(Winter 1976), pp. 119-121; Blanche H. Gelfant, "Fiction Chronicle," *Hudson Review*, 28(Summer 1975), esp. pp. 312- 314.
23. See Janet Karsten Larson, "A Man Out of the Cloth," *Christian Century*, 30 April 1975, pp. 445-447; Joan Joffe Hall, "A Month of Sundays," *New Republic*, 22 February 1975, pp. 29-30; Paul Gray, "Ring Around the Collar," *Time*, 17 February 1975, p. 82; Ronald De Feo, "Sex, Sermons, and Style," *National Review*, 20 June 1975, pp. 679-680; Benjamin De Mott, "Mod Masses, Empty Pews," *Saturday Review*, 8 March 1975, pp. 20-21.
24. Peter J. Prescott, "The Passionate Cleric," *Newsweek*, 2 March 1975, p. 72; Hunt, "John Updike's 'Sunday Sort of Book,' " p. 477. The response in British journals is largely laudatory. John Carey praises its "depth and seriousness," and Peter Ackroyd, in a glowing notice, says that "this novel is far more inventive and more substantial than anything which is currently being written and praised in England." See John Carey, "Desert Father," *New Statesman*, 4 July 1975, pp. 21-22; Peter Ackroyd, "Wittery," *The Spectator*, 28 June 1975, p. 781.
25. Gado, p. 109.
26. John Updike, "Faith in Search of Understanding," *Assorted Prose* (New York: Knopf, 1965), pp. 273-274.
27. Prescott, p. 72.
28. John Gardner, "Moral Fiction," *Saturday Review*, 1 April 1978, p. 32.
29. Suzanne Henning Uphaus, "The Unified Vision of *A Month of Sundays*," *University of Windsor Review*, 12 (Spring-Summer 1979), p. 15.
30. Detweiler, p. 619.

# Marry Me: A Romance

*"Any romance that does not end in marriage fails."*
—*Marry Me*

Reverend Tom Marshfield's reconciliation with the mysterious Ms. Prynne in *A Month of Sundays* underscores Updike's recognition of Nathaniel Hawthorne as the first great American author to examine the often baffling relationships among sex, sin, faith, and art. That he grins at the tradition even as he honors it is part of the fun. Marshfield's mess is not so devastating as Hester's plight.

Neither is Jerry Conant's in *Marry Me* (1976). But because Updike takes the trouble to stress the subtitle *A Romance* on the title page, he suggests that in this novel he still has an eye on the Hawthorne tradition. Jerry is a distant cousin of the hypocritical Arthur Dimmesdale, but unlike the minister's, his predicament is more comic than grim. Updike enjoys the difference. His comments about *Marry Me: A Romance* in a two-page "special message" for an edition published by the Franklin Library indicate the difficulty he had writing it:

It has been a long time making. Chapter II, "The Wait," was published in *The New Yorker* of February 17, 1968, and it was not newly written then. But *Marry Me* was always a book in my mind, not a collection, or collage, and was written pretty much in a piece, with the five chapters symmetrically alliterative as I have them, and their lengths in the proportion of a diadem. The central chapter, cut down from the length of a novel in itself, is flanked by two longish, less inward, more spoken chapters, and these in turn by brief idylls, partaking of the same texture, between real and unreal.[1]

He also argues that the book is about religion and the potential of love. The religions of the four principals—Lutheran, lapsed Catholic, Unitarian, and Atheist—offer various ecumenical possibilities, and comfort at the beach and congestion at the airport suggest Heaven and Hell. In limbo between the extremes, the characters nourish the illusion of love, what Updike calls "a component of our daily lives, wherein air and dreams are as essential as earth and blood." Recognizing the flaws that give a kind of charm to anything built by man, be it a bookcase or a book, he knows that part of love is the emotion that any creator brings to his handiwork, to the seams and cuts that glare at the eye of the maker but that other viewers may note or ignore as they will. The author's duty is not, in other words, to point out adjustments made in the name of harmony. Like reality, a novel has its own opacity. What counts, says Updike, is the finished product, and in the case of *Marry Me* he is satisfied: "The artist's effort perhaps is not to bring a work to perfection but to bring it to the point where the creation, not the creator, takes the active part in the sentence; the question then becomes not whether I am content but whether the book, or the bookcase, is finished. It is."

Some readers do not think so. As will be discussed later, they worry about the reality of the characters and the fantasy of the ending. The dust jacket to the first trade edition explains that Updike added the subtitle "A Romance" because "People don't act like that any more."[2] It is not that adultery is unusual but that the moral agony and incessant talk about domestic responsibility make these characters seem to be refugees from another era. The subtitle shows that verisimilitude is not the issue in this novel.

Maureen Howard wishes that it were. Calling *Marry Me* "a curiously bad book," she argues that Updike's allusion to the idea of romance is no more than an intellectual prop. Without the complexities necessary to place a novel in the tradition of romance, "the combination of the actual and the imaginary is fatal for him. . . ."[3] Similar complaints have been made about American fiction since the first novelist took the first step away from realism. Nearly every reader of American literature recalls, for example, Hawthorne's explanation of what he was up to in *The House of the Seven Gables* (1851). That he felt the need to explain at all illustrates awareness that his fiction challenged the limited expectations of his readers. The opening sentence of his famous preface is both a defense of the book and an appeal to the reader, and it applies as much to Hawthorne's classic tale as to Updike's *Marry Me:* "When a writer calls his work a Romance, it need hardly be observed that he wishes to claim a certain latitude, both as to its fashion and material, which he would not have felt himself entitled to assume, had he professed to be writing a Novel." The problem, as Hawthorne and Updike realize, is that it *does* need to be observed. Too many readers expect realism when they pick up a novel. For those who do not recall Hawthorne's well-known definition of the

Romance, the following quotation from his preface may be helpful: "The latter form of composition [Novel] is presumed to aim at a very minute fidelity, not merely to the possible, but to the probable and ordinary course of man's experience. The former [Romance]—while, as a work of art, it must rigidly subject itself to laws, and while it sins unpardonably, so far as it may swerve aside from the truth of the human heart—has fairly a right to present that truth under circumstances, to a great extent, of the writer's own choosing or creation."[4]

The point, of course, is not fidelity to external details but allegiance to internal concerns. Since so many readers equate the novel with realism, Hawthorne asks that his fiction be judged by other criteria. Two years after Hawthorne published his preface, William Gilmore Simms expressed a similar opinion in the second edition (1853) of his 1835 tale *The Yemassee: A Romance of Carolina:* "The romance is of loftier origin than the novel. . . . It does not confine itself to what is known, or even what is probable. It grasps at the possible. . . ."[5] These famous statements in defense of the American romance have led to several penetrating studies of American fiction. Two of the best are Richard Chase's *The American Novel and Its Tradition* and Joel Porte's *The Romance in America.* Offering a distinction between British and American novels, Chase proposes a working definition of the romance that he expands as his study progresses: ". . . since the earliest days the American novel, in its most original and characteristic form, has worked out its destiny and defined itself by incorporating an element of romance . . . that freer, more daring, more brilliant fiction that contrasts with the solid moral inclusiveness and massive equability of the English novel."[6] He goes on to stress the author's right to assume freedom from the usual novelistic qualities of verisimilitude and continuity, and he acknowledges the romancer's tendency toward formal abstractness. Porte agrees. His definition of romance as it pertains to American fiction is interesting because it touches on Hawthorne's and Updike's concerns to write novels in the native tradition of romance that are also literally about romance. Stressing the use of archetypal characters, symbol, dream, and fantasy, he suggests that "the American romance is characterized by a need self-consciously to define its own aims, so that 'romance' becomes frequently . . . the theme as well as the form of these authors' works."[7] Finally, Brook Thomas argues that such authors as Hawthorne—and I would add the Updike of *Marry Me*—create their peculiar brand of fiction not to avoid the rigors of verisimilitude but to show that social order is a human construct, that it does not inhere in society: "that to be interested in society is not necessarily to describe what is already there but to show how a possible world could be organized if human beings had the freedom to choose."[8]

Updike's subtitle is thus crucial to a reading of *Marry Me.* Jerry Conant has the freedom to choose but not the will to make the choice. Like many of Updike's characters, he hesitates on the border between the possible and the probable. In other words he does not know whether to make of his life a romance or a novel because the reverence he finds in Sally is balanced by the duty he feels toward Ruth. One offers imagination; the other promises the real. Sympathetic to the problem, Updike turns Jerry's dilemma inward to the book itself and supplies multiple endings, not because, like Jerry, he cannot make up his mind as Maureen Howard charges, but because he wants to invite the reader to participate in the text. Active reading is called for, just as Hawthorne asks his readers to "perhaps choose to assign an actual locality to the imaginary events of the narrative." Jerry must learn that despite his religious sureties the realm of the social contract does not innately hold an order that he can discover if only someone makes the right choice for him. Updike shows that Jerry needs to create his own pattern, that he needs to live actively. In urging his readers to help Jerry choose, he hints that they face similar dilemmas in their own lives. One recalls the resonant line at the conclusion of "The Music School": "The world is the host; it must be chewed."[9] Jerry fears to take the final bite.

Many reviewers claim that in his case the bite is not worth taking. It is fair to say that *Marry Me* was widely criticized when it appeared in 1976. Timothy Foote, for example, calls Jerry Conant the "twerp of twerps" and declares that despite Updike's effort to pose a moral dilemma "it is difficult to care very much one way or the other." Peter Wolfe dismisses the novel because of its ending which, he insists, maroons everybody— "author, reader, and characters." But their criticisms pale beside the hysterically negative response of Brigid Brophy. Brophy just cannot handle the implications of the subtitle: "John Updike subtitles his new book 'A Romance.' That would have been a classy claim in the fourteenth century and a still reputable one, from the literary point of view, in the eighteenth. Presumably, however, the label is couched in modern English and is meant to declare that the book has a high saccharin content. . . . John Updike aspires no higher than the written equivalent of kitsch wallpaper for the nursery."[10] Presumably, Brophy has not consulted nineteenth-century American romances.

Other commentators have, even though their responses to *Marry Me* are lukewarm. Calling the novel "elaborate and ingenious," for example, Alfred Kazin says that it is "as original in its development as it is familiar in its situation." Walter Sullivan likes Updike but wonders if this novel is empty: ". . . and though from *Antigone* to *Anna Karenina* and beyond, the sanctity of family ties has informed much of our greatest literature, for Updike a broken marriage is only that—a shift in relationships, a trading off of bedfellows." William Pritchard, usually an Updike supporter, calls

Jerry "abominable" and the book itself a "wan sequel" to *Couples*. And Thomas LeClair complains that Updike is too self-indulgent, that he "takes his characters much more seriously than he makes them."[11]

Yet for all the carping, *Marry Me* has its defenders. Peter Prescott calls it "quite simply, Updike's best novel," and he defends his comments by showing that he understands the implications of the subtitle: " 'Romance' is the word that Updike applies to this story: clearly he is aware of the continuity. Like Chrétien de Troyes, he uses the narrow confines of an illicit affair to explore problems of choice, will and responsibility, the problem of a kind of love that is mostly pain, that precludes rational thought and, by becoming an obsession, threatens social order."[12] Bruce Allen is not quite so convinced, but he praises Updike's "compassionate scrutiny of some unlovable people." Similarly, Greg Johnson calls *Marry Me* "an immensely likable novel," but he wonders if Jerry Conant can bear the thematic weight that Updike asks him to carry. George W. Hunt argues that Jerry can, and he insists that the relatively shallow characters and repetitive dialogue are deliberate ploys to draw the reader into a complex moral debate on the nature of goodness and sin.[13]

Heated disagreement among reviewers is by now standard fare for an Updike novel, but the debate that activates readers paralyzes Jerry. The year is 1962 in an atmosphere of moral twilight, a moment before President Kennedy's murder signals the plunge from Camelot to chaos, a time when the ethics of an older generation have weakened to the point where they both torment with their ties and liberate with their loosening. Discontent sneaks into the garden of suburbia. The jacket cover is a photograph of "The Garden of Eden" from the sarcophagus of Valerius Adelphia (4th century). The toad on the jacket of *Couples* is now a full-fledged snake, and Eve, demurely covering her genitals, tempts Adam with the most famous bite in history. That Adam holds his hand in a position that may be either a blessing or a warning illustrates the dilemma that has faced every couple since Eden. Love and death, the Garden and the sarcophagus, are intertwined as securely as the tree and the serpent.

A quatrain by Robert Herrick serves as the epigraph and urges lovers to bite the apple before death intervenes:

> Choose me your valentine,
>   Next, let us marry—
> Love to the death will pine
>   If we long tarry.

Not love but death is forever. Fearful for his soul, cognizant of death, Jerry Conant freezes before the contrast of the ephemeral and the eternal. Updike is correct: People do not act like that anymore. The constraint of

Herrick's "tarrying" seems lifted in Updike's romance of the early 1960s, but moral inhibitions still linger on the edges of Eden.

Jerry thinks of himself as the last religious man, but he carries the assumption on his own. Unlike *Couples* in which Updike builds a foundation of general religious symbolism with such means as resonant names (Piet and Angela) and apocalyptic events (a church fire lit by God's "own" lightning), *Marry Me* tends to undercut Jerry's insistence that his existential dread in a community of unbelievers warrants sympathetic consideration from the women and children he betrays. His faith lacks the committed aspiration that one often admires in Rabbit Angstrom and Piet Hanema, and it seems rather an expression of his pride. It is not that his fear of death or his guilt over adultery is faked but that neither is reinforced by the symbols or narrator of the book. The result is that Jerry's passivity isolates him both in his community and the novel, and the reader joins the characters in wondering why he should sympathize with a man whose genuine faith projects more of his ego than his belief. Jerry is an adulterer who wants God or women to make decisions for him. When they refuse, he fancies himself a victim of Kierkegaard's either/or. His crisis is finally not so soul-rending as Rabbit's or Piet's or even Marshfield's. Updike's gentle undercutting makes him more comic than his fictional fellow wanderers.

Josephine Hendin's description is appropriately amusing: "This superb, irresistible novel is a subtle exposure of what you might call tender malice."[14] No one has done more than Updike to explode the myth of male freedom that dominates American fiction from *The Last of the Mohicans* through *Deliverance*, and Hendin knows that men, especially Updike's men, are molded from cradle to grave by women. Pondering the situation, Updike does not join Hawkeye or Huck and light out for the territory. He grins. Hendin calls *Marry Me* the "most sophisticated comedy imaginable," and she correctly notes that Updike's "wit blooms in the gap between the euphoric outburst 'marry me,' and the failure of those magic words to change one's soul." Paralysis results from the tension between man's ties to his mother at one extreme and to his wife at the other. Mistresses are always tangents.

When Jerry finds the sexual princess of his fantasies in Sally Mathias, he freezes rather than comes alive because he fears that his all but asexual wife will stop mothering his guilt and dread. As Hendin suggests, sex may be a tonic only for Updike's women. His men are too busy trying to find heaven between a female's thighs. Their bodies require one thing, their spirits another. This is why Jerry gazes so often at the stars. He wants heaven to shine on him while he passively maneuvers his sexual mistress and his mothering wife to fight it out between themselves, thereby absolving him of all responsibility. Jerry has taken lessons from Joey

Robinson *(Of the Farm)*, and like Joey he hurts both women, withholding marriage from Sally, upsetting marriage to Ruth.

The bottom line for Jerry is that he longs to think well of himself. How can he, he worries, if God disapproves at one end, wife and mistress at the other? Hendin may be correct: "The greatest love in *Marry Me* is Updike's. It is evident in his lavish unsparing skill in creating Ruth. Her acid accuracy about her husband's flaws is unaccompanied by any desire for revenge, any critical bent, any interest in throwing him out. . . . Ruth has more insight into her man than into herself."[15] That insight, of course, is Updike's. Few other American novelists are as grateful for the grace of women, as decisive about the indecisiveness of men.

The first chapter "Warm Wine" (also published in a slightly different format as "Warm Wine: An Idyll" in a limited, signed edition of 250 copies by Albondocani Press in 1973) sets the scene of the snake of desire easing into the idyll of suburban America—Connecticut by the beach. Although this land of commuters is crowded, the beach is obscure, all but secret, just the place for romance. But it is also a place to hold back mortality, to trick time by indulging the illusion that the joy of adultery, the lure of new love, creates new life: ". . . it was the taste of his renewed youth, his renewed draft on life. Since the start of their affair he was always running, hurrying, creating time where no time had been needed before; he had become an athlete of the clock, bending odd hours into an unprecedented and unsuspected second life" (4).

In Updike's parody of the romantic idyll, the lovers' speech reverts to adolescent slang and monosyllables. Even language slows down. Because time seems to stop in their garden by the sea, Jerry and Sally dream that they are the original couple. She likes Camus and Moravia, warm wine, and lovemaking; he worries about morality and acts like a husband. His belief in God inhibits her effort to teach him about love and recklessness. When Jerry says "hell," Sally knows that he means a real place. She takes Robert Herrick's quatrain literally. Restraint and waiting rankle her because she does not have world enough and time. Disobeying Jerry's caution, flying to him in Washington, she becomes, she believes, a heroine: ". . . Jerry and Sally made love lucidly, like Adam and Eve when the human world was of two halves purely" (33). Like Eve, she proudly shows him how to bite the apple.

Jerry is a willing student, but he cannot keep Ruth and Richard, the other wife and husband, out of the garden. Yet rationalization of his love for Sally is simple because the affair boosts his spirit. He even quotes St. Paul for support. As Richard says, Jerry has never suffered because he believes in God and the avoidance of pain. He is a comic portrait of Updike's religious man, more articulate than Rabbit, more intelligent than Piet. Sally, on the other hand, believes only that "things happened." Curiously, her lack of religious scruples attracts Jerry.

A lapsed Roman Catholic, she has been married a decade and has had other lovers, but she always seems virginally innocent. Committed to an adulterous affair with Jerry, she wonders if she has lost her identity as well as her faith: "What sense did it make? Who had made these arrangements? He had gotten her so confused, her husbandly lover, she didn't even know if she believed in God or not. Once she had had a clear opinion, yes or no, she had forgotten which" (35). Sally's problem is that she has a bad man for a husband and a good man for a lover when she needs the opposite. Updike understands the dilemma well enough to describe her longing to be accepted as her lover's wife, her resentment at being obviously her lover's mistress.

As Updike writes in "Giving Blood," "Romance is, simply, the strange, the untried."[16] When Sally offers to abandon her children for Jerry, he counters that she would then tire of him in three weeks. The shock of the new, not the promise of fulfillment, lures Jerry. In Updike's many fictions about successful love, radiance is a necessary factor, a blessing of sorts that keeps the serpent at bay. Unlike Sally, Jerry admits the need for radiance, the necessity of maintaining the illusion of the strange, the untried: "I want you and I can't have you. You're like a set of golden stairs I can never finish climbing. I look down, and the earth is a little blue mist. I look up, and there's this radiance I can never reach. It gives you your incredible beauty, and if I marry you I'll destroy it" (46). These are the words of an aspiring but selfish man. He longs to have his feet in the real and his eyes on the ideal. In other words, he wants both Ruth and Sally, both the novel and the romance, and he bases his rationalization of guilt on the fantasy that Sally will always be his mistress but never his wife. Like a chivalric lover in a medieval romance, he believes that ideal love should not be realized. But realization for him means not sexual consummation but wedding vows. Marriage to Sally would make her a wife, and courting a wife, Updike writes in "Wife-wooing," takes "tenfold the strength of winning an ignorant girl."

Jerry lacks the strength to commit either way. Adultery is one thing, but abandoning a wife is quite another. Ecstasy and guilt are a pair. Updike observes in an interview, "I wonder if twentieth-century man's problem isn't one of encouragement, because of the failure of nerve, the lassitude and despair, the sense that we've gone to the end of the corridor and found it blank. . . . I don't want to say that being passive, being inactive, being paralyzed, is wrong in an era when so much action is crass and murderous."[17] The blank at the end of his corridor, Jerry believes, is death. Passivity is his means of avoiding the final walk down the hall.

When Sally accepts her role as mistress, Jerry insists on believing that mistresses are material for European novels while wives are the blessing of the American dream. His key line in the novel—though it sounds pompous—fixes him as another of Updike's men caught on the border between the conceivable and the inconceivable: "Maybe our trouble is that we live in the twilight of the old morality, and there's just enough to torment us, and not enough to hold us in" (53). He honestly believes that his predicament traps him between death and death; death of his spirit if he gives up Sally, death of his faith if he abandons Ruth.

Jerry lacks Piet Hanema's longing to fall from a false Eden to a coarse world. Everywhere he turns he sees sin or feels guilt. Unfortunately, some of his lines are silly: "You were given to me in Heaven, and Heaven won't let me have you" (56). One can picture him joining Piet and Foxy in the bathroom, with Ruth and Angela rattling the knob. Jerry is like a child indulging his pain, stating the worst in order to be contradicted, exaggerating his guilt in order to don the sackcloth of God's sinner. At the same time that Updike stresses the seriousness of the predicament, he undercuts Jerry by placing him on stage as if he were a high school heart throb hoping to take two girls to the dance. Knowing Jerry, one expects him to glide to the dance floor, glance at the spotlight, and grin to receive the applause.

Needless to say, Ruth is not clapping. She is perhaps Updike's finest character, surely the heroine of *Marry Me*. Although Sally calls her a "blameless wife," matters are not so simple. Learning about the complexities in her life, the reader understands that Updike is much more interested in Ruth than in Jerry and Sally. The daughter of a Unitarian minister, she thinks of religion in terms that are bound to clash with her husband's orthodox views. She is an art student before her marriage, a painter of "remarkably unafraid" pictures. Since she knows color and Jerry knows line, their love carries itself more on mutual admiration than mutual possession. Between them they appear to have everything, but their "merger," as the narrator calls it, is too aesthetic for the harsher light of the long years of marriage: ". . . unexpected shadows deepened, emphasizing differences overlooked in the ideal overhead light they had once painted by" (77). They even quarrel over which church, Ruth's Unitarian or Jerry's Lutheran, will baptize their children.

Although for some reason Updike does not show us, he tells the reader that Jerry has recently experienced a fear of death and that only religion, especially the theology of Barth, Marcel, and Berdyaev, has helped him cope. Surviving the crisis, he becomes cocky in his faith and begins to hate what he calls the pale belief of Ruth's lapsed Unitarianism: "Once, wakened from sleep to hear him protest that some day he would die, Ruth had said, 'Dust to dust,' and rolled over and gone back to sleep. Jerry never forgave this" (78). Yet he feels duty-bound to Ruth, and he finds in her an ally for the mixture of attraction and repulsion he senses toward Sally and Richard Mathias.

In one sense Ruth and Jerry are drawn to the mysterious in the Mathiases, to Richard's undefined source of money, to Sally's undisguised glow of grace. He is rich and she is beautiful, and the Conants look on with a kind of disapproving awe. It is a sign of Jerry's immaturity that he hates Richard just because his neighbor is an atheist. His childishness persuades him that all atheists are sadistic toward their wives. But Ruth knows that Richard is too good to Sally, that he has a practical sense of family that Jerry lacks: "He saw the raising of children as a kind of problem, where Jerry saw none: he was the original, and in the children God had made some reproductions which in time would be distributed" (83). The point is that Ruth's painter's vision, her sense of color and proportion, grants her a wider view of domestic life in America than Jerry's. One does not read a third of the novel before realizing that Ruth might enjoy a fling with Richard. While her husband worries about guilt and faith, her neighbor discusses Piaget and Spock with her, strokes her buttocks when dancing, and notices her hair and clothes. She becomes his mistress without too much effort.

For Ruth, too, needs the new, the untried. Richard gives her his worldliness; Jerry offers his fear. Richard tells her that she is "a great piece"; Jerry calls her "a spiritual cripple." Caught between loss of her vision with Jerry and loss of her stability with Richard, she feels life all but stumble to a halt. The affair with Richard over, the life with Jerry on hold, she returns to her marriage for a rest. It is not forthcoming. Despite her skill with color and shape, Ruth is not sure who she is. For one thing, she believes that "any romance that does not end in marriage fails," a dubious proposition at best (97). Worse, however, is that rather than bring her solace, religion gives her nothing: "She was a Unitarian, and what did this mean, except that her soul was one unit removed from not being there at all?" (96). Updike skillfully places Ruth in an ironic position that only the reader recognizes. Afraid to confess her affair with Richard—Sally and Jerry never do find out—, she totters for much of the novel toward an even deeper abyss of fear, the chasm of the unsuspecting wife. She looks in the mirror of her marriage and sees a void. It is to Updike's credit that he presents the wife's point of view in such depth. As he explains in an interview, he sympathizes with housewives, with their "devastating sense of emptiness—their ear is somehow held closer than most ears to the steady ticking of time."[18]

After mapping Rabbit's flight from Janice, Piet's from Angela, and Marshfield's from Jane, one is refreshed to have Ruth's perspective on such inane comments from her husband as "tell me who you like." In

*Marry Me* the woman's pain is real rather than a reflection of the husband's panic, and Ruth's musing on the dead end of her life is the center of the novel. Expected by everyone to be calm and patient and wise, she cannot define the germ of her discontent. Thus when the specter of divorce slithers out from under the bed, Ruth has no way to react except further self-laceration at being so blind. Updike's depiction of her bafflement is superb: "At first she thought that, having gazed so long at her own guilt, she mistook for an afterimage what was in truth a fresh development. She admitted to herself, then, what she could never admit to Jerry, that she did not think him capable of it" (103). The idyll of her own adultery turns to a nightmare of nothingness. The mirror of her marriage once more gives back the void.

Her husband's childishness exacerbates the tension. Typical of his self-righteousness, Jerry goes to church before asking Ruth for a divorce, returns home to slap his baby and throw a fork at his wife, and screams at his family that he would rather say grace in a pigpen than let his children come to the table in bathing suits. When Ruth reacts to protect the family, he calls her a "pathetic frigid bitch." Of all Updike's wayward husbands, Jerry is the most unsympathetic because he is the most immature. But since Updike refuses to show us Jerry's crisis of mortality, his fear of death seems more a curiosity of uncertainty than a leap toward despair. No wonder Ruth is baffled by his peculiarities; the reader is too. Rather than a man confronting nothingness, he is like a little boy afraid of the dark.

Jerry's rationalization for divorce is that he and Ruth have been "protect-ing" each other from living. When Ruth tries to match his frontal attacks by telling him that she has also had an affair, he responds, "That's won-derful!" He is not honest; he is not brave; he is not wise. One wonders why Ruth bothers to hang on except for the children. Maturity lets her admit that it is harder to be a husband than a lover, and her comment echoes the famous line in "Wife-wooing" about courting a wife. The irony is, however, that Jerry wants not a wife but a combination mistress-mother. His announcement to Ruth that he will marry Sally to "protect" her sounds more like a threat than a proposal, and in his weakness he hopes that the two women will settle the problem and relieve him of the decision.

Jerry loves the idea of his erotic mistress more than that of the literal woman. Looking at Sally, he projects his need of completion onto her.[19] His inability to choose wife or mistress is based in part on his belief that obstacles are the heart of romance, that marriage to Sally would wither their love. The other part of his hesitation is fear of God, fear of breaking commandments and sacramental vows. Yet one finally wonders whether his paralysis is more a matter of excusing himself, of dodging adult responsibility by appealing to God's love.

The problem for Jerry is freedom; the crisis for Ruth is life. This is a classic dilemma in Updike's fiction—one thinks of Janice and Harry Angstrom or of Joan and Richard Maple—and in each case the predicament represents an attempted balance of the conceivable and inconceivable. Confronting Sally about the adultery, for example, Ruth feels defensive in the face of her rival's will to live: "It would be so easy, Ruth thought, to lie down and die, to sacrifice herself to this other woman's vitality. Sally had no doubts of her right to live" (129). Sally makes a point which Ruth acknowledges, that emotional starvation squeezes a marriage, that a romance cannot be built on children alone. Yet behind the parry and thrust of mutual accusation rests Jerry's inability to act, his cowardly hope that his women will resolve the issue. Even Sally tells Ruth that she is waiting for him to make up his mind, that "he has to be man enough to come for me" (133). Ruth's retort that *they* must decide shows how much better she knows her husband, his weaknesses and whims, his boyishness, his fear. Sally lumps Ruth and Jerry together and calls both immature, but we know better. Jerry is the one who cannot cope. Between tantrums and tears, he pleads for understanding.

Updike perhaps loads the dice against Ruth by portraying her as evaluating the domestic crisis in aesthetic rather than human terms. It is as if he wants to question Ruth's claim to a stable marriage. Jerry assumes the same tactic, telling her, "You married me because—I could draw. I'd make the outlines—and you'd put in the—colors" (142). But by this point the reader puts little faith in Jerry's explanations. It is more significant, then, when Updike has Ruth describe in similar terms a possible resolution to the tension: ". . . reaching into herself, Ruth found something akin to his strange inner wall, for her imagination could not quite grasp the need to let him go. She saw that he was determined to punish her if she did not, and that her dignity lay with the immediate sacrifice of their marriage. Such sacrifice would be simple, bold, pure, aesthetic" (142–143). One suspects Updike of maneuvering the reader to understand that Ruth may recover her imagination, her artistic vision, only if she frees Jerry from her bedroom to the world. After she admits that she might divorce him, for example, she glances at the mirror that had previously shown only the void and sees an erotic image of herself: "hip outthrust, elbow cocked, lips pursed as if having bitten a fruit too succulent" (146). An additional implication is that if she grants the divorce her greatest aesthetic triumph would thus be both herself and Jerry, that by leaving him she would create two lives.

Jerry longs for the creation. One of his silliest statements is that Ruth is his death: "Nothing I can do will really change you. . . . I'm married to my death" (144). It is not that the sentiment is silly—Rabbit has a similar fear with Janice—but that the reader never sees Jerry attempt to act his way out of the terror as Rabbit does on the drive south, on the basketball court, on the golf course. Rabbit is a hero of sorts because he aspires rather than accepts. Jerry would like to aspire, but he is bogged down in letting others do much of it for him. His immaturity is the reason why the reader does not take his declarations of faith and belief as seriously as Rabbit's or Piet's or Marshfield's. Karl Barth's theology, a staple of Updike's wandering men, seems awash in Jerry's tears of self-pity. His solution is not to shore up his faith but to nurture Ruth's illusion that marriage to him blocks her entry to a livelier world. Fantasy shapes his vision of the future.

No wonder Updike subtitles the novel "A Romance." One reads of Jerry's whining and Ruth's strength and thinks of Dimmesdale's hypocrisy and Hester's endurance. Like Hawthorne's weak minister, Jerry longs for Ruth to betray him, to panic into a confession of their plight; and like Hawthorne himself, Updike arranges his doomed couple so that the betrayed woman has only her "assassin" to confide in. Because they are isolated in a fallen Eden, their sex life improves as if they were Hawthorne's mythic pair, wandering into Mistress Hibbins' dark forest. But where Hester returns from the forest intact, Ruth crashes through the trees in an auto accident. Once again, her training in art makes the experience weirdly aesthetic: "It seemed a Rousseau." Yet what she describes as the "Edenlike beauty and intensity" of the woods shakes her to the core, because unlike Hester she might have died there.

Jerry's accusation that Ruth indulges a death wish is finally baffling. Unable to deal with the complexities of adulthood, he decides the accident is God's sign that nothing will happen unless they make the moves themselves. In his eyes, anyone who does not share his view of God is an atheist, and atheists are despicable. Christ's message of love is not his way. Yet he does not want to cause pain. All he asks, cowardly but directly, is that Ruth *tell* him to go. She does. But the children peer around the corner of his dream, and he freezes on the threshold of escape: "Jerry devalued himself by not acting on the strength of his unhappiness. . . . It was humiliating; a man shouldn't stay with a woman out of pity, or if he did he shouldn't tell her. Jerry neither told her nor told her otherwise, or rather, he told her both at various times. What he said lost all specific point. . ." (182). Faced with such waffling, Ruth can only question whether their mutual misery is her fault for refusing to die. In Updike's domestic world, Ruth represents all the women who suffer the indignity of no longer understanding themselves because of guilt they do not deserve, fear they have not earned: "She was a prisoner; the crack between her mind and the world, bridged by a thousand stitches of perception, had quite closed, leaving her embedded, as the white unicorn is a prisoner in the tapestry" (186). Her guilt eases only when Jerry finally walks toward the door, leaving her feeling empty, leaving her staring at nothing.

The snake of Genesis sneaks out of Eden, and Sally's husband Richard is the last of the foursome to be warned. Facing him, Jerry has a "craven fear of losing." No wonder. Jerry has manipulated all concerned. His response that the four of them must now love one another seems absurdly naive beside Ruth's fear for such concrete matters as the children: "He felt now that all four of them had been pressed into a single family and he, an only child, at last had sisters and a brother. He was happy and excited. He wanted never to leave them" (220). Yet Updike wants us also to disapprove of Richard for his boorishness, his vague connection with mobsters, his apparent dislike of children. In addition to his unattractive behavior, Updike saddles Richard with one good eye and then lets Jerry criticize his warped vision of the eternal: "It was the world, he realized, as seen without the idea of God lending each thing a roundness of significance. It was terrible" (225). Since Jerry has a childlike faith in God, presumably his view of domestic particulars is round. But Updike exposes Jerry's faults too, and in an interesting parallel he suggests that Jerry's assessment of the mess is likewise warped: "Having seen too much, he was as good as blind, and possibly it was they, Richard and Ruth, who saw her accurately" (226–227). His pie-in-the-sky solution is that he and Sally must be "better" than other people for the rest of their lives because they have asked so much of their spouses. Richard's solution is more direct. He moves out of the house. All the while he and Jerry bicker, however, the reader, Richard, and Ruth know what Jerry never knows, that Richard has been Ruth's lover.

Jerry's inability to decide between attractive alternatives inhibits him and thus cruelly affects the others. When, looking at Sally, he confesses that hers is not the face he wants at his death bed, he calls off their affair. Having all but lost Ruth, he now fears to marry Sally. This is a nice twist to the tale. Concern for the soul overwhelms desires of the body. Either way he turns, he loses—yet also wins. The knight fork, a chess metaphor he falls back on, is not so devastating as he fears. Returning to Ruth, he clasps himself to Christ, or so he thinks. The unexpected conclusion to *Marry Me* is one of the triumphs of the Updike canon. Just as Jerry remains undecided at the end, so does the novel.

Nathaniel Hawthorne would have approved. He hovers in the wings once again, especially in his ironic conclusion to *The Marble Faun:*

There comes to the Author, from many readers of the foregoing pages, a demand for further elucidations respecting the mysteries of the story.

He reluctantly avails himself of the opportunity afforded by a new edition, to explain such incidents and passages as may have been left too much in the dark; reluctantly, he repeats, because the necessity makes him sensible that he can have succeeded but imperfectly, at best, in throwing about this Romance the kind of atmosphere essential to the effect at which he aimed. He designed the story and the characters to bear, of course, a certain relation to human nature and human life, but still to be so artfully and airily removed from our mundane sphere, that some laws and proprieties of their own should be implicitly and insensibly acknowledged.[20]

Like Hawthorne offering several endings to *The Marble Faun* to placate readers who demand realism in the face of romance, Updike transfers the burden of his tale from the characters to the technique. He presents three conclusions and, with an ironic bow to reader expectations, invites the reader to choose his own.

As he explains in another context, his novels rarely tie up the loose ends: "One has this sense that the old-fashioned novel, and indeed films and television plays, are falsifying life terribly by making events happen, by creating tensions and then resolving them, by setting up trials and then handing down the verdicts—for in fact verdicts don't usually get handed down. All my books end on a kind of hesitant or ambiguous note."[21] This kind of open-endedness is true to the spirit of the romance, for it allows Updike to avoid the neat conclusion, the verdict, that realistic novels and too many readers require. The people who wanted to limit Hawthorne are still buying books. *Marry Me* is not, after all, a novel of manners, a "mirror" of domestic society; it is a romance.

The first ending—Jerry and Sally and Sally's children in Wyoming—is illusory because the gorgeous Western sky is described as "mythic" and the distant mountains as "unreal." They drive into the Wyoming desert and vanish, their "mutual illusion" complete. The second ending—Jerry and Ruth and their children in Nice—is also illusory because a young Marlene Dietrich meets them at the airport.[22] But whereas Jerry's lungs are free in Wyoming, they are congested in France. Thinking of Sally in Nice, as he does not think of Ruth in Wyoming, he climbs toward a hotel with a wedding cake façade and disappears. Finally, the third ending— Jerry alone in St. Croix—is illusory because it glides through the astonishing light of the islands and merges with duller possibilities: Jerry and Ruth in Haut-de-Cagnes, Jerry and Ruth back home in Connecticut. This illusion may be his most acceptable because in his isolation Jerry finds a visionary place that makes him happy. Here amid the color and the beauty and the light, he may detach himself from everyone, indulge his greatest fancy, and, like a character in a romance, turn to an imaginary Sally and say, "marry me."

## NOTES

1. John Updike, *Marry Me: A Romance* (Franklin Center, Pennsylvania: The Franklin Library, 1976). Although not the first trade edition, this special edition was used for copyright registration.

2. John Updike, *Marry Me: A Romance* (New York: Knopf, 1976). Further references will be noted in the text.

3. Maureen Howard, review of *Marry Me: A Romance*, New York *Times Book Review*, 31 October 1976, p. 2.

4. Nathaniel Hawthorne, Preface, *The House of the Seven Gables* (Columbus: Ohio State University Press, 1965), p. 1.

5. William Gilmore Simms, *The Yemassee: A Romance of Carolina* (New Haven, Conn.: College and University Press, 1964), p. 24.

6. Richard Chase, *The American Novel and Its Tradition* (Garden City, N.Y.: Doubleday Anchor, 1956), p. viii.

7. Joel Porte, *The Romance in America* (Middletown, Conn.: Wesleyan University Press, 1969), p. x.

8. Brook Thomas, *"The House of the Seven Gables:* Reading the Romance of America," *PMLA*, 97(March 1982), p. 196.

9. John Updike, "The Music School," *The Music School* (New York: Knopf, 1966), p. 190.

10. See Timothy Foote, "Uncouples," *Time*, 15 November 1976, p. 97; Peter Wolfe, review of *Marry Me*, *Saturday Review*, 13 November 1976, p. 41; Brigid Brophy, "Love in the Garden State," *Harpers*, 253(December 1976), pp. 80-82.

11. See Alfred Kazin, "Alfred Kazin on Fiction," *New Republic*, 27 November 1976, pp. 22-23; Walter Sullivan, "The Insane and the Indifferent: Walker Percy and Others," *Sewanee Review*, 86(January 1978), pp. 153-154; William H. Pritchard, "Merely Fiction," *Hudson Review*, 30(Spring 1977), pp. 157-158; Thomas LeClair, "Updike & Gardner: Down from the Heights," *Commonweal*, 4 February 1977, pp. 89-90.

12. Peter S. Prescott, "To Have and to Hold," *Newsweek*, 8 November 1976, p. 103.

13. See Bruce Allen, "Dream Journies," *Sewanee Review*, 85(October 1977), pp. 691-692; Greg Johnson, "Updike's Infidelities," *Southwest Review*, 62(Spring 1977), pp. 208-209; George W. Hunt, review of *Marry Me*, *America*, 8 January 1977, pp. 18-19. The British reaction is largely laudatory. Malcolm Bradbury, for example, admits that the book is not Updike's best, but he points out that in *Marry Me* Updike is "superb at intersecting between the revelation and the void." Calling Updike a "very eerie writer," Peter Ackroyd says that the book is "not really a romance, rather a perpetually interesting postponement of one." Louise Collis is not as pleased; she praises the wit but wonders if the characters are bloodless. Finally, Neil Hepburn damns the novel as coming "close to turning" his stomach. See Malcolm Bradbury, "Made in Heaven," *New Statesman*, 29 April 1977, pp. 568-569; Peter Ackroyd, "Paradise Lost," *Spectator*, 23 April 1977, pp. 22-23; Louise Collis, review of *Marry Me*, *Books and Bookmen*, 22(May 1977), pp. 61-62; Neil Hepburn, "Blank Looks," *The Listener*, 21 April 1977, pp. 526-527.

14. Josephine Hendin, "Updike as Matchmaker," *Nation*, 30 October 1976, p. 437.

15. Hendin, p. 439.

16. John Updike, "Giving Blood," *The Music School* (New York: Knopf, 1966), p. 31.

17. Eric Rhode, "Grabbing Dilemmas: John Updike Talks about God, Love, and the American Identity," *Vogue*, 1 February 1971, p. 184.

18. Jane Howard, "Can A Nice Novelist Finish First?," *Life*, 4 November 1966, p. 74-A.

19. For an overview of Updike's union of religion and sex through *Marry Me*, see Victor Strandberg, "John Updike and the Changing of the Gods," *Mosaic*, 12(Fall 1978), pp. 157-175: "For the Updike hero, the unattainable lady represents that part of the self which continues to reside in that transcendent realm, having never participated in the soul's earthly incarnation. By the grace of her sexual favor, the Updike heroine affords her lover access, or even 'ascent,' to that higher dimension of reality" (p. 171). Needless to say, Updike's women do not like being thought of in such metaphysical terms.

20. Nathaniel Hawthorne, *The Marble Faun* (Columbus: Ohio State University Press, 1968), p. 463.

21. Rhode, "Grabbing Dilemmas," p. 140.

22. See Strandberg, p. 171: "At the end of the book, Updike affirms de Rougemont's system one last time by bringing into his text that classic movie archetype of the unattainable lady, Marlene Dietrich, whose most famous film, *The Blue Angel*, bears a title that happens to suit Updike's purpose to perfection."

# BECH: A CONCLUSION
*Bech: A Book*

# Bech: A Book

*"Now what?"*
—*Bech: A Book*

"Now what?" Henry Bech muses at the conclusion of *Bech: A Book*(1970).[1] Perusing an ever expanding canon, many of Updike's readers might echo Henry's question. What may they expect next from an author who publishes poetry, short stories, essays, reviews, plays, children's literature, drawings, romances, novels, and *Bech: A Book*? No answer is possible. Predictions about someone as eclectic as Updike are risky. Conclusions about someone as productive as Updike are presumptuous. Yet following an examination of his novels to date, it is instructive to discuss a few of his ideas about fiction and about the problems facing the fiction writer, especially as they are personified in that folk hero of the literary establishment, Henry Bech.

Let me confess at the outset that I do not know what *Bech: A Book* is—a tightly constructed cycle of stories or a loosely constructed novel—but in either case it is a delight to read. Updike himself seems content to leave *Bech* described as, simply, a book. The list placed opposite the short title page of *Marry Me* names his books in chronological order and provides a brief description. Note, for example, the following:

> *Midpoint* and other poems
> *Bech: A Book*
> *Rabbit Redux*, a novel
> *Museums and Women* and other stories
> *Buchanan Dying*, a play
> *A Month of Sundays*, a novel
> *Picked-Up Pieces*
> *Marry Me*, a romance

All one knows for sure is that Bech is an ironic alter ego and that *Bech* is a book.

The book grew out of Updike's travels to the Soviet Union and Eastern Europe on behalf of the State Department in 1964. Placed in the role of the visiting fireman, Updike became aware of the dilemma involved when the private author is asked to be the public man. More important, he found the predicament to be especially threatening to American writers. What happens, he wondered, when the role absorbs the artist? Although he enjoyed the trip to Russia, he now hesitates to be a spokesman for anything. During his visit to the Soviet Union he was "everything I'm not here, a public figure, toasting this and that all the time." He explains, "A writer shouldn't take himself too seriously. I don't think it's a very fruitful state of mind for him to consider himself any sort of a spokesman."[2] Several years later, following a reading at the University of Iowa, Updike developed his reservations: "I had a fine time and loved mouthing my words into the microphone and getting a lot of applause at the end, but you wonder how much of this one should allow oneself. There's a kind of false excitement at being a public person and a public performer. An illusion of wisdom and worth that I don't think is what really makes people write or makes writing good, so without being entirely reclusive I have tried to keep an inexpensive private life and do my work in a more or less plodding and steady way. . . . it's not as if we have an establishment or literary tradition like that of France, or to a lesser extent, England. I think that for whatever deep cultural reasons or inadequacies, the public role is a burden for the American writer in general, and he really shouldn't be asked to shoulder too much of it."[3]

Bech cannot balance the burden. It is not that he has nothing to say to his public but that he is not convinced of the value of his saying it beyond the ephemeral effect of entertainment. Books are all that should matter to an author's reputation, but Bech's audience wants to adore the man. Updike's awareness of the problem is one of the factors behind *Bech: A Book:*

As a writer, I made use of the capital I have acquired—the peculiar sensation of being a literary person. In that respect, I knew Bech intimately before I started. His background, of course, is not at all mine, but he became fairly real to me as, in story after story, he filled out a little more of his past. "The Bulgarian Poetess" is the first written of the stories, and there I gave the titles of his main books, which was meant to represent the curve of his rise and fall. He rises with *Travel Light*, which is his *On the Road*, then passes on to a book which, I suppose, is his *Barbary Shore*, and so on. Being specific in this way helped me to see him as a concrete character and, in addition, to make a joke.[4]

The laughs continue, for Updike has kept up the charade of Henry Bech as active author by publishing bogus interviews between Bech and himself in the New York *Times*.[5]

In other words, even as he extends the joke, Updike raises the question of what happens when a novelist stops writing novels and becomes a cultural object: "Don't laugh—most American writers *are* over the hill by thirty. . . . We're anxious in America to package our things quickly and the writer can become a package before he's ready to have the coffin lid nailed down."[6] To avoid the nailing down, Updike packaged not himself but his anxieties as a writer. He explains that an author suffers strange happenings and that the best way to deal with them is to invent another writer. Bech is that writer, but only at the beginning is he merely an alter ego: "At any rate, I have used the writer in *Bech* as a subject in order to confess sterility in a truthful way. It was an effort, but an effort you can't keep making. Once you've written a book saying how hard it is to write and to describe, in one way or another, the way the facts of fiction creep into your own self, it makes your self and the enterprise seem unreal. . . . In my book, I tried to—and I believe I did—package and dispose of a certain set of anxieties and tensions which I have as a practicing writer. . . . Mine is merely a kind of complaint about the curious position that the American writer now finds himself in; he is semi-obsolete, a curious fellow without any distinct sense of himself as a sensible professional."[7]

European authors, he argues, do not face the same crisis because they have been able to maintain a belief in authorship as a true profession. Even in the relatively recent time of Ernest Hemingway and Scott Fitzgerald, the leading American writers were confident of an authentic literary establishment that helped to define their commitment to fiction. Today, however, the academic sphere has encroached, and writers like Bech face what Updike calls "a fall from the grandeur of a lusty transaction with the ideal reader" to a place on the seminar syllabus. *Bech: A Book* specifically addresses that problem: "My book, morally, is about this situation: a little bit about the way in which it's hard to be an American writer. The Europeans, in contrast, have retained the professional sense. Over the years, they've had more opportunity than we. There, writing has been thought of as a respectable craft that could be learned, whereas in America, as soon as it becomes a craft, it's thought of as really uninteresting."[8]

Part of the problem is the increased whining from critics who call for the "big" book. Henry Bech has heard the cry, the insistence that the author write a book that "equals" his talent. So has John Updike. As long ago as 1966 (Updike's first book was published in 1958), Jane Howard made fun of the uncalled for critical uneasiness that already plagued Updike: "But where does Updike's hyperdeveloped Sense of Wonder get him or us? Is he capable, to paraphrase an early reviewer, of 'thought rather than language'? Does he indeed, as another accuses, 'shun the major sorrows and calamities' ?"[9] Aware of this ridiculous situation, Updike lets Bech write his "big" book, *The Chosen*, and then discover that the critics do not like it. The irony is that they do like *Bech*. Many of the consistently negative commentators, those who, as Updike says, try hard to "puncture" him, find something to praise: "*Bech* has been strangely successful. I have never written a book that has received so few bad reviews as this one. Even some of the critics who haven't had much use for me in the past seemed not to be able to screw themselves up to write nasty things about it."[10]

Generally well received, *Bech: A Book* was conceived in bits and pieces.[11] "The Bulgarian Poetess," which won an O. Henry short story award, was written first. It was followed by "Bech in Rumania," and "Rich in Russia." With the next story, "Bech Takes Pot Luck," Updike suspected that he was creating not individual tales but a book. He then wrote "Bech Swings?," "Bech Panics," and "Bech Enters Heaven." The excerpts from Bech's Russian journal, which serve as an appendix, were salvaged from a chapter that did not work. The foreword, a letter to Updike from Bech himself, suggests the delicacy of the author's ego: "Well, if you must commit the artistic indecency of writing about a writer, better I suppose about me than about you" (v). Bech needs the attention because he suffers from writer's block, and he is convinced that America is to blame for reducing "her writers to imbecility and cozenage. . . . we veer between the harlotry of the lecture platform and the torture of the writing desk. . ." (vi). Worse, he adds, the American author's sweat drips only to support a parasitic conglomeration composed of publishers, agents, editors, reviewers, and media personnel. Despairing that "the contents of a book count as little as the contents of a breakfast cereal box," Henry seems nevertheless secretly pleased by the attention *Bech: A Book* will bring to him (vii). One wants to say, "But, Henry, other professions suffer similar humiliations," but one suspects that Henry would not listen. Updike listens, however, and in *Bech: A Book* he takes a heartfelt but often ironic look at the profession of authorship.

One myth about writers that Updike exposes through Bech is that contrary to popular opinion, successful serious authors are not rich. "Artistically blocked but socially fluent," Bech is, as Updike undoubtedly knows, a perfect candidate for the role he abhors outwardly but needs financially, the visiting writer, the cultural exchange, the big city intellectual deigning to tour the hinterlands. Henry's amusement at his status is funny, especially when, visiting Russia for the State Department, he lets Voznesensky and Yevtushenko indulge their reputations as literary lions while he pretends to be a "graying, furtively stylish rat" (15). The account of Bech's stay in the Soviet Union takes the form of a lecture to students so that Updike may smile at all of us busily commenting on his books. The charm is not only the sharp-eyed humor but also the amused way Updike lets Bech play down his reputation even while he takes pride in it. Updike grins at both author and audience, exposing the writer's need to "evade, confuse, and mock" his American readers.

Yet Updike is also upset about the way Bech, for all his befuddlement, is used: ". . . his success has thrown him into a very baffling world of the wrong kind of praise, or being used by younger people as in the London story, or being asked to join dead people, as in the last story, or of women constantly trying to lure him out of his monkhood. . . . We're not going to get anybody like Hemingway for a while, who so intensely and instinctively cared about language. . . . Instead you get showmen and professors. Bech becomes a showman against his will. A display piece. A toy."[12] Left relatively free in Russia as long as he plays the role of display piece or toy, Bech is manipulated by his own officials in Rumania. American bureaucrats in Bucharest remind him of literary agents. Laughter is the frustrated author's saving grace.

Much of the humor in *Bech: A Book* is directed at *Commentary*, a real journal of some pretension which supplies the imaginary Henry Bech with an editor, a ready market for his essays, and a forum for his ideas. The bogus bibliography to *Bech: A Book* lists many essays by and about Bech in *Commentary* (for example, "The Importance of Beginning with a B: Barth, Borges, and Others"), and one of them, attributed to Norman Podhoretz, the true editor of the journal, carries the imposing title "Bech's Noble Novel: A Case Study in the Pathology of Criticism." Pushing in the needle even farther, Updike has Bech write in his Russian journal: "I say I know Norman Podhoretz and they ask if he wrote *Naked and Dead*" (196). Needless to say, Updike is making fun of the critic and journal that have consistently and maliciously tried not to review his books but to demolish his career. His point is that authors have little opportunity to respond to negative critics. Making Henry Bech the star of *Commentary* is an irony that Updike's mosty knowledgeable readers will appreciate: "I've never been warmly treated by the *Commentary* crowd—insofar as it is a crowd—and so I made Bech its darling. Norman Podhoretz has always gone out of his way to slam me, and this was my way of having some fun with him."[13]

For all the fun, however, Bech learns in the Iron Curtain countries that books do make a difference. His Russian guide presses books on him; his Rumanian guide asks for them. Despite the betrayal into show biz, the good writer does touch the eternal. By his own admission, Bech is the author of "one good book and three others, the good one having come first"—hardly Updike's problem—and he despairs of regaining his momentum. Updike catches the middle-aged author's plight, the debilitating tension created by increasing homage and decreasing creativity. The following passage seems more angry than amused, as if Bech (and Updike?) truly does resent the hoopla:

As he felt himself sink, in his fiction, deeper and deeper into eclectic sexuality and bravura narcissism, as his search for plain truth carried him further and further into treacherous realms of fantasy and, lately, of silence, he was more and more thickly hounded by homage, by flat-footed exegetes, by arrogantly worshipful undergraduates who had hitchhiked a thousand miles to touch his hand, by querulous translators, by election to honorary societies, by invitations to lecture, to "speak," to "read," to participate in symposia trumped up by ambitious girlie magazines in shameless conjunction with venerable universities. (49-50)

As Updike well knows, the irony is that the confident author need not accept the invitations or the handshakes, but fearful of writer's block, Bech receives the applause as a way of jettisoning "the burden of himself."

Updike realizes the author's need of audience. The alternative is silence, not always simple writer's block, but a deliberate refusal to offer one's creations to the world. Bech asks Updike in the foreword: ". . . am I paranoid to feel my 'block' an ignoble version of the more or less noble renunciations of H. Roth, D. Fuchs, and J. Salinger?" (v). Apparently, paranoia is not an issue, but, Updike explains, Salinger is the most important model: Bech "began as a kind of war correspondent, a soldier who wrote stories with gung-ho titles for magazines like *Liberty* and *Collier's*. He was intellectualized in New York in the post-war period. And now he has fallen into silence. There are a number of careers like this, but Salinger's best fits the pattern."[14] Yet for all the parallels with Salinger, Bech's contrast between ignoble silence and noble renunciation hits the mark. Salinger rejected the hoopla and retreated into himself. Bech accepts the applause and stops writing. Unlike Bech, Updike would write about anything to break out of the dilemma: "I would write ads for deodorants or labels for catsup bottles if I had to."[15] He goes on to explain that when he is stuck he leaves the study and moves through the day. Motion clears the air: "It's hard to hold a manuscript in your mind, of course. You get down to the desk and discover the solution you had arrived at while having insomnia doesn't really fit."[16] Thus while Updike distances himself from Bech through irony, he sympathizes with the blocked writer's crisis. Admitting in 1966 that he had no faith in himself as a novelist, he commented that in the process of composition novels seem endless. The struggling author feels trapped in the "belly of a big thing" that will not allow him to remember his characters' middle names or the color of their hair. The only escape is to hold on to the imagined shape of the novel and then write the next word.[17] The artist who rejects Salinger's noble renunciation must endure the increasingly irritating trappings of fame, but Bech and Updike clearly find their resentment more and more difficult to conceal. In one sense, then, writing about writing displaces frustration. Bech takes a crucial step when he admits the "decay" of his own career.

The reader thus understands why one of Henry's concerns is nostalgia. When he thinks of his "big" novel that the critics demanded and then dismissed, he considers its "epic theme, by showing a population of characters whose actions were all determined, at the deepest level, by nostalgia, by a desire to get back, to dive, each, into the springs of their private imagery" (67). Although in some ways Updike describes here the shape of his early short stories as well as the nostalgic drives of Rabbit Angstrom, Peter Caldwell, and Joey Robinson, he also touches on the novelist's desire to cling to his material. Bech's grasp at the moment is precarious. His condition is as poignant as it is comic. For Bech is the last of the moderns, those writers who, along with his gods T. S. Eliot and James Joyce, believed the written word to be sacred. This is what Updike means when he says that we will not see a writer like Ernest Hemingway for a long time. Bech's distractions are many: The former student who wants Bech to look at his "stuff"; the polite interruptions by the curious and worshipful when he seeks privacy at the beach; the mistress who asks for LSD and marriage; the inane charges of racism by tense blacks. But the most nagging distraction is the realization that he will never be so good as James Joyce. The triumph of modernism has faded. Nostalgia will not bring it back.

Yet Bech is a writer, and a writer is, in one sense, a performer. If he cannot offer new words to the public, he will read old ones to it. Something has to break his slump. Motion is an antidote to lethargy. His current mistress is indignant when he agrees to give a reading at a college for women in Virginia: "You won't speak at Columbia when it's two subway stops away and full of people on your own wavelength, but you'll fly a thousand miles to some third-rate finishing school on the remote chance you can sack out with Scarlett O'Hara" (105). She may be correct, but his panic has deeper roots. When the lovely coeds in their heels and hose escort him around the magnolia-filled campus, he glimpses what no author wants to face, the probability that his best work is behind him and that death owns the horizon. This fear makes Rabbit Angstrom his cousin, Piet Hanema his contractor, Tom Marshfield his pastor, and Jerry Conant his neighbor. Like their crises, Bech's panic is crucial to the Updike canon. He performs for the coeds as if in a trance, as if the celebrated artist on stage is a faked copy of the real thing. He probably is. Although he is witty and charming with the lovely Southern girls of the Lanier Poetry Club, "to himself his tongue seemed to be moving strangely, as slowly as one of those galloping horses he had seen from a mile in the air, while his real attention was turned inward toward the swelling of his dread, his unprecedented recognition of horror" (110). Death and nullity threaten the artist's spirit. Writer's block is the physical manifestation of inward terror, for looked at from the perspective of death, fame and excellence mean nothing. No wonder Bech panics. So do Rabbit, Piet, Marshfield, and Jerry Conant. Backed into a corner, he even wonders if his critics could be correct, if his fiction is not life-serving and real but "flimsy, unfelt, flashy, and centrifugal. That the proper penance for his artistic sins was silence and reduction. . . . Who was he?" (118, 124). The sad fact is that he does not know. Words may be maggots. Peace may be silence.

Yet silence can also exacerbate the tension. What he needs, he realizes, is something to stimulate him to create, something to justify his sense of himself as a valuable man. Perhaps love is the key. In one of Updike's finest descriptions of the fame all authors crave, Bech thinks, "one more woman, one more leap would bring him safe into that high calm pool of immortality where Proust and Hawthorne and Catullus float, glassy-eyed and belly up" (135). But sex is an inadequate substitute and the words do not come. Updike knows the risks of authorship, the tendency of the adoring public to fashion an image of the artist that it can manipulate with interviews and parties and thereby trap the author inside the mold. The creator becomes, in a sense, a character created by himself. All he has left is self-parody.

Ironically, writers want it both ways, want simultaneously to be applauded and left alone. What Updike calls "the haven of lasting accomplishment" exempts successful authors from the incessant demand for growth and the inexorable creeping of decay, but Bech lacks the confidence that he has reached that point. Inspiration, the mistress he needs, seems forever fled, but the academy of writers honors him anyway along with other authors whom Bech had thought dead. The parallel is too noticeable to ignore. His fame now official, his creativity gone, he asks at the end the one question that all writers, including presumably Updike himself, must eventually pose, "Now what?" Bech does not know. The final entry in the bogus bibliography all but answers the query. Attributed to fem-libber Gloria Steinem, the title cuts deep: "What Ever Happened to Henry Bech?"

That question will not be asked about John Updike. Although he is not Henry Bech, it seems likely that many of the uncertainties and fears that immobilize the aging Bech have touched him. Rather than panic, however, Updike writes. His writing is so varied and of such high quality generally that he has all but achieved "the haven of lasting accomplishment." The lure of immortality is always there: "I think anybody in the arts who can say 'this is mine, this is something I've made and it has an existence outside of me,' is sort of one step up in combatting our sensations of perishability. The creative impulse surely is to some extent the itch to make something that survives or might survive."[18] Unlike Henry Bech, Updike could accept the invitation of silence, stop publishing today, and still be guaranteed the kind of survival he describes.[19]

The pleasures of John Updike continue. They are likely to do so for a long time. Perusing Updike's comments about himself, Henry Bech, and the general profession of authorship in this conclusion, I jotted down my subjective reactions to some of the novels, just as Bech thinks back over his own accomplishment. The most impressive novels are *Rabbit, Run* and *The Centaur;* my favorite is *Of the Farm;* the novel I least want to reread is *Couples;* the most difficult novel is *A Month of Sundays;* and the most unexpected novel by Updike is *The Coup.* Further surprises are surely forthcoming from this astonishing artist of lyrical prose and intellectual vigor. For one thing, he has promised to see Rabbit Angstrom into old age.

Now what? John Updike is so gifted, so intelligent, and so committed that one is grateful to be unable to answer the question.

## NOTES

1. John Updike, *Bech: A Book* (New York: Knopf, 1970). Further references will be noted in the text.
2. Jane Howard, "Can A Nice Novelist Finish First?," *Life,* 6 November 1966, p. 81.
3. Richard Burgin, "A Conversation with John Updike," *John Updike Newsletter,* 10 and 11(Spring and Summer 1979), p. 61.
4. Frank Gado, "Interview with John Updike," *First Person: Conversations on Writers and Writing* (Schenectady, New York: Union College Press, 1973), pp. 105-106.
5. The most recent mock interview appeared when *Rabbit Is Rich* was published (New York *Times Book Review,* 27 September 1981, pp. 1, 34-35). The first may be found in Updike's *Picked-Up Pieces* (New York: Knopf, 1975), pp. 10-13.
6. Charles Thomas Samuels, "The Art of Fiction XLIII: John Updike," *Paris Review,* 12(Winter 1968), p. 99.
7. Gado, p. 83.
8. Gado, pp. 83-84.
9. Howard, p. 74 C.
10. Gado, p. 105.
11. For Updike's comments on how *Bech* was written, see "One Big Interview," *Picked-Up Pieces,* pp. 505-506.
12. "One Big Interview," p. 508.
13. Gado, p. 105.
14. Gado, p. 105.
15. Samuels, p. 95.
16. Samuels, pp. 96-97.
17. Howard, pp. 81-82.
18. Burgin, p. 7.

19. For the further adventures of Henry Bech, see "Three Illuminations in the Life of an American Author," *New Yorker*, 21 August 1978, pp. 24-32. Now collected in *Bech Is Back*, this story has been published in a limited, signed edition of 350 copies: John Updike, *Three Illuminations in the Life of an American Author* (New York: Targ Editions, 1979).

## SELECTED CHECKLIST OF JOHN UPDIKE'S NOVELS

The primary bibliography of John Updike's novels is mildly complicated by the presence of revised editions, paperback editions, limited signed editions, and British editions. The following list may help the interested reader. I have noted with asterisks the editions quoted in this study. A helpful source in preparing a list of Updike's novels is Ray A. Roberts, "John Updike: A Bibliographical Checklist," *American Book Collector*, 1, Nos. 1 and 2, new series(Jan.-Feb., March-April, 1980), pp. 5-12, 40-44; 39-47.

THE POORHOUSE FAIR
   1.a. First edition:
      New York: Alfred A. Knopf, 1959.
 *1.b. First edition, sixth printing (revised):
      New York: Alfred A. Knopf, 1977.
   2. First English edition:
      London: Victor Gollancz, 1959.
   3. First paperback edition:
      Greenwich, Connecticut: Crest, [1964]; # d677.
   4. Fourth edition (revised); published with RABBIT, RUN:
      New York: Modern Library, [1965].

RABBIT, RUN
   1. First edition:
      New York: Alfred A. Knopf, 1960.
   2. First English edition:
      [London]: André Deutsch, [1961].
   3. First paperback edition:
      Greenwich, Connecticut: Crest, [1962]; # R538.
   4. Fourth edition (revised):
      [Harmondsworth]: Penguin Books, [1964]; # 2097.
 *5. Fifth edition (revised): published with THE POORHOUSE FAIR:
      New York: Modern Library, [1965].

6. Sixth edition:
Franklin Center, Pennsylvania: The Franklin Library, 1977
(signed).

THE CENTAUR
*1. First edition:
New York: Alfred A. Knopf, 1963.
2. First English edition:
[London]: André Deutsch, [1963].
3. First paperback edition:
Greenwich, Connecticut: Crest, [1964]; # R682.

OF THE FARM
*1. First edition:
New York: Alfred A. Knopf, 1965.
2. First English edition:
[London]: André Deutsch, [1966].
3. First paperback edition:
Greenwich, Connecticut: Fawcett Crest, [1967]; # R993.

COUPLES
*1. First edition:
New York: Alfred A. Knopf, 1968.
2. First English edition:
[London]: André Deutsch, [1968].
3. First paperback edition:
Greenwich, Connecticut: Fawcett Crest, [1969]; # P1252.

BECH: A BOOK
*1.a. First edition:
New York: Alfred A. Knopf, 1970.
1.b. First edition limited signed issue:
New York: Alfred A. Knopf, 1970.
2. First English edition:
[London]: André Deutsch, [1970].
3. First paperback edition:
Greenwich, Connecticut: Fawcett Crest, [1971]; # M1563.

RABBIT REDUX
*1.a. First edition:
New York: Alfred A. Knopf, 1971.
1.b. First edition limited signed issue:
New York: Alfred A. Knopf, 1971.
2. First English edition:
[London]: André Deutsch, [1972].

3. First paperback edition:
   Greenwich, Connecticut: Fawcett Crest, [1972]; # Q1753.
4. Fourth edition:
   Franklin Center, Pennsylvania: The Franklin Library, 1981 (signed).

## A MONTH OF SUNDAYS
*1.a. First edition:
   New York: Alfred A. Knopf, 1975.
1.b. First edition limited signed issue:
   New York: Alfred A. Knopf, 1975.
2. First English edition:
   [London]: André Deutsch, [1975].
3. First paperback edition:
   Greenwich, Connecticut: Fawcett Crest, [1976]; # C2701.

## MARRY ME: A ROMANCE
1. First edition:
   Franklin Center, Pennsylvania: The Franklin Library, 1976.
*2.a. Second edition:
   New York: Alfred A. Knopf, 1976.
2.b. Second edition limited signed issue:
   New York: Alfred A. Knopf, 1976.
3. First English edition:
   [London]: André Deutsch, [1977].
4. First paperback edition:
   Greenwich, Connecticut: Fawcett Crest, [1977]; # 195.

## THE COUP
*1.a. First edition:
   New York: Alfred A. Knopf, 1978.
1.b. First edition limited signed issue:
   New York: Alfred A. Knopf, 1978.
1.c. First paperback printing (Quality Book Club):
   New York: Alfred A. Knopf, 1978.
2. First English edition:
   [London]: André Deutsch, [1979].

## RABBIT IS RICH
*1.a. First edition:
   New York: Alfred A. Knopf, 1981.
1.b. First edition limited signed issue:
   New York: Alfred A. Knopf, 1981.

2. First paperback edition:
   New York: Fawcett Crest, [1982]; # 395.
3. First English edition:
   [London]: André Deutsch, [1982].

# Index

The index does not include references to material in the footnotes and checklist.